eah

Bullying in Secondary Schools

Bullying in Secondary Schools

What It Looks Like and How to Manage It

**Keith Sullivan, Mark Cleary
and Ginny Sullivan**

P·C·P
Paul Chapman
Publishing

CORWIN
PRESS

© Keith Sullivan, Mark Cleary and Ginny Sullivan

First published 2004

Paul Chapman Publishing
A SAGE Publications Company
6 Bonhill Street
London EC2A 4PU

Corwin Press, Inc
A SAGE Publications Company
2455 Teller Road
Thousand Oaks, California 91320

Library of Congress Control Number: 2002115860

A catalogue record for this book is available from the
British Library

ISBN 0 7619 4192 4
ISBN 0 7619 4193 2 (pbk)

Typeset by Dorwyn Ltd, Rowlands Castle, Hants
Printed and bound in Great Britain by the Cromwell Press, Trowbridge

Contents

List of Tables and Figures .... *viii*

Foreword .... *ix*

Authors' Preface .... *xi*

Acknowledgements .... *xiii*

About this Book .... *xv*

PART I INTRODUCTION **1**

1   What We Know about Bullying in Secondary Schools 1

    The waiter's story 1

    The chaos theory of bullying 3

    What is bullying? 3

    What we know about bullying 7

    The bullying triangle: bullies, victims, and bystanders 15

    The effects of bullying 20

2   Adolescence: "It Was the Best of Times; It Was the Worst of Times" ... 27

    A case study: six set off on an adventure 27

    Changes in adolescence: flying through turbulence with no safety belt ... 31

    Problems and disorders 41

    The end of the adventure 43

3   The Social Climate of the Secondary School 45

    Arriving at secondary school 45

    The culture of the secondary school 46

    Peer relations at secondary school 48

PART II WHY "BAD" THINGS HAPPEN TO "GOOD" SCHOOLS ... **55**

4   Let's Be Honest about What Schools Do 55

    The whole-school approach 55

    What we know/what we do 56

    How some schools respond to bullying 58

    The case studies 62

5   How Teachers Contribute to a Bullying Culture   72
      Introduction   72
      Teachers who contribute to a bullying culture   73
      Conclusion   81

6   Parents, the Other Victims   82
      Silence and marginalization   82
      Case study: a real "worst case" scenario   85

PART III MAKING THE WHOLE SCHOOL SAFE   93

7   Developing a Whole-School Approach   93
      What is a whole-school approach?   93
      The six stages of the whole-school approach   94
      Making the approach work   94
      Case study: implementing the whole-school approach at Pounamu
        High School   100

8   The Power of the Bystanders   109
      Introduction   109
      Participant roles in bullying   111
      A case study: entrenched roles in a bully culture   115
      Understanding the bullying dynamic   119

9   Authoritative Teaching Practice   130
      Introduction   130
      The foundations of authoritative teaching   131
      Taking the No Blame Approach into unchartered waters   134
      The teacher as team leader and community builder   139

PART IV THE SAFE SCHOOL IN ACTION   141

10   What to Do When Bullying Happens   141
      Taking a step back   141
      Applying policy   142
      Diagnosis   146
      Choosing the interventions   148

11   Using the Curriculum to Understand and Deal with Bullying: 150
        "In the Cafeteria"
      Introduction   150
      Lesson 1: understanding bullying   151
      Lesson 2: defining bullying   153
      Lesson 3: developing a deeper understanding of bullying—   154
        "In the Cafeteria"

12 Harnessing Student Leadership   165
    Introduction: a tale of two schools   165
    Leadership in today's schools: "we don't need no other heroes"   166
    The leadership program   169
    Jonah enters the leadership program   178

13 Experiential Learning through Social Theater   181
    If bullying needs an audience, let's put on the play   181
    Using social theater in the school. a case study   182

14 Supporting Students through Peer Mentoring   199
    What is peer mentoring?   199
    Peer mentoring and recovering from bullying   199
    A peer mentoring program   201
    A case study of a peer mentoring training workshop   206

15 Changing the Social Dynamic: The No Blame Approach   216
    What is the No Blame Approach?   216
    Why does it work?   217
    How do teachers feel about it?   218
    The five steps of the No Blame Approach   218
    Golden rules of the No Blame Approach   226
    Two No Blame Approach case studies   226

APPENDICES
1   Useful Websites   233

2   School Bullying Questionnaire   236

3   An Example of a School Anti-Bullying Policy   240

4   Student Charter   242

References   245
Index   251

List of Tables and Figures

List of Tables

8.1   The percentages of children and adolescents in different
      participant roles among sixth (n=573) and eighth (n=316) graders   113

List of Figures

1.1   What we know about bullying   4
1.2   The ripple effect of bullying   22
1.3   The downward spirals of bullying   25

2.1   Tumultuous yet invigorating: the passage through adolescence   28

3.1   The changing nature of peer groups and individual-
      ization during secondary school years   49

4.1   The blocked drain syndrome   57

8.1   The passive–active continuum   120
8.2   Self-perception   121
8.3   Influence   122
8.4   Leadership   122
8.5   Involvement/inclusion   123
8.6   Submission   123
8.7   Empathy   124
8.8   Prosocial skills   124
8.9   Selfishness   125
8.10 Manipulation   125
8.11 Combined continuum and Strathclyde triangle   126
8.12 Distribution of students on the triangle   127
8.13 Changing positions on the triangle   128

9.1   Characteristics of authoritative teachers   134
9.2   Changing the emphasis during the school year   135

12.1 Deep structure and surface manifestations of negative and positive
      leadership   167

14.1 Requirements for an effective peer mentor   200

Foreword

Around the world, there is an emerging awareness of the problems associated with bullying. This is not just a normal part of growing up nor something that kids grow out of. It is a problem that a substantial proportion of young children and adolescents experience—as perpetrators, victims, or bystanders, and at some point they may have been involved in each of the three roles. Recent data from 35 countries participating in the World Health Organization Survey of Health Behavior in School-aged Children (2003) confirm the ubiquity and magnitude of the problem of bullying.

Once a problem, such as bullying, comes to the forefront of social consciousness, there is a logical call for strategies to address the problem. This book is unique in that it provides an understanding of bullying in adolescence and provides direction for intervention. To date, the majority of the literature has focused on elementary school-aged children. Recognizing the problem of bullying in adolescence as well as childhood is an important step. The authors of this book, Keith and Ginny Sullivan and Mark Cleary, make a strong contribution to the field by providing a critical developmental understanding of the problem. They address the important issue of the salient developmental challenges in adolescence (e.g., developing intimacy, autonomy and identity) and relate these processes to the relevant social systems that influence bullying. The consequence is that the complexity of bullying is revealed, and an understanding of the complexity of bullying is essential to any successful intervention.

The authors base the book on a central tenet: bullying at any age interferes with the normal developmental process. As such, in order to promote healthy development, we need to address these problems long before any negative consequences develop. Drawing upon cogent case examples, the authors have put a spotlight on the nature of bullying during adolescence and developmentally appropriate interventions to stop the bullying behavior. A key feature of this book is the sensitivity with which the authors portray victimized youth, and the effective ways in which they frame the problem not as a defect in those who are bullied, but within the systems that permit the abusive behaviors to take root.

This book not only sheds light on understanding bullying in adolescence, but also on designing and implementing interventions that are both developmentally relevant and systemically appropriate. It provides an overview and understanding of the important social systems that impact on development such as the family, peer group, school, and community. For example, in adolescence the role and influence of the peer group becomes increasingly important, while the role and influence of parents changes. The authors highlight how certain children may fall prey to the aggressive tendencies of their peers and how their low social status and power in the peer group context place them at risk of ongoing torment through bullying. At the same time, there are normal dominance processes that are continually unfolding in the lives of adolescents. Some teenagers find it socially beneficial to establish and reinforce their social power through bullying vulnerable school mates. The challenge in recognizing the changing importance and salience of these social contexts is to design interventions that match these significant social changes. This is what this book does and encourages others to do within their own creative and cultural contexts.

We have here a book that sheds much light on the nature of the problem of bullying in adolescence, the systemic factors that underlie bullying, and specific directions for the design of interventions with developmentally appropriate strategies for responding to the problems. The majority of interventions to date have focused on bullying as a problem in childhood and in primary schools. With this volume, the authors give us information and strategies that are essential for dealing with bullying in adolescence but are often also applicable to bullying in other contexts. While the physical, social, emotional, and cognitive changes that typify adolescence give bullying at secondary school its special character, the underlying factors of abuse, coercion, cruelty, and the wielding of power are of relevance when considering bullying of any type.

This book presents a clear, well-constructed and useful account of bullying in adolescence and marks an important starting point in understanding bullying and designing age-appropriate interventions. Bullying is a form of abuse in youth-to-youth relationships. The time has come to ensure that all individuals have the right to be safe at school and in our communities and this book makes a valuable contribution to that goal.

Associate Professor Wendy Craig, Department of Psychology, Queen's University, Kingston, Ontario, Canada

Professor Debra Pepler, Director, LaMarsh Research Center for Research on Violence and Conflict Resolution, York University, Toronto, Ontario, Canada

Authors' Preface

In this book we are describing a new approach to dealing with bullying. Whereas much bullying research examines how often it occurs, who bullies, and who is bullied, our approach, firstly, sees bullying as part of a social dynamic and, secondly, as part of an unsafe school culture. If the dynamic changes so that the bystanders cease to watch from the sidelines but intervene and show their rejection of the bullying behavior, then the bully will no longer have power over the group and, more specifically, the victim. A change in the bullying dynamic means that individuals are not trapped into their roles and the whole power base upon which bullying relies crumbles. We are also advocating the creation of safe schools that provide positive and enabling learning environments. Reducing bullying is the tool.

Planning for a bullyfree school needs to be done with creativity, imagination, and commitment. And it needs to include as many people as possible from within the school community—students, teaching and other school staff, parents, and others from the wider community. The ideal that these people come up with does not have to stay an ideal; it can become a reality.

In any school, bullying will erupt from time to time. That is a fact of life. But in safe schools, social relationships are founded on respect, students can confidently talk to staff about difficulties, and the school provides a clear set of strategies for teachers to use and offers complete and systemic support. And in such schools, learning can take off and become as enjoyable as it should be.

We have all experienced bullying. We have personally experienced it as children, as parents, and as teachers. It is because we have seen the harm it can do, but also because we have seen that it can be successfully dealt with, that we have chosen to write this book.

Keith Sullivan
Mark Cleary
Ginny Sullivan

Acknowledgements

The authors would like to thank the following people: Gaylene Denford-Wood of Wellington, New Zealand for her careful and caring reading and feedback; Barbara Maines and George Robinson of Bristol, England, for their generosity and openness in allowing us to use their wonderful work; Alan McLean of Glasgow, Scotland, for the free use of his inspired materials; Tina Salmivalli of Turku, Finland, for allowing us to reproduce some of her important research findings; Margaret Anderson, of Victoria University of Wellington, for her crucial and unfailing help in finding articles, books and resources; and Margaret Wheeler of Rangiora High School, Canterbury, for her support and insightful feedback.

We are very grateful to all those who have shared their stories of bullying and being bullied, most of whom wish to be nameless. We would all like to thank the students and staff of Colenso High School, Napier, New Zealand, for trusting Mark with their stories and for helping him develop his anti-bullying practice.

Keith would like to thank the President and Fellows of Wolfson College, University of Oxford, for electing him to the Charter Fellowship in Human Rights in order to study anti-bullying research and initiatives in the UK; and Professor Richard Pring and members of the Department of Educational Studies who hosted him during his time at Oxford. Mark would like to thank the generous support of the Nuffield Foundation for financing a visit to the UK; and Peter Smith, members of the Education Department of the Strathclyde Local Area Authority and the Tayside Anti-Bullying Team who all helped him develop a depth of understanding into the bullying dynamic.

We would also like to acknowledge the important work of Owen Sanders, Maurice Cheer and Gill Palmer from the New Zealand Police Youth Education Services who have provided ongoing support and encouragement to our work.

We are very grateful to Oxford University Press for permission to use two figures and a questionnaire from Keith Sullivan's book, *The Anti-Bullying Handbook* (2000).

Many thanks to colleagues around the world who have shared insights into how to understand and deal with bullying and whose work has been both inspirational and helpful. In the UK: Professor Peter K. Smith of Goldsmiths College, University of London; Professor Helen Cowie, Roehampton Institute, University of Surrey; Sonia Sharp, Senior Psychologist, Nottingham; Dr Val Besag, Gateshead; The Tayside Anti-Bullying Team, Dundee, Scotland (wherever you now are). In Norway, Elaine Munthe, Professor Erling Roland and their team of researchers at Stavanger University College. In Finland, Professor Kaj Bjorkvist and Dr Karen Osterman of Åbo Akademi University, Vaasa; and Dr Tina Salmivalli and Dr Ari Kaukiainen of the University of Turku. In Canada, Professor Debra Pepler, Director of the LaMarsh Center for Research on Violence and Conflict Resolution, York University, Toronto; Dr Wendy Craig, Department of Psychology, Queen's University, Kingston; Dr Claudia Mitchell of McGill University; and Professor Shelley Hymel of the University of British Columbia. In the US, Dr Nan Stein of Wellesley College, Boston. In Australia, Professor Ken Rigby of the University of South Australia and Professor Phillip Slee of Flinders University, Adelaide.

We are also grateful for the support of our places of work and our colleagues, Professor Cedric Hall, Maggy Hope, Phil Kay, Professor Helen May, and Marilyn Wright, and the staff of the School of Education, Victoria University of Wellington, and Colenso High School. Mark would like to thank Barbara for forbearance and support, and Ginny and Keith would like to thank each other. Our greatest debt is to our own children, who have taught us about bullying in their progressions through school.

About this Book

The book is divided into four parts. Part I, "Introduction," consists of three chapters. Chapter 1, "What We Know About Bullying in Secondary Schools," is based upon research and scholarship from around the world and provides a summary of the most useful information about the nature of bullying in the secondary sector. Chapter 2 entitled "Adolescence: 'It Was the Best of Times; It Was the Worst of Times'" describes the various changes that occur during the turbulent teenage years of secondary school from the point of view of biological, social, emotional, and cognitive development and also examines the nature of relationships, peer pressure, and problems and disorders. Chapter 3, "The Social Climate of the Secondary School" describes how secondary schools confront students with a massive cultural change at a time when they are changing in a variety of other ways. The authors map out three stages through which students evolve on their passage through secondary school (the first-year students, the middle students, and the finishing students).

Part II is entitled "Why 'Bad' Things Happen to 'Good' Schools" and is the most challenging part of the book. It argues that although schools often agree philosophically with the intentions of anti-bullying policies and practice, there are a number of obstacles within schools that make this difficult. This is termed the blocked drain syndrome. Chapter 4, "Let's Be Honest about What Schools Do," provides an overview of issues that schools need to address honestly and fully in order to make things work. It provides case studies of situations where bullying has had insidious and tragic results. Chapter 5 examines "How Teachers Contribute to a Bullying Culture" and Chapter 6 "Parents, the Other Victims."

Part III, "Making the Whole School Safe," responds to the difficult issues raised in Part II and builds on the useful information from Part I. Chapter 7, "Developing a Whole-School Approach,"describes how to initiate and implement an effective whole-school program; and Chapter 8, "The Power of the Bystanders," describes how the third parties to bullying, the bystanders, can be involved to help reduce bullying. In response to the criticism about teachers who either directly or inadvertently encourage bullying (Chapter 5),

Chapter 9, "Authoritative Teaching Practice," discusses how teachers can carry out their professional practice in a way that is effective for countering bullying and that is supportive of them as well.

Part IV, entitled "The Safe School in Action," provides a set of interrelated strategies and solutions designed to counter bullying effectively and create safe school environments. It builds on the concepts of a properly constructed whole-school approach, the need to involve the bystanders/peer group, and the development of nonpunitive problem-solving mechanisms. "What to Do When Bullying Happens" (Chapter 10) provides a plan of action to show school staff how to deal with bullying events. Chapter 11, "Using the Curriculum to Understand and Deal with Bullying: 'In the Cafeteria,'" provides useful and practical curriculum materials for teaching lessons about the nature of and how to deal with bullying. Chapter 12, "Harnessing Student Leadership," provides an overview of a leadership program that has been used to help both prosocial and antisocial year 9 students to become school leaders who take on a variety of positive roles in the school including being promoters of a safe school. Chapter 13, "Experiential Learning through Social Theater," demonstrates how to give students a better sense of the bullying dynamic through the use of social theater. "Supporting Students through Peer Mentoring" (Chapter 14) gives a template for creating a program that involves older students in providing support and encouragement to those who have been involved in bullying (largely, victims, bullies and, sometimes, bystanders) so that bullying stops and its effects are ameliorated. Chapter 15 ("Changing the Social Dynamic: The No Blame Approach") gives an overview of a humane and very practical program for reframing student culture and breaking cycles of bullying.

The book finishes with several useful appendices: an overview of key anti-bullying websites, a bullying questionnaire, a typical anti-bullying policy, and materials to supplement information for Chapter 8 (on leadership).

Throughout this book, pseudonyms are used and locations fictionalized where necessary to protect identities.

This book is designed for the use of teachers, parents, students, administrators, counselors, psychologists, youth and social workers, university lecturers, and teacher education students.

PART I

INTRODUCTION

1

What We Know about Bullying in Secondary Schools

> In a report prepared for the New Zealand Office of the Commissioner for Children, Lind and Maxwell (1996) found that when the secondary school students in their study described the three worst things they had ever experienced, the death of someone very close (a mother or father, brother or sister) was mentioned most often. Being bullied by other students came second.

The waiter's story

Ask anyone anywhere about bullying, and they will have a story to tell. Each one of these stories tells us a lot about bullying and the pain it causes, and each one of them is unique. These stories have led us to take a long hard look at bullying and how it can be dealt with.

In the midst of writing this book, we visited our favorite café in central Wellington. It was a beautiful sunny late afternoon, and we sat outside under an umbrella. When the waiter arrived, Keith was indecisive and, explaining his behavior as a result of the heat and the lateness of the day, he then corrected himself and said, "No, the reason I'm a bit unfocused is that we're writing a book and we're just taking a break." The young man asked what the book was about, and Keith told him, "Secondary school bullying." He referred to a recent case of violent school bullying that had been reported in the newspapers, and the young man responded, "That was nothing. You should have been at *my* school and experienced *my* bullying." When Keith talked about our intention of writing a deep and compelling account of secondary school bullying that also offers solutions, the young waiter wavered between being positive and being dismissive. He had attended a single-sex denominational boarding school in another city. He said that although the school had an anti-bullying policy, a culture of bullying and intimidation flourished there. He described how those who were bullies sat at the back of the class and laughed to themselves, because all the tut-tutting about bullying made no difference at all to what went on in the school. In this young man's class, there were three particular victims: he is still recovering from his experience of being bullied, one is a drug dealer, and the other committed suicide.

The waiter's story highlights the fact that when schools pay lip service to an anti-bullying stance, they place their students in jeopardy. The message is very clear: schools have to be totally committed to developing a safe environment. What schools do is more important than what they say, and that is why this book is practical rather than theoretical.

Over the last 20 years, there has been a massive amount of interest in bullying among psychologists and educators, and new and useful insights into this complex behavior are added to this growing body of work every year. Taking into account this collective knowledge, reevaluating the bullying literature, and using our own observations and research, some basic tenets about bullying emerge. These are:

• Bullying is unpredictable behavior that appears to strike without pattern and to become a difficult problem for about one in six students.
• It occurs in all types of schools.
• It is not restricted by race, gender, class, or other natural distinctions.
• It is at its worst during early adolescence.
• There is compelling evidence that the impact of bullying has lifelong debilitating consequences.

This book focuses on bullying in secondary school. For adolescents, one of the most important, urgent and affirming requirements for growth and survival is the need to be part of a group, to be accepted, defined, and mirrored by a cohort of peers. We are focusing on the 12–18 age group, and while bullying occurs before and after this, it is at this time that the pivotal questions, "Who am I?," "What is the meaning of life?," and "Where do I fit in?" are asked. It is a time when each child moves toward adulthood, passing through various processes of individuation.

What bullying does at whatever age it occurs is to interfere with normal developmental processes. If children have a smooth passage through adolescence, they are likely to experience a growing awareness that they are part of a community, whereas bullying isolates, excludes, and pushes individuals to the periphery. It is the job of teachers and school administrators to make sure that their students are kept well inside this periphery so that they are able to learn and to develop.

Teachers tend to be very practical. They typically say words to the effect that, "Bullying researchers carry out research and provide interesting information and statistics about bullying. They can tell me more precisely, perhaps, what I already know. What I *need* to know, however, is what to do in my classroom and school tomorrow to deal effectively with bullying." With this in mind, our purpose is to provide fundamental information and a new interpretation of bullying behavior, as well as practical and useful strategies and solutions.

The chaos theory of bullying

There is a mass of empirical research that gives us a picture of what bullying is, but every time someone is bullied, it is *their* story that is important, and the circumstances and context of *this particular event.*

Bullying is a fact of life. Research on bullying tends to focus on rates of bullying, identifying and predicting victims of bullying, and school types or settings where bullying is most likely to occur (Figure 1.1). Empirical evidence is essential and very useful, but isolating and identifying causes will not eliminate bullying; nor can it be used predictively. While we may be able to generalize about the rates, characteristics, and causes, statistical indicators are less important than how bullying affects individuals. In New Zealand, a zealous focus on single-sex boys' boarding schools in the 1990s had the effect of making other types of schools dismissive of their need to be vigilant about bullying: when high-risk contexts appear to be identified, everyone else puts anti-bullying protection on the back burner. However, being bullied at a co-educational school is every bit as bad as being bullied at a single-sex boys' school. The message is that *all* schools should be vigilant.

Bullying is random. What we are arguing is that it can happen to anyone at any time: while there is some predictability, there is also a massive element of chaos. Most research suggests that in year 10, for example, 25 percent of the school population is going to be bullied regularly. But in any sample of students, the victims are unlikely to add up to 25 percent. In one sample, there may be none, and in another, there may be a large number. This brings us back to one of our main points: that however statistical, descriptive, or quantitative research is, it cannot address individual stories, which are the crux of the issue.

What is bullying?

Definition

Bullying is a *negative* and often *aggressive or manipulative* act or series of acts by one or more people against another person or people usually over a period

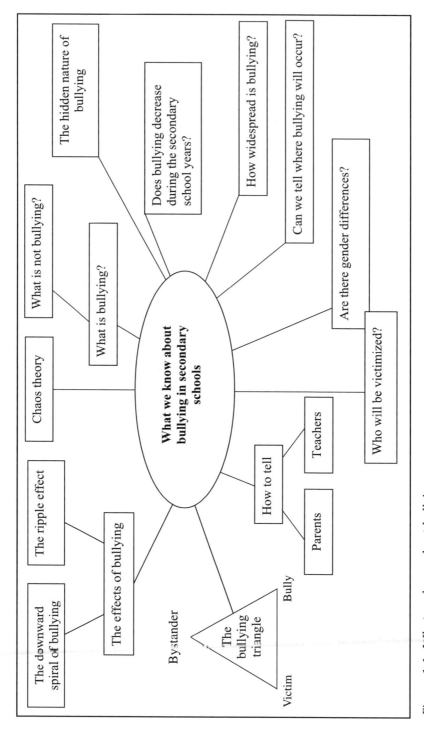

Figure 1.1 *What we know about bullying*

of time. It is *abusive* and is based on an *imbalance of power.*[1]
  Bullying contains the following elements:

1 The person doing the bullying has more power than the one being victimized.
2 Bullying is often organized, systematic, and hidden.
3 Bullying is sometimes opportunistic, but once it starts is likely to continue.
4 It usually occurs over a period of time, although those who regularly bully may also carry out one-off incidents.
5 A victim of bullying can be hurt physically, emotionally, or psychologically.
6 All acts of bullying have an emotional or psychological dimension.

Forms of bullying

Bullying can be *physical* or *non-physical* and can include *damage to property*.

1 *Physical* bullying is the most obvious form of bullying and occurs when a person is physically harmed, through being *bitten*, *hit*, *kicked*, *punched*, *scratched*, *spat at*, *tripped up*, having his or her hair pulled, or any other form of physical attack.
2 *Nonphysical* bullying (sometimes referred to as social aggression) can be verbal and nonverbal.
  (a) *Verbal bullying.* This *includes abusive telephone calls, extorting money or material possessions, general intimidation or threats of violence, name-calling, racist remarks or teasing, sexually suggestive or abusive language, spiteful teasing or making cruel remarks,* and *spreading false and malicious rumors.*
  (b) *Nonverbal bullying.* Nonverbal bullying can be direct or indirect. Direct nonverbal bullying often accompanies verbal or physical bullying. Indirect bullying is manipulative and often sneaky.
    (i) *Direct nonverbal bullying.* This includes making *rude gestures* and *mean faces* and is often not regarded as bullying as it is seen as relatively harmless. In fact, it may be used to maintain control over someone, and to intimidate and remind them that they are likely to be singled out at any time.
    (ii) *Indirect nonverbal bullying.* This includes: purposely and often systematically *ignoring, excluding,* and *isolating*; sending (often anonymous) *poisonous notes*; and *making other students dislike someone.*
3 *Damage to property.* This can include *ripping clothes, damaging books, destroying property,* and *taking property (theft).*

Bullying can be any *one* of the above or a *combination* of them.
  Bullying is a *cowardly* act because those who do it know they will probably

get away with it, as the victimized person is unlikely to retaliate effectively, if at all, nor are they likely to tell anyone about it. Bullying often relies on those who are marginally involved, often referred to as bystanders, doing nothing to stop it or becoming actively involved in supporting it.

Most bullying is *indiscriminate* and is not caused by or the result of obvious differences between students: "Victims are not different—the group decides on the difference" (Robinson and Maines, 1997: 51).

Physical bullying often *causes visible hurt* in the form of cuts and bruises. *All bullying causes invisible hurt in the form of internal psychological (or emotional) damage*. When the hurt is invisible there is a sense that there is no proof that anything bad has happened.

Victims of bullying may feel *alone, angry, depressed, disempowered, hated, hurt, sad, scared, subhuman, trampled on, useless,* or *vengeful.*

At the extreme end of the spectrum of physical bullying is behavior that moves into the realm of criminality and involves the use of weapons. The *carrying and use of weapons* in schools is a growing phenomenon internationally and is a major cause of concern in American schools in particular. Killings in American high schools in the last few years have occurred across a wide age range. However, a major study of violence in American schools by Kingery, Coggeshall and Alford (1998), that was published before the Columbine and Santee shootings, suggested that the carrying and use of weapons in high schools mostly involved only grade 12 students and was often linked to students who took part in neighborhood violence.

The differences between these findings and the Columbine and Santee attacks should alert us to the fact that statistical results may bear little resemblance to what actually happens. However, research by the US Secret Service on high school shootings, while saying there is no single "typical" school shooter, did suggest that the majority of such students had previously drawn attention to themselves in some way and complained of being bullied (BBC News website, "Education," July 18, 2001 http://news.bbc.co.uk/1/hi/education/1445005.stm). The carrying and use of weapons can thus be a hidden part of a larger culture in which bullying may be endemic.

> While statistical results may give us indications of trends, they can never mitigate against actual bullying events, can never predict who will bully and how, and cannot determine who will be a victim and why.

What is not bullying

In the same way that it is important to be clear about what is bullying, it is also important to be clear about what is not bullying (Sullivan, 2000: 13).

Bullying is hidden, opportunist, mean-minded, and recurrent, and involves an imbalance of power. There are other types of behavior that are sometimes mistaken for bullying but which occur in the open and do not involve an imbalance of power. For example, two individuals (or groups) may get into an argument or fight (verbal or physical) as tempers flare up and things get out of hand. While such conflicts need to be dealt with in schools in a transparent and fair way, they do not constitute bullying. Rather, they are simple cases of conflict.

In some instances, however, individuals or a group set out to create a situation where it appears that those involved have equal responsibility, but this may be part of a plan to discredit a targeted person (or group). They may blame the victim for starting the fight and may even pose as victims themselves to deflect punishment and maintain their hidden status as bullies. It is important that schools are able to distinguish between conflict and bullying, and to see through the web of deceit that typically surrounds bullying.

What we know about bullying

The hidden nature of bullying

One of the major issues to come out of several major research projects (Adair et al., 2000: 211; Smith, 1999: 83, for instance) is that most victims of bullying are reluctant to tell anyone about it. Part of the bullying dynamic is the power imbalance between the bully and victim, which is a guarantee that the bullying is unlikely to be reported. Like other forms of abuse, bullying is hidden. The reasons people do not tell are very complicated:

- Victims are afraid and fear further retribution and harm.
- They think they will be singled out even more, and secretly hope that if they do not tell, the bully may like them after all.
- They do not believe teachers can or will do anything to make the bullying stop.
- They do not want to worry their parents.
- They are afraid that if their parents tell the school authorities, the bullying will get worse.
- Telling on peers is regarded as a very bad thing to do.
- They feel they are somehow to blame.

Research tends to indicate that around 30 percent of victims do not tell (for example, Rivers and Smith, 1994). Differences have been detected in who tells, who is told, and what sort of bullying generally gets reported.

For example, Peterson and Rigby found that "reluctance to tell teachers is particularly marked among male adolescents, for whom 'dobbing' (an Australian term for 'telling') is seriously un-Australian" (1999: 482). Smith and Shu (2000) suggest that students are reluctant to tell largely because adults (particularly teachers and administrators) talk about protecting those who tell, but this is actually difficult to guarantee. It is not surprising, therefore, that researchers from the University of Otago (Nairn and Smith, 2002: 18–19) reported that *teachers consistently underestimated the level of bullying that students identified as occurring.*

Adair et al. (2000) found that of the 81 percent of students in their survey who stated they had witnessed bullying, only 21 percent had reported it to an adult. Nearly half indicated they were just as likely to ignore bullying as to take action. A similar percentage did not believe it could be stopped and had no strategies for dealing with it.

The UK Department for Education and Employment anti-bullying package, *Bullying: Don't Suffer in Silence* (2000), underlines the need to bring the issue of bullying out into the open. This is part of the change that needs to occur in a safe school, so that bullying does not remain hidden and is thus divested of much of its power.

Does bullying decrease through the secondary school years?

There are certain identifiable patterns in the epidemiology of bullying in secondary schools:

1 There is a steady decrease in bullying and victimization between the ages of 12 and 18.
2 Bullying tends to be at its worst at the beginning of secondary school.
3 While bullying decreases as a whole as children get older, within this, direct physical aggression becomes less, and direct and indirect verbal and nonverbal methods increase.
4 But if bullying does continue into older adolescence, it can become more severe.
5 Adolescents show less empathy towards their victims than younger children.

Research generally indicates clearly that bullying reaches a peak in early adolescence and then tails off throughout secondary school (see Kingery, Coggeshall and Alford, 1998; US Department of Justice, 1998, for instance). The steady decrease in bullying and victimization is a result of several factors. At the beginning of secondary school new arrivals are prey to older more experienced children (many of whom have previously "run the gauntlet").

New students do not know the rules in the generally much bigger and less friendly environment of the high school and, as a result, are more vulnerable. Physically they tend to be smaller than everyone else and psychologically to be less confident. The peer group at this stage is in a state of flux and bullying may become more frequent as power relationships are established. As they become older, adolescents become more resistant both to being victimized and to tolerating the bullying of others. Those who bullied them earlier may turn their attention to younger students, and as classes above them leave school the cohort of potential bullies becomes smaller.

Peterson and Rigby's Australian research found that in a school where an anti-bullying program had been introduced, bullying was highest for boys and girls in year 9. While there was some decline in years 10 and 11, year 9 boys were particularly resistant to attempts to reduce bullying. Peterson and Rigby argue that the macho image of "toughing things out" makes it much harder for anti-bullying strategies to work:

> In a relatively extreme bullying environment, aspects of the school ethos may serve to encourage many mid-adolescent boys to engage in bullying as an admirably tough way of behaving or as a means of survival in a school jungle. Arguably, anti-bullying programs could be seen as a direct attack upon prevailing "masculine" values of this group. This may explain why, after 2 years of exposure to anti-bullying information, reported peer victimization among Year 9 students appears to have increased together with greater reluctance to seek help from others. (1999: 491)

There are certain settings in which the normal fall-off that occurs in bullying throughout adolescence is less likely to occur. For instance, if a school champions and privileges one group above all others, it is easier for a bullying culture to take root and less likely that bullying will decline in the way that it usually does throughout adolescence.

Elite groups are sometimes given license to be abusive because of the status they bring to the school. In Mark's school, he uses the Maori concept of the warrior as protector (and the idea of *kia kaha*[2]) to teach those with power to use it for positive rather than abusive leadership purposes (see also Chapter 11).

How widespread is bullying?

Research tells us that consistently from country to country and from school to school bullying is widespread.

In a recent study of 4,236 middle school students in Maryland (Haynie et al., 2001), 30.9 percent of the students reported being victimized three or more times over the past year. A further 7.4 percent reported having bullied others three or more times over that past year. More than half of those who reported bullying others also reported having been victims of bullying. Simanton, Burthwick and Hoover's (2000) study of bullying in small town America found that nearly one in three students experienced some degree of peer victimization and that one in five participated in bullying of peers.

In the UK, Smith and Shu (2000) carried out research targeting years 6 to 10 (10–to–14–year–olds) in 19 English schools, and found that, overall, 55.5 percent of pupils stated they had not been bullied, with 32.3 percent having been bullied once or twice, 4.3 percent two or three times a month, 3.8 percent once a week, and 4.1 percent several times a week. Sweeting and West's Scottish study (2001) found 44 percent of students reported some experience of being teased or called names and 17 percent reported having bullied. Fourteen percent said that they were teased weekly or more frequently, and 4 percent bullied others weekly or more frequently.

An Australian survey of more than 38,000 children (Peterson and Rigby, 1999) found that approximately one child in six is bullied at school at least once a week. *In a class of 30 this would mean five of the students would be victims of bullying and in a school with a population of 1,000, this would equate to 166 students.*

Adair et al. (2000) carried out a survey of 2,066 New Zealand secondary school students. When the researchers provided a list of behaviors that counted as bullying, 75 percent reported having been victims of bullying during the current year and 44 percent said that they had bullied others at some time during their schooling.

An examination of these results shows us that bullying does not conform to stereotypes. It is not restricted to poverty-stricken areas, ethnic or other minorities, dysfunctional children, or gang warfare. Instead, the events touch us strongly because they show us that bullying occurs widely and indiscriminately.

Can we tell where bullying will occur?

An examination of violence-prone locations in American schools comes up with two concepts that are useful in analyzing the socially and organizationally complex secondary school context:

1 undefined public spaces (locations that are dangerous or violence prone because no one takes responsibility for monitoring and/or maintaining them); and
2 territoriality (by which crime and violence can be reduced if people are appointed to safeguard spaces so that they become owned by the school) (Astor, Meyer and Pitner, 2001).

Undefined public spaces tend to be unowned by school community members (students and staff) and are therefore more prone to violence. They include hallways, cafeterias, playgrounds, bathrooms, and routes to and from school. Although members of the school community are aware of the violence-proneness, neither students nor teachers think it their personal or professional responsibility to monitor them. A solution is that, from a territoriality perspective, students and teachers (for school spaces), and the community (for coming to and from school) should reclaim these spaces (see also Astor, Meyer and Behre, 1999).

Smith and Shu (2000) found that in British secondary schools most bullying takes place in the school yard. It occurs to a lesser extent in classrooms and corridors. But again, it needs to be stated that bullying can and does occur anywhere. The research of Adair et al. (2000: 211) indicates that bullying most often goes on very close to the teacher.

Are there gender differences in bullying?

In general, research into gender differences in bullying examines the nature of inter-gender and in-gender bullying, and the issues of whether girls and boys react differently to bullying and being bullied. Particular attention is paid to girls' involvement in manipulation and what is called social aggression.

While it has consistently been found that girls fight less than boys, an Australian study by Peterson and Rigby (1999: 483) found that although girls were involved as victims in less than half the amount of physical bullying than boys, boys were as involved as girls in the various forms of emotional/ psychological bullying:

1 being called hurtful names (boys 14.4 percent, girls 11.2 percent);
2 being unpleasantly teased (boys 14.2 percent, girls 11 percent);
3 being hit or kicked (boys 13.7 percent, girls 6.7 percent);
4 being often threatened (boys 12.9 percent, girls 5.3 percent); and
5 being often left out (boys 9.7 percent, girls 9 percent).

An American study by Galen and Underwood (1997) found girls experienced social aggression (aimed at hurting by damaging relationships) as being as hurtful as physical aggression. They point out that because victims of social aggression are not recognized as such (because the damage is internalized and not immediately visible) then victims of this type of bullying often do not receive teacher, parental, or peer support or intervention, and are by implication doubly victimized.

Owens, Slee and Shute's study (2000) also found girls were affected by both physical and indirect aggression. Those who were easy targets:

1 were new;
2 had few friends; or
3 were unassertive.

The first two characteristics mean that there is not a network or group of friends to provide support and protection, and the third means that the person in question does not have the social skills to help defuse or sidetrack initial bullying forays.

In the study by Adair et al. (2000), victims of bullying reported that boys were involved in 76 percent of incidents and girls in 45 percent. Going by these percentages, it appears that boys bully significantly more than girls. But it may be the case that the nature of much of girls' bullying is more subtle and better hidden or that the type of psychological bullying girls often take part in is not recognized as bullying. Lloyd (1994) talks of girls as "hidden bullies". She argues that while boys use physical means, girls rely on a range of psychological weapons, such as persistent teasing, isolation from the group, and spreading malicious rumours. Besag suggests that girls bully for reassurance and affiliation, "a feeling of belonging and shared intimacy expressed in exchanging confidences and gossip" (1989: 40); and she describes boys' bullying as displays of power and dominance.

Shakeshaft et al. (1995) identified three gender types particularly at risk of being bullied: girls seen by their peers as exceptionally attractive; girls regarded by their peers as unattractive; and males whose behavior style does not fit gender-based expectations, that is, students who are or appear to be gay. It was observed in a high school in the North Island of New Zealand, for example, that every year the names of what were described as the four ugliest girls were written on a toilet door, and updated every year. In another school, the students were aware that every Tuesday night was "gay-bashing night."

How can you tell if someone is being bullied?

For parents
The teenage years are often very turbulent and adolescents can become upset for all kinds of reasons. If young people are in distress, it is sometimes hard to know whether this is "normal" or because they are having difficulty with issues such as bullying. The following are some of the symptoms that may be exhibited if they are being bullied:

1 They have physical injuries.
2 Some of their clothes are missing or ripped.
3 They steal money (to give to their tormentors or to replace what has been stolen from them).
4 Their belongings disappear.

5 They have extreme mood changes.
6 Their schoolwork declines.
7 They are reluctant to go to school.
8 They seem to have no friends.
9 They come home very early from "dates" and meetings with friends.
10 They are evasive and noncommunicative.

For teachers

Teachers also need to be vigilant about the presence of bullying, especially as it is often hidden. The following characteristics may be indicators that bullying is occurring:

1 Members of a class titter, snigger, or nudge each other when a particular student comes in, answers a question, or draws any attention to him or herself.
2 A student appears despondent, listless, or unhappy.
3 A student is mostly alone, and/or is actively left out of activities.
4 A student is never chosen for joint activities.
5 A student who is working well and getting good grades seems to work less well and gets worse grades.
6 A student is frequently absent.

Can you tell who will be victimized?

The fact is that *anyone* can be victimized. Once a bullying culture is operating, those who are somehow different or stand out in some way are likely to be singled out, but the random and indiscriminate nature of bullying means that no one is immune. Having said that, many studies rightly address bullying that does target certain individuals, as a way of addressing questions of inequality, prejudice, and stereotyping within society.

It is significant that the young man in the story with which we opened this chapter is gay, and says that this was why he was bullied. We felt it was important to present his story without this information first of all, because the fundamental point of what he told us is that he was bullied, and that he was not supported by peers or teachers. To say that he is gay and that is why he was bullied is to find a reason within him for the fact that he was bullied, when the truth is that the reason lies outside him in the bullies and the bullying culture of which they were a part. That is one of the key themes of this book—shifting the focus from the victim to the bullying behavior.

Racist bullying

Minority groups are often picked on because they look different, they have different values, and their languages, customs, and food are unfamiliar. "Racist bullying is where racism and bullying meet. It is an abuse of power involving physical or psychological bullying, or both, to demean or cause harm. The most common form of racist bullying is racist name-calling, which is widely experienced by ethnic minority children" (Sullivan, 2000: 12). Racist bullying is a particular problem because of the injustices involved and the wanton cruelty of its jibes and actions.

Bullying of special needs students

These children stand out in a classroom and school as a result of physical or psychological differences (such as Asperger's, autism, blindness, or deafness). These students may not be able to defend themselves or may act in ways that make them vulnerable to the predations of an intolerant peer group. Such children are often singled out and intentionally humiliated and ridiculed (see Whitney, Smith and Thompson, 1994).

Sexual bullying

Sexual bullying can take various forms. It most commonly involves coercion and unwanted, suggestive, and lewd attention paid by boys to girls; and includes obscene or suggestive demands, gestures, remarks, or teasing. Girls in early adolescence sometimes humiliate their smaller male peers through sexual bullying; and adolescent girls also denigrate particularly pretty girls whom they see as threats, or can become vicious with a girl whom they feel has "stolen" a boy from them.

Homophobic bullying

This occurs when individuals are singled out and bullied because of their actual or perceived sexual orientation (gay, lesbian, or bisexual) (see Rivers, 1995; 1996; Warwick, Aggleton and Douglas, 2001). Some students label other more vulnerable students whom they know to be heterosexual as gay so as to put their sexuality in question and to humiliate them.

Who else?

Many reasons are given for why adolescents get bullied: there is certainly no shortage of excuses for the behavior. For example, poverty (Fonzi et al., 1999), and physical unattractiveness and being overweight (Sweeting and West, 2001: 225) are cited frequently. Some researchers have found that students who do poorly academically are likely to be targeted (Berthold and Hoover, 1999). More importantly, Sharp suggests that poor academic achievement can in fact be a result of bullying, that is, that students with impaired concentration who are anxious about their next encounter with the bullies are "unlikely to achieve their full potential academically or socially" (1995: 86).

Underlying all these descriptions of who gets bullied and why they are sin-gled out, there is one overriding fact, which is that ultimately anyone is a vic-tim. A study carried out in Australia found that "Children who have little or no support from others are clearly more vulnerable to attack from those who may wish to bully them" (Peterson and Rigby, 1999: 65). The very dynamics of the bullying culture mean that anyone singled out, however momentarily, is immediately in more danger, and as their separation from the peer group continues, so does their vulnerability.

The bullying triangle: bullies, victims, and bystanders

Very often people think of bullying being a one-to-one relationship, but in fact there are three main roles: bullies, victims, and bystanders.

The bullies

How to deal with bullying is a major concern of this book, and it is helpful to have a good idea of who the bullies are and where they are coming from. But as with our approach to other issues, we feel it is important not to create hard and fast rules; instead, it is better to understand the *process of bullying*.

The most important characteristic of bullies is that they know how to use power. We would argue that people who are in leadership positions often have a similar sort of power: the central issue is how the power is used.

Taking into account the research, we would suggest that there are three types of bullies:

1 the clever bully;
2 the not-so-clever bully; and
3 the bully victim.

The *clever bully* often masks his or her bullying behavior, and when teachers are told that this person is a bully, they say, "Are you sure you're not mistaken?" Clever bullies may be popular, do well academically and socially, and have the ability to organize people around them to do their bidding. Often they are egotistical and confident. The main characteristic that makes them bullies is that they fail to put themselves in the place of those they victimize: they do not have empathy or they just do not care how the other person feels. They take a position of arrogance or ignorance. This type of person may have a lot of power with teachers as well as other students and often has much more appeal than those he or she chooses to victimize. The hardest part of dealing with clever bullies is being able to identify them.

These bullies are prime candidates to be prosocial leaders in a school (see Chapter 12, "Harnessing Student Leadership").

The *not-so-clever bully* may not be an entirely appropriate term for this sort of bully. They tend to attract others because of their antisocial and at-risk behavior, and at the same time to intimidate and frighten their peers. Their cleverness may have been distorted by their life experiences so that they operate in socially dysfunctional ways. They might consider those who support them as friends, but while peers may feel obliged to go along with their behavior, they do not usually like them as people. Not-so-clever bullies are often mean-minded and have a negative view of the world. They are frequently failures at school and direct their anger at people they see as weak. Sometimes these bullies are cruel and possibly irretrievable, but their anger and bullying behavior is often a displacement of their own lack of self-esteem and self-confidence. Mostly they are lost souls who do not know how to feel comfortable in the world. Their experience has been of failure, rejection, and lack of ability to function well. Although their behavior is negative and hurtful, this is something they do well—they get results. The main result is that they are given a role and status in the peer group through their bullying behavior.

Unlike clever bullies who are more easily able to mature and change as they progress through the secondary school, this type of bully usually has limited resources, does not progress, loses popularity, gets left behind, and tends to drop out.

Our argument here is that with a great deal of support, for example, through peer mentoring, leadership programs, and anti-bullying strategies (see Part IV), the not-so-clever bullies can learn that they have leadership skills and that they can use their power in a more positive way. The truth is that often such bullies are not "not-so-clever;" it is just that they have not been supported to achieve their potential. In making this statement, we are not being woolly and unrealistic: our experience has been that, when given proper guidance, such students can become very positive forces in a school.

We would also argue (and this is based on speculation and observation rather than research) that, untended, these students often drop out and probably contribute through their absence to the reduction in bullying in the later years of secondary school. It is better to get to them earlier rather than later: they are likely to contribute to the crime statistics in the wider community if they are not "picked up" while they are at school.

The *bully victim* is a bully in some situations and a victim in others. They victimize those younger or smaller than them and they are victimized by their peers or those older than them. They are sometimes bullies at school and victims at home. The research shows that a lot of bullies fall into this category.

Bully victims are the hardest type of bully to deal with because they exhibit behavior that is aggressive and unacceptable as bullies, but they are also vulnerable and easy to undermine as victims. Because they tend to bully mercilessly, it is often difficult to empathize with them when they themselves are bullied. Teachers and peers find it hard to treat them fairly as they see them inciting victimization on the one hand, and victimizing others as well.

In a recent study, students identified as bullies and victims were described as "particularly high risk," having higher rates of problem behavior and depressive symptoms, and lower self-control, social competence, and poorer school functioning (Haynie et al., 2001: 44). They were at greater risk of deviant peer group involvement, less able to form positive peer friendships, and had a greater chance of antisocial adult behavior.

In medicine, when a doctor is dealing with one illness, then the symptoms facilitate an accurate diagnosis. When there are two illnesses occurring at the same time, then the symptoms that present may be confusing and contra-dictory, and it can be difficult to see what is in fact going on. It is similarly very difficult for school staff to make correct diagnoses and to "treat" bully victims. While it is not easy to deal with bully victims, it is important that one set of behaviors (that is, bullying) is not used to decide how another set of behaviors (that is, victimization) is treated. In the case of bully victims, both the bullying and the victimization need to be addressed and stopped.

When students have been bullied and feel angry about it, they sometimes bully others. In doing so, they feel they are reclaiming their power and gain-ing a sense of closure to their experience of bullying. They are not chronic bullies, but do what appears normal in this microculture. When bullying is passed on from cohort to cohort in this way, it is dysfunctional and the cul-ture needs to be changed.

In early adolescence, teenagers are usually dependent on peer approval and acceptance to the exclusion of all else. As they progress through adolescence their sense of individuality usually strengthens. What happens to many bullies is that their social development becomes stuck at the point where they win power and prestige through bullying, and they tend not to progress toward individuation and empathy as adolescents usually do. They get left behind.

As Haynie et al. state, "In the short term, bullying might allow children to achieve their immediate goals without learning socially acceptable ways to negotiate with others, resulting in persistent maladaptive social patterns" (2001: 31). In other words, if bullying is the primary mechanism whereby individuals maintain status and dominance, and nothing is done to change this dynamic, then a bullying culture is likely to take hold.

The victims

Anyone anywhere who shows vulnerability and does not have the support of a group can become a victim of bullying. These roles are not fixed: a confident person in one environment can be very vulnerable in another. This is why children who are in transition from one school to another (as at the start of secondary school) are always at greater risk.

When someone is a victim, they are often on the periphery of the social group. They may also be different in some way from the other children, or they may be rejected because of provocative behavior. They may be at the bottom of the pecking order and be unable to change their status simply because the culture dictates that someone has to occupy this space.

Victims of bullying are in a very poor situation academically, socially, and emotionally. They tend to think that they are responsible for their bullying because they are inadequate, and this is made worse because they are unable to deal with the bullying. Through the ongoing abuse, they lose their sense of worth and frequently experience depression. If they are subjected to ongoing bullying, the depression can become worse, and the extremes of victimization and low self-esteem are self-harm and suicide.

When children are bullied, they are on the lookout all the time, waiting for the next attack, trying to avoid it, and feeling helpless and hopeless. In order to avoid it, they may start staying away from school. Because of the stress and fear, doing academic work seems unimportant and loses its meaning, and they begin falling behind. The further they fall behind, the more difficult it is to catch up. There is a sense that they are failures anyway, and their academic work simply reflects this.

In the teenage years, social development is extremely important because adolescents find out who they are, how they express themselves, and what their values are. They learn to build relationships with friends and potential sexual partners, and to experiment with and make judgments about the boundaries of behavior. Victims of bullying are shut out from many of these experiences: it is as if they have had a door slammed in their faces, and they retreat, their development atrophying and withering. Being a chronic victim means that they take on all the attributes of a victim. As such, they may swing in the other direction and take chances that are more risky than is normal in adolescence. This comes from a sense of hopelessness.

There are usually three types of victims identified in the literature:

1 the passive victim;
2 the provocative victim; and
3 the bully victim (see above).

The *passive victim* has few defenses, is an easy target, and takes up a position at the bottom of the pecking order. He or she may try to please the bully, who typically plays him or her along and then does something nasty.

The *provocative victim* is different from the bully victim. Provocative victims behave in ways that are annoying, immature, or inappropriate. In some cases, they do not mean to provoke but have just not figured out how to behave; in others, they deliberately set out to irritate those around them. By drawing attention to themselves, they at least get some attention: they may feel negative attention is better than no attention at all.

The behavior they exhibit causes their peers to react adversely toward them. They are regarded as irritating, stupid, or silly. Some choose to ignore or avoid them, and they are less likely than anyone else to be supported when they are bullied: no one is there to rescue them or be on their side. It is also the case that their peers may go out of their way to provoke them to react in an angry or irrational way as a means of ridiculing them and putting them down. If challenged by a teacher, the bullies in this case can always claim that the victim is the perpetrator, or at least is partially to blame. It is very easy to provoke a reaction in these victims: it is a little like waving a red flag in front of a bull.

The aggravating behavior exhibited by provocative victims can also cause teachers to react toward them with impatience and annoyance. Teachers are likely to dismiss parental complaints as false, and the students in the back row can chuckle to themselves. The victim therefore has no recourse for support. It is very important that teachers understand this complex dynamic and keep a watch out for provocative victims. Counseling, mentoring, and being taught assertive rather than provocative responses can help provocative victims to change their behavior. At the same time peers can be taught to stop their normal derisory and dismissive responses, and to allow the provocative victim to become part of the group.

The bystanders

In our construction of bullying, bystanders are more important in the end solution than either the bully or the victim (see Chapter 8 for more detail). Without the positive participation of the bystanders, there is no solution to bullying; and at the same time, bullying can only go on if the bystanders let it.

The bystanders typically take on various roles in the bullying dynamic:

1 the sidekicks;
2 the reinforcers;
3 the outsiders; and
4 the defenders.

The sidekicks are closest to the bully and are sometimes called lieutenants or henchmen; the reinforcers are next in line and act in ways that also support the bullying. The outsiders try not to draw attention to themselves, but in their apparent neutrality they appear to condone the bullying and to be immune to it themselves. The defenders are those who are furthest from the bully and may have the courage to step out of the bystander role and become active in their support of the victims and condemnation of the bully.

Bystanders tend to depersonalize and dehumanize the victim, and ignore how they feel about what they see. In the first three of these roles they abdicate involvement and responsibility. They are quite clearly susceptible to being bullied as well, and it is possible that they hang back because they are afraid they could be next in line as victims.

Adolescent groups try to establish hierarchies. No matter what the group, there is a group-forming process, with tensions, energies, and power relationships. In this process there is the potential for those wishing to demonstrate their power to do so at the expense of those with less power. The least powerful may be deserted by those around them: if they do not have enough prosocial friendship-making skills, then they are likely to be bullied.

The defenders have to do very little to make a difference. They may not want to be burdened with being the victim's friend, but if they actively show their rejection of the bullying behavior it is likely to stop. Bullies are only allowed to be bullies because the bystanders appear to support them. To change the bullying dynamic, all the bystanders have to do is to demonstrate that they support the victim.

The effects of bullying

All the research on the effects of bullying shows how damaging and destructive it is.

Victims of bullying tend to have lower levels of self-esteem, can be depressed, insecure, anxious, oversensitive, cautious, and quiet (Berthold and Hoover, 1999; Craig, 1998; Olweus, 1995; Rigby and Slee, 1991a; 1991b). They are usually more withdrawn, worried, and fearful of new situations (Byrne, 1994), showing extreme introversion (Slee and Rigby, 1993).

They are less happy at school, more lonely, and have fewer good friends (Boulton and Underwood, 1992; Slee, 1995; Slee and Rigby, 1993). They are therefore also more likely to drop out of school (Olweus, 1993b).

Victims, particularly girls, are very badly affected by being avoided socially or being negatively evaluated by their peers (Slee, 1995).

Kumpulainen et al. (1998) linked bullying with psychosomatic symptoms, depression, and psychiatric referral. Kaltiala-Heino et al. (1999) and Rigby and Slee (1999) found that those involved in bullying showed the highest risk for suicide ideation, that is, thinking about suicide, and suicide. In relation to school bullying, Smith and Shu (2000) state that in part because of bullying several young people in England commit suicide every year.

When they carried out research in an Australian high school over a two-year period, Peterson and Rigby (1999: 483) found there were negative after-effects to being bullied:

1 31 percent of boys and 46 percent of girls felt worse about themselves;
2 40 percent of boys and 60 percent of girls reported feeling angry or miserable; and
3 14 percent of boys and 12 percent of girls reported staying away from school as a result.

Rigby (2000) argues that there is a causal relationship between peer victimization and poor mental health, and that students who have been bullied report a loss of self-esteem afterward. Children who are victimized and isolated often have no effective way of dealing with the problem of bullying. Rigby's research found adolescents who reported high levels of victimization in their first two years of high school also reported relatively low levels of personal well-being three years later.

Olweus's (1993b) study found that victim behaviors can continue into adulthood, with young adults exhibiting more symptoms of depression and lower self-esteem. There is plenty of evidence everywhere we turn that bullying has repercussions for many people throughout their lives.

In a seminar on the No Blame Approach,[3] Barbara Maines described two scenarios and asked the participants (teachers and educationalists) which event would have a worse effect on the victim: in the first, a girl was made fun of by her peers and kept out of the group; in the second, a girl was made to kneel and drink from a can of Coke that one of her peers had spat into. Everyone at the seminar thought the Coke can incident was easily worse, but in fact the effect on the first of these students was far more devastating and damaging. She lacked friends or support and was kept on the outside of the group, whereas the second girl had support but was picked on in this instance.

Most attention that is paid to the effects of bullying looks at how it affects the victims, but there are also indications that it may adversely affect the bullies and bystanders as well. Bullying in adolescence stunts growth towards individuation and is like a disease that distorts the development of the self and the formation of healthy relationships. When it emerges in the chaos of the first few months of secondary school, it occupies a void in the power base or takes a foothold while the dominant players jockey for position. If it is not eradicated at this point, a bullying culture develops in which the destructiveness takes hold and dominates the entire social culture of the school. It is crucial, therefore, that we identify it for what it is and learn how to deal with it.

The ripple effect of bullying

Bullying occurs in a social context. It affects the person or persons being bullied most of all, but it affects others as well. It is like a stone that is thrown into the middle of a pool: the ripples that come from the point of impact spread outwards toward the edges of the pool (see Figure 1.2 and Sullivan, 2000: 32–3). More specifically, this occurs as follows.

Level 1

This is where the act of bullying occurs and is most intense. The bullied person is subjected to humiliation and feels the brunt of the bullying not only when it occurs but beyond.

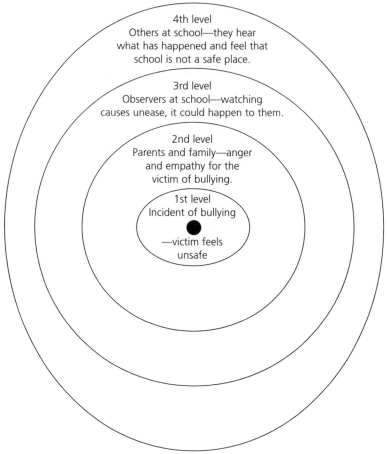

5th level
The wider community—if students are not safe in school, why should they be safe in the wider community? The school is a microcosm of the community.

4th level
Others at school—they hear what has happened and feel that school is not a safe place.

3rd level
Observers at school—watching causes unease, it could happen to them.

2nd level
Parents and family—anger and empathy for the victim of bullying.

1st level
Incident of bullying

—victim feels unsafe

Although bullying most affects those being victimized, there are second, third, fourth and fifth level effects. Bullying can be said to have a ripple effect.

Figure 1.2 *The ripple effect of bullying*
Source: Sullivan (2000: 32)

Level 2

Parents and families are the secondary victims of bullying. They will have a mixture of feelings. Very often they feel anger that their child has been bullied and want to know why it was not handled earlier. They may also want revenge, to make sure that the bully suffers as their child did ("An eye for an eye ..."). On the other hand, they may be unable to support their child, be loath to contact the school, or be unsure what to do.

When parents approach the school, it is important that they are listened to, kept informed, and involved in the solution. The fact that the bullying occurred at school when the school was *in loco parentis* means that the school must take responsibility for what happened.

Level 3

The bystanders will have played a role in the act of bullying and will have various feelings about what occurred. Some will have aided by giving support. Others will have sat on the fence, neither supporting nor defending, feeling unclear or uncomfortable ("she deserved it," "she didn't deserve it," "I'd better shut up or they'll turn on me"). There will be some who will get involved (and some who would like to but are not brave enough). Those who are intimidated are tertiary victims of bullying. Their world is seriously threatened and they may behave fearfully as a result.

What a school does in response to the bullying is a symbolic statement for this group. If they feel that the school cares enough to act effectively and is truly aware of how bullying works (including knowing the precarious positions of individuals in this group), then they may feel able to show disapproval of the bullying (or at least to tell an adult—parent or teacher).

Level 4

The school's response to bullying sends a message to others in the school. If the school handles it well, it gives a clear message that bullying will not be supported or allowed to hide in the school; if it handles it poorly, it sends a message to bullies that they can continue to bully with impunity and to everyone else that they may not be safe. If the school does not act, then it is a direct (albeit not obvious) contributor to the culture of bullying.

Level 5

There are several things that can happen in relation to the community. If a school does not safeguard its vulnerable students, it gives those who bully a free hand to bully whom they please on the way to or from school, or in chance (or planned) meetings at the shopping mall, the youth club, the cinema, or anywhere in the community. If a school handles bullying and has told its students to report anything that occurs outside school (that could then be investigated as a youth or criminal offence), then the school contributes in a significant way not only to the well-being of its students, but also in its responsibility towards the wider community.

The downward spiral

The downward spiral (see Figure 1.3) is a useful model for understanding how bullying works and to illustrate the effects it may have in the short, middle, and long term. The model underlines that there are three parties to bullying: the victim, the bully, and the bystanders. Figure 1.3 is self-explanatory and shows that bullying is a dynamic and organic process. It goes through five stages (which can be more salient or less, depending on the circumstances):

1 watching and waiting;
2 testing the waters;
3 something happens;
4 the bullying escalates; and
5 there are various impacts, the worst of which can end in tragedy.

Those who bully sometimes get a sense that their power is greater than it is and, as Olweus has shown (1993b), they are much more likely to end up committing criminal offences. They can draw others into their web of menace and deceit, and can cause irreparable damage. In the end, if the bullying is not halted, like their victims, they end up in a place that is very negative and harmful to them.

A common theme that haunts many people is that of someone attacked in the street when bystanders turn away because they do not want to get involved. In an ongoing bullying scenario, if the bystander is passive and does nothing, then the downward spiral is likely to come to its expected and tragic conclusion. We argue in this book that it is the role of the bystanders, individually, collectively, or with reference to the adults in the school (and at home), to find a way to stop the bullying from having a life in the school. In doing this, bystanders not only support the victim (and sometimes the bully), they also contribute to their own safety and that of their schoolmates. What is more, the sooner in the downward spiral process the bullying is stopped, the better.

If bullying is treated like an illness or an injury, then the person who has been targeted could be reframed as traumatized. If the bullying is physical, there will be external (and visible) injuries, but the bullying will also have caused internal (and hidden) psychological and emotional damage that will need attention. The extent of the trauma will depend on a number of factors, including the length of time the bullying has been going on, the nature of the bullying, and the personal qualities of the individual (some individuals are more resilient than others). The use of a medical model underlines

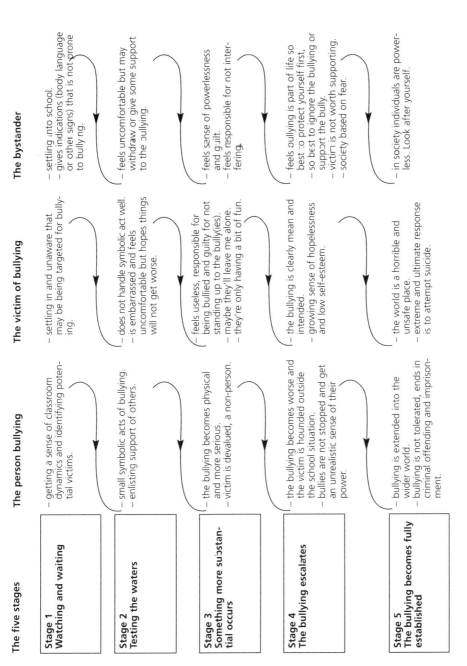

The five stages

The person bullying

The victim of bullying

The bystander

Stage 1
Watching and waiting
– getting a sense of classroom dynamics and identifying potential victims.

– settling in and unaware that may be being targeted for bullying.

– settling into school.
– gives indications (body language or other signs) that is not prone to bullying.

Stage 2
Testing the waters
– small symbolic acts of bullying.
– enlisting support of others.

– does not handle symbolic act well.
– is embarrassed and feels uncomfortable but hopes things will not get worse.

– feels uncomfortable but may withdraw or give some support to the bullying.

Stage 3
Something more substantial occurs
– the bullying becomes physical and more serious.
– victim is devalued, a non-person.

– feels useless, responsible for being bullied and guilty for not standing up to the bully(ies).
– maybe they'll leave me alone.
– they're only having a bit of fun.

– feels sense of powerlessness and guilt.
– feels responsible for not interfering.

Stage 4
The bullying escalates
– the bullying becomes worse and the victim is hounded outside the school situation.
– bullies are not stopped and get an unrealistic sense of their power.

– the bullying is clearly mean and intended.
– growing sense of hopelessness and low self-esteem.

– feels bullying is part of life so best to protect yourself first,
– so best to ignore the bullying or support the bully.
– victim is not worth supporting.
– society based on fear.

Stage 5
The bullying becomes fully established
– bullying is extended into the wider world.
– bullying is not tolerated, ends in criminal offending and imprisonment.

– the world is a horrible and unsafe place.
– extreme and ultimate response is to attempt suicide.

– in society individuals are powerless. Look after yourself.

Figure 1.3 *The downward spirals of bullying*
Source: Sullivan (2000: 38)

the fact that once the bullying has stopped, its effects still have to be attended to.

Notes

1 Much of the information in this section is from Sullivan (2000).
2 *Kia kaha* is Maori for "stand strong," and exemplifies the warrior as protector rather than aggressor. It is also the name of the New Zealand Police's anti-bullying program.
3 This approach was developed by George Robinson and Barbara Maines (see Chapter 15). The seminar referred to was delivered on February 3, 2003, in Wellington, New Zealand.

2

Adolescence: "It Was the Best of Times; It Was the Worst of Times"

Never at any stage of human development is change so rapid, extreme, and unpredictable as it is in adolescence.

During these turbulent years, individuals go through a process that varies from person to person, but inevitably causes rapid physical development, changes of mood, crises of identity, skirmishes into peripheral and extreme areas of human behavior, and a progression in various forms and at differing speeds of leaving the bounded and secure world of childhood and the family and entering the unbounded and insecure world of adolescence and adulthood.

The onset of adolescence largely coincides with students' shift into secondary school.[1] Transitions are always problematic, and in most cases children face the two major transitions of entering puberty and starting a new school at the same time. Many also suddenly have a new peer group and a different school system. (See Figure 2.1.) After being the oldest students in their schools, they suddenly find themselves the youngest, smallest, and least powerful in this new setting.

A case study: six set off on an adventure

We begin this chapter with a snapshot of six students on their first day at high school, setting off on an adventure that will take them out of childhood and into adulthood. We zoom in on them right at the start, not because they are unusual or different from their peers, but because they are fairly typical of the diversity that teenagers display in early puberty.

Simon is a physically immature small boy, an only child of a single mother, who is awkward with his peers but gets on well with his mother's friends.

Saul is tall and heavily built. He is socially inept, poor at making and maintaining friends, often depressed, angry or stoned, and usually isolated.

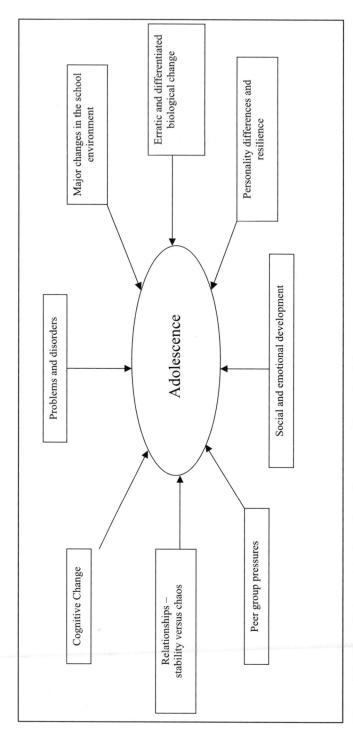

Figure 2.1 *Tumultuous yet invigorating: the passage through adolescence*

Jon is bigger than average, socially competent, and athletically and academically proficient.

Celeste is physically mature, precocious, disinterested in school, unambitious, and "hangs out" with older boys. She has a sharp wit and is clearly intelligent, a fact that is shown in her test scores but not in her schoolwork.

Sylvia tries hard to please, wears ill-fitting and unfashionable clothes, has bad posture, does not make eye contact with people, and has a poor sense of boundaries. She is quite slight for her age and physically immature.

Marianna is well dressed, effervescent, surrounded by friends, good at sports and school, and confident.

The students have been told to be at school at 9 A.M. on the first day and to gather in the assembly hall. As they start to converge on the school, a few walk with their mothers. One of these is Simon. Oblivious to the looks of the other children who find his behavior "uncool," Simon says farewell to his mother and makes his way alone into the hall. He goes up to a teacher and says "Hi" in an overly friendly way and asks where he should sit. The teacher tells him to "sit anywhere over there" and he goes and sits in the front row.

Meanwhile, Marianna is seen speaking in an animated fashion with a group of four other girls. They have clearly arranged to meet under a tree outside the hall. They are discussing what they are wearing and taking a great deal of interest in the students around them. Marianna looks at her watch and says it is time to go in. Sylvia is on the outskirts of the group, standing nearby. They ignore her and make their way to the hall. Sylvia is very nervous and unsure what to do, and follows them. When they sit in the second row, she tries to sit with them but they wriggle along so there is no room for her. Marianna turns around looking for other friends and waving to them.

Celeste has been dropped at the school gates by an older boy in a fast car. Heavily made up, she saunters across the forecourt and two girls run over and join her. They are all physically mature, dressed in black, and have no schoolbags. They are told to go into the hall and are directed to the row where Sylvia is sitting on her own. Celeste sits next to her, and Sylvia smiles shyly at her, but is virtually ignored. Celeste laughs for no apparent reason and nudges the girl on the other side.

Jon arrives at the school and a group slowly forms around him. This has not been prearranged and the conversation is monosyllabic. Jon pulls a hackysack[2] out of his bag and they start playing. They move into the hall and sit near the back when one of the senior teachers announces that it is time to get under way.

When the teacher in charge of the first-years starts talking, she is interrupted by Saul who accidentally bangs the door as he comes in late. He is directed to sit in the front row next to Simon. When he sits down he looks as if he is standing because he is so big. Whereas Simon is neat and tidy, Saul looks scruffy and dishevelled.

As the class lists are read out, five of these students end up together and know no one else in the class. Saul has to remain behind as he has not been registered, but once this is sorted out he is put into the same class as the others.

They arrive at their form classroom. Celeste sits half-turned towards the door, and appears to look wistfully at the exit sign. Marianna and Simon both volunteer to help the teacher, Ms Brown, hand out books. Jon follows instructions and asks a question for clarification. Saul ambles in late, sits once again next to Simon and "borrows" some paper and a pen from him. Simon acquiesces and is happy to please a potential friend. When the teacher is explaining the timetable, Sylvia puts up her hand and asks, "Is it true we have to have our bags inspected at high school?"

It is a month later. Marianna has quickly established a group of supportive friends, and is losing contact with her other friends from primary school. Although Sylvia has tried to make friends with this group, she has not been accepted. Simon and Saul appear to be friends, but this is a relationship of convenience for Saul. Simon's mother is concerned about the friendship and has already banned Saul from her house because she suspects him of stealing money and does not like the fact that he smokes. Jon has not found any natural friends in the class and has adopted a disinterested onlooker's approach to peer relations. At the same time, he has joined several sports teams and appears self-confident and self-contained. Celeste has befriended a girl in the class, but is already causing concern because she has missed several days of school. She does not pay any attention to the males in the class because she sees them as "little boys."

We are now going to look ahead three years. Celeste was expelled from school halfway through her second year for her extreme abusive behavior toward students and teachers, and for nonattendance. She goes to live with a 19-year-old gang member. She has begun to smoke marijuana regularly, is often drunk, and has started to use hard drugs. To support this habit, her boyfriend arranges for her to "dance" at the local strip joint. She is now living in an abusive relationship with another gang member and working part-time in a fast-food restaurant, still supporting a drug habit. She has scars up her arm from cutting herself, and has made one serious suicide attempt that hospitalized her.

Simon is still at school. He grew 4 inches in his second year, and since his growth spurt has become more aggressive. He is indiscriminate in his aggression and has been in a number of physical fights in which he has come off worst. He remains isolated, is easily provoked, and is unsure where he fits in. He is confused about his sexuality and is wounded by homophobic taunts, while he displays homophobic behavior himself. He is unable to establish friendships with peers, and is no longer friends with Saul. Simon has been unsuccessfully doing an anger management course run by the school psychologist because his mother complained about his increasingly aggressive behavior at home. Academically, he is performing very poorly and is floundering.

Halfway through the first year, Saul was sent to a boarding school in another city when his uncle inherited money and decided to look after him. Teachers at his first school found him lazy and unresponsive, always without the correct materials and frequently stoned. At boarding school, Saul is excelling. The routines and sports programs suit his temperament, and the special interest in him of his math teacher has brought out abilities that no one had ever identified before. He wants to be a professional athlete and is working hard academically in the hope of gaining a university sports scholarship. He has stopped smoking dope.

Jon continues to find school easy and now has a group of friends. He has been going out with one of Marianna's friends for three months. Apart from one occasion during a weekend stay at a beach when he succumbed to peer pressure, he does not regularly drink alcohol and he does not use drugs. He is heavily involved in a range of sporting and extracurricular activities.

Marianna is still attractive and popular, with many friends of both sexes but no boyfriend. She is very busy with her life. She cares very deeply about how she looks, and works on Saturdays in a beauty salon so she can buy nice clothes. She does well at school and plays basketball and field hockey.

Sylvia has found school difficult and has made few friends. She has always believed she is ugly and overweight and by her second year was clearly suffering from anorexia. In her first two years at secondary school, she latched onto new students but was quickly dropped once they were socialized by the peer group. She was often bullied and was the victim of practical jokes. In her third year, she has sought sanctuary in the school library where she has been made a book monitor. This new responsibility appears to be having a positive influence on her, with the school librarian introducing her to new ideas and interests. The librarian goes with Sylvia to see a doctor about her eating disorder. Sylvia is referred to the local eating disorders clinic. During subsequent counseling sessions, Sylvia discloses early sexual abuse within her family. By the end of the year, her anorexia is abating and she is beginning to make friends. This new-found confidence is being reflected in academic improvement.

Changes in adolescence: flying through turbulence with no safety belt

Biological changes

During adolescence children's bodies are undergoing tremendous change. Puberty occurs largely in early adolescence (although it can start between 11 and 16 years of age), and usually about two years after the onset of puberty, young people experience massive growth spurts, sometimes gaining 5 inches in height over one year. At the same time, they are undergoing rapid sexual development, which is one of the most visible signs of adolescence, that is accompanied by hormonal activity which is apparent in emotional change. During puberty, boys are sexually transformed into young men, girls into young women.

Puberty usually starts two years earlier for girls than for boys and, in early adolescence, girls tend to be larger and more mature than boys their own age, which further complicates peer relations and school learning. By around 14, however, boys have usually caught up and become taller and heavier than girls of the same age.

As 13-year-olds, our group of six is typical of the range of physical development that occurs in early adolescence. At the extremes are Saul, who is tall and heavily built, and Celeste, who has the body of woman; and Simon, who is small and underdeveloped, and Sylvia, who seems physically like a pre-pubescent girl.

The physical identities of these students have a great impact on their perceptions of themselves within their peer groups. At one extreme, Celeste is aware that she is more sexually mature than her peers. This, coupled with the fact that she lives in a home that provides little guidance or social support, means that she enters into sexual relationships for which she is not emotionally equipped. Although she seems confident, even arrogant, the truth is that she gets into difficult situations and is actually unsure of herself. Not only do adolescents have no control over their physical development, there is no reference point against which they can check their normality because of the huge variation in the onset, pace, and range of biological change. Body image is a major issue, but it is not a map they can safely read; instead, it is confusing, and has no key and no compass points.

An outcome of the process of adolescence is that everyone apart from the most resilient will feel abnormal at some point, in relation to how they were before, how they are now, how they thought they would be, how their contemporaries look, the general physical trends of those dominant in the peer group, and whether they have supportive friends. As recounted in Santrock (2001: 297–305), if a child's development is out of synchronization with their social context this can cause sexual, psychological, and social problems. Adolescents are therefore at one of the most vulnerable stages of their lives, that is also unpredictable in duration and character. Clearly for children who have other disorders, such as autism spectrum disorders, conduct disorders, sexuality confusion, ADHD[3] and personality disorders (including schizophrenia), this period is even more fraught.

At the same time, many physical and psychological functions appear to be at their best during adolescence, for example, strength, speed, and the ability to learn (Csikszentmihalyi and Schmidt, 1998, cited in Santrock, 2001: 72–3). Adolescents who are in safe, supportive environments and who have a clear sense of identity and self-worth are therefore likely to be able to match their physical with their intellectual and social development.

Individuals and temperaments

As well as undergoing the ravages of adolescent physical and emotional change, teenagers bring with them their conditioning, their innate senses of self, and their temperaments. There are many educational, philosophical, and psychological approaches to temperament. For example, Chess and Thomas (1977) have classified three basic types of temperament. The easy child is generally positive, well organized, and adapts well and easily to new situations. A difficult child is generally negative, disorganized, lacks regular routines, and does not adapt easily to new experiences. The slow-to-warm-up child is largely inactive, negative to some degree, does not easily adapt to new experiences, and does not react with much enthusiasm to stimulus.

Rudolf Steiner's insights into temperaments can be very useful for understanding adolescents. He identified four different temperaments that are meant not as definers but as ways of understanding the innate character and disposition of each person. The choleric can be fiery, reacting sometimes with anger and with bursts of unreflective energy. At the same time, they are warm and attractive people, and are often leaders. The melancholic tends to introspection and often feels very deeply, sometimes tuning in to negativity more readily than to positivity. Logical thinking, however, is a strength. The phlegmatic tends to be sluggish, an observer rather than a doer but also tolerant, careful, and well organized. The sanguine child is cheery, optimistic, and sociable, though sometimes disorganized, having difficulty finishing tasks. One of Steiner's most important applications of this analysis was to argue that teachers should be aware of the temperament of each person, so that they are taught in ways that are not obstructed by temperament, but rather draw on their positive qualities. Steiner recommends ways of balancing out the negative aspects of each temperament through positive social interaction (Trostli, 1998).

Steiner also believed that while each individual may display a predominant temperament, there are different elements in every one of us that take turns in revealing and asserting themselves. Sometimes this may be because of mood, but more often it is to do with social approbation and emotional environment. If temperament therefore becomes a determinant of success, as it is in many school systems, then a huge number of students are selected out before they have had a chance to shine, and temperament becomes as iniquitous as ethnicity, religion, class, or appearance as a determinant of acceptability.

The research of Galambos and Turner (1997), for example, suggests that an adolescent's ability to adapt works best when there is a fit or similarity between the adolescent's temperament and the expectations of teachers, peers, or parents. Children with good social skills who are active, appealing, cooperative, and responsive, and who smile more, tend to receive more encouragement and support than passive and quiet children. Those who are athletically inclined tend to get support and succeed more than those who are not athletic. On the other hand, children who are less cooperative and more easily distracted do not appeal as much.

This type of response does not allow for or encourage diversity. It does a disfavor both to those who are excluded and also to those who are included, who can think of themselves as superior, divest themselves of empathy and social responsibility, and fail to develop appreciation of those who are different from themselves.

Social and emotional development

When students go to secondary school, they are moving toward a closer affiliation with their peer group. During the primary school years, the family provides love, support, role-modeling, and safety (when the family is functional, at least), whereas adolescence is a time when the process of growing up necessitates a move away from the nest that the family has provided. Biologically, teenagers change radically, and as they develop their critical thinking skills and their individual identity they push away from all that they know in order to say, "I am me, I am not you." All that they have believed in ceases to be "holy" and parents are seen as the fallible human beings that they are. In this discovery the adolescent often dismisses them, and finds them dictatorial, dishonest, embarrassing, hypocritical, and totally reprehensible. Some adolescents manage to separate out in a way that is benign, making it clear to their families that they still love them but that they are becoming adults, while others do it violently and damage themselves and their families.

While adolescence can be a time of healthy exploration, it is also a time of social and emotional turmoil, and the line between what is healthy and unhealthy often becomes blurred. Adolescents can and do make bad decisions, often based on a sense of their own infallibility that is linked to their individuation and growth of ego. This is made more difficult by the fact that they can be very emotional, illogical, and unreasonable. A hallmark of this phase is extreme egotism and narcissism. Adolescents are plagued by mood swings that in an adult may seem like manic depression: "I look at myself in the mirror, I see that my body is changing, I am becoming an adult and I'm really cool and good looking. I feel sexually mature but, oh my God, I've got zits, I'm so ugly, I wish this wasn't happening to me, everything is out of control. I wish I was dead."

Peer relations

As in primary school, the peer group plays an important role for each child. But in the secondary school, the peer group comes into its own. The safety net of the family is challenged and the values of the peer group take over to the extent that family and peers may become like two foreign and warring cultures existing side by side. Teenagers often do not want adults to know what they are doing and will lie to them: they want to hold onto the two parallel universes between which they travel without having to make compromises. They often feel they have to "protect" their parents from worrying about what they are doing, who they are seeing, and the decisions they are making.

Various studies (for example, Brown and Lohr, 1987; Prinstein, Fetter and La Greca, 1996) have identified different ways of grouping students, and there are many kinds of sorting processes going on in the secondary school. Students sort themselves out into various peer groupings; and schools do as well. From our observations in the New Zealand setting, we can identify the following groups.

The *athletes* are those who are chosen to represent the school. They are usually physically very strong and are admired by both the student population and the staff. Within the school, they have (and exert) the most power as individuals and as a group, and are probably the most conservative of all the students and the least susceptible to bullying. They tend to dominate, especially in single-sex boys' and coeducational schools.

The *academics* are students who do well in their school subjects and are likely to earn places at prestigious tertiary institutions. This group is generally well regarded by the school but does not usually command the same respect as the athletes, especially in single-sex boys' and coeducational schools. In single-sex girls' schools, this group may receive the most approbation.

The *alternatives* are nonconformist and colorful students who maintain a degree of success and are attractive to a wide group because of their dance with the extremes of appearance and behavior. They are characterized by reasonable-to-high healthy functioning and are often good academically.

The *at-risk* students may sit first of all alongside the alternatives, but whereas the alternatives have fairly widespread kudos, the at-risk students have gone so far out on a limb that they are eventually rejected by most of the school population. Staff try their best for them and then usually give up, and students distance themselves from them as they fall further and further into risk.

The *glamorous* students are conscious mostly of appearance, are conformist and stringent in their dress, personal hygiene and image, and are more concerned about how they present and how they are seen than how they perform.

The *general* is a grouping of students who do not belong to any identifiable group but who blend in, perhaps changing appearance, style, and affiliation, but drawing no special attention to themselves.

Among our six students, Jon straddles the academic and athletic groups, and Marianna fits mainly into the academic group but is also comfortable among the athletes and the glamorous students. Whereas Saul begins as an at-risk student, he becomes successful academically and athletically. Celeste begins the year by thinking of herself as an alternative student, but rapidly becomes dysfunctional and at risk. Sylvia, who flits from group to group at the start (one of the general group), becomes an academic during her third year as her identity and confidence coalesce. Simon declines throughout his schooling and ends up firmly in the at-risk group.

This analysis shows not only that individuals can shift, re-form, and change allegiance, application, and style, because of circumstance, context, influence, and social reinforcement; but also that they can change over time as the peer group develops and adolescence progresses. Brown et al. (1995) (cited in Santrock, 2001: 204) found that in the ninth grade, the rules of cliques in high school are rigid and clique differentiation is great, whereas by the twelfth grade it is easier to have friendships across groupings and with a greater number of people. It appears that the rigid nature of groupings changes as students mature and are able to be more flexible.

Relationships in adolescence

The move to secondary school parallels the movement from the family to the peer group that occurs in adolescence. For every generation this involves going into unchartered waters. In the process of this passage, children leave behind their families and parents to varying extents and also the other significant adult in their lives, their home-room teacher from primary school. The foundations and skills laid by families in preadolescence are vital for students' survival as they forge ahead, despite the fact that they expend so much energy rejecting parental values.

Parenting styles tend to fall into one of three major types: authoritarian, permissive, and authoritative (Baumrind, 1971 and 1991, cited in Santrock, 2001: 155). Essentially, authoritarian parenting entails children being controlled by parents (sometimes through the use of force) without reason or explanation. Children are told what to do and are not encouraged to think about their actions. Such parenting is usually punitive and leads children to think of our complex world in simplistic black and white ways. It is suggested that such parenting leads to behavior in adolescence that is socially incompetent.

Two kinds of permissive parenting are described: neglectful and indulgent. Neglectful parents are uninvolved in their children's lives. They do not provide adequate guidance and role-modeling and neither control nor encourage independence. Adolescent behavior in this type of setting is socially incompetent and children from these sorts of families often lack self-control.

Indulgent parenting, on the other hand, occurs when parents are over-involved in their children's lives. Although intentions may be good, the child is submerged beneath overconcern, overprotection, and a lack of controls, expectations, or demands. This approach to child-rearing does not prepare the child for the world. Children raised in such settings are often incompetent socially as adolescents and lack a sense of boundaries and self-control.

Authoritative parenting encourages individuals to think about their actions and to act with consideration, responsibility, and respect. Independence is encouraged but clear limits are set. Verbal interchange and warm and nurturing relationships are established between parents and their children. Authoritative parenting is synonymous with socially competent behavior in adolescence.

Our group of six students, as well as having different peer relationships and rates of individualization, also have different types of relationships with their families. While Simon has been nurtured by his mother, he has also been indulged by her. He has no siblings and no male presence, and his eventual abusive relationship with his mother and others is partly a result of the way he was brought up. He is unable to function well in his peer group.

Sylvia's childhood was betrayed by sexual abuse and, consequently, the foundations which should have been laid for her in her family are shaky. While Celeste's parents were caring, she was born when they were very young. They were permissive because they did not know how else to parent, and indulged her to make up for their inability to give her time or material possessions. They were unable to cope and soon split up, with Celeste being raised by her grandmother and then her aunt.

In Saul's case, there was no functioning family and he was a latchkey adolescent. He is the youngest of six siblings, all of whom left home by the time he was 7. His mother died of cancer when he was only 5, and his father is an alcoholic. In his uncle who sends him to boarding school he finds a family, and in his math teacher there he finds encouragement and faith in himself.

All six of our students are heavily influenced by their peers. Sylvia and Simon are isolated by the exclusive approach taken by their classmates. Celeste defines herself mainly in opposition to her immediate peer group and chooses to associate with a much older group. Saul is able successfully to become part of his peer group only after he feels personally validated at boarding school. Jon and Marianna form normal friendships with their peer groups and to some extent set the tone of these groups.

The dynamics of what occurs in the peer groups of these six students echo our understanding of the nature of secondary school peer groups. In the first year, they emerge out of chaos and tend to be quickly established, rigid, inflexible, and unforgiving toward those who do not fit. Communication within the peer group is typified by inference, unclear messages, and no spoken rules: it is full of misunderstanding and misinterpretation. The adolescent world also tends to be hidden from the adult world: everything outside it is "other."

As adolescence progresses, the strength of the peer group lessens as individuals gain confidence, physically and emotionally, and become more sure that they are normal, thus losing their earlier pubescent uncertainty.

Of our six students, Celeste bypassed her chronological peer group and chose relationships outside the school with disastrous consequences. Her social and emotional development were retarded. She survived neither with the older group nor with her peers, so she psychologically left the school before physically leaving it.

By the end of their third year, four of the six students were establishing themselves as individuals. Saul had his future clearly mapped out and was enjoying success in a supportive environment. Marianna and Jon continued to cope with normal developmental processes, while Sylvia, although having had a traumatic childhood and a difficult transition, was gaining confidence in herself thanks to the support of the librarian and her new role in the library. The future was not so bright for either Celeste or Simon who would find it difficult to function in the adult world.

During adolescence, social, emotional, and gender identity form and solidify. At the same time that adolescents struggle with personal identity and friendships, dating also begins, which is first of all a process for sorting out social acceptability and hierarchies. Dating in young teenagers has little to do with intimacy, communication, and caring, and more to do with attractiveness, belonging, and acceptability. It tends to be experimental, superficial, and short-lived in early adolescence.

Initially, the play for dominance is physical and in-your-face for boys and more subtle for girls. Antisocial peer relations in adolescence waver in the face of hierarchies, dominant behavior, and the creation of groups, norms, and cliques. The "success" boys have in bullying other boys in early adolescence is sometimes transferred later to abusive relationships with girls. While most students display risky behavior at some time, these students and the minority who follow them push it a long way beyond the bounds. As teenagers begin to think critically and to individualize, this behavior becomes less attractive to the majority.

Through mid and later adolescence, teenagers tend to move away from group relationships to individual friendships, and presexual and sexual relationships. Generally, they become more confident about who they are, and are likely to be more comfortable with their sexuality and to have established a preferred relationship style. They may have developed a sense of empathy and social responsibility. The values laid down during early childhood are able to come to the surface because of their increasing confidence. Ideally, adolescents move from being scared conservative children to altruistic, free-thinking adults.

Cognitive changes

Some secondary schools make purposeful efforts to create cultures that reproduce the friendly and supportive nature of the primary school so that children who would otherwise fail can achieve to their potential. There are factors that may seem determinants of individual success, such as parental support, school size, and class size, all of which, along with ethnicity, class, and cultural capital, are variously cited as reasons for success or failure. However, there are other determinants that also need to be considered.

In most school systems in Western countries, going from primary to secondary school is a move from an essentially child-centered approach that values diversity, toward a form of learning that rests on the assessment of academic achievement. At a time when students are developing cognitively and their potential is great, the curriculum tends to be restrictive and focused on qualifications. The point at which the one road stops and the other begins is the juncture at which a number of students heading toward academic success suddenly head toward failure.

Adolescents go through changes in various areas of cognition. The way they process ideas changes, and they also learn to reason and think in different ways. Piaget's theory of formal operational thought is based on the idea "that adolescents are motivated to understand their world because doing so is biologically adaptive" (Santrock, 2001: 102). They organize their experiences to make sense of the world. They learn to think in more abstract terms, not of what is but of what could be; that is, they are idealistic in their thinking. They develop the ability to problem-solve and use the logical thinking method of hypothetical deductive reasoning. They are able to think more abstractly, idealistically, and logically than they could during childhood (Santrock, 2001: 102–10).

At the secondary school level there is a great potential for stimulating critical creative thinking. However, students who have missed out various developmental steps may have potential but not demonstrated ability. They may fail or perform poorly, and while they can do better, they do not know how. They may feel cheated as a result and can be disruptive in all kinds of ways. As they cannot effectively take on the establishment, that is, the school and its teachers, they may look toward members of their peer group whom they see as weak in order to assert their power. Realizing that this is going on, and that it is in fact a complex problem involving the learning as well as the social environment, is the first step to finding a solution that works.

This type of situation may be addressed by the application of knowledge about cognitive development. Sternberg (1986), for example, argues that there are three types of intelligence: analytic thinkers, creative thinkers, and street-smart (practical) thinkers (Santrock, 2001: 127–9). Just as the concept of temperaments may be useful in finding ways to access individual strengths, so may theories about intelligence and learning. In addition to applying knowledge about cognitive "styles," it is also useful to know about theories such as Vygotsky's concept of cognitive development that focuses on what he calls zones of proximal development. He identifies tasks that may be too difficult to be dealt with by an individual that can be mastered with the assistance of someone else such as a teacher, parent, or older member of the peer group (Santrock, 2001: 110–12).

Particular attention has recently been paid to the concepts of emotional intelligence (Goleman, 1995) and social cognition (Flavell and Miller, 1998, cited in Santrock, 2001: 134–8). Emotional intelligence involves being able to understand how one reacts to situations, how those around react, what emotions emerge, what they represent, and how understanding and skills can be used to function effectively in relationships. Social cognition involves understanding how relationships with groups and individuals work, and how people choose to take particular actions in the social world.

Studies of cognitive development draw our attention to two almost oppositional stances in terms of social development. On the one hand, individuals experience extreme egocentrism—adolescents are very self-conscious and believe that everyone else is as interested in the minutiae of their lives as they are. They also have a sense of being unique. On the other hand, they grapple with what Robert Selman calls "perspective-taking," which is essentially being able to put oneself in another's shoes and understanding what they may be thinking or feeling. Selman (1980: 135) sees individuals as going through five stages of perspective-taking from the egocentricity of early childhood to the perspective of late adolescence when the other person's point of view is able to be seen. In relation to bullying, those who bully often cannot see the other person's point of view, and they do not empathize or feel the pain that individual may be feeling. It may be in the area of perspective-taking that they are actually immature.

Similar to the idea of perspective-taking is the sense of moral development. As adolescents progress through secondary school and develop their abilities to see others' perspectives, hone their critical reasoning skills, and become more comfortable with their increased ability to think in an objective fashion, they learn to stand outside situations that occur and to make moral judgments about them. In relation to bullying, the power of the peer group in the early stages of secondary school is such that although students may feel uncomfortable about what is happening to one of their classmates, they do not have the power, skills, or sense of responsibility to intervene. As they become more able to see the other person's perspective and that others feel as they do, they can act more responsibly. Students who are several years older can support and encourage them to take on these responsibilities at an earlier age.

Our six students illustrate the complexity of the relationship between successful individuation, emotional intelligence, and the development of social cognition. While Saul clearly had the thinking ability to be successful, it was only when he was placed in a nurturing environment where his other needs were being catered for that this became apparent (Maslow, 1970). Celeste had no connection with school at all and was sabotaged by many influences and events. She had no structure in her life, and was sexually active and provocative from a very young age. She had ability but her intelligence was not accessed by the school. Instead, she remained disengaged, and opted for what she thought was a fun, risky, attractive lifestyle. Sylvia found an escape from her past in study, and used it as a shield until she had the strength, encouragement, and confidence to take on her identity as an intelligent, thoughtful student. Marianna and Jon continued to enjoy academic success, and were able to marry survival within the peer group with the maintenance of a good level of achievement at school. Simon made no academic progress because of his refusal to comply—his personal difficulties prevented the development of his cognition and learning. He found schoolwork hard and actively resisted attempts to give him remedial support. On the one or two occasions when he made a serious effort with his schoolwork, the lack of recognition for his improvement saw him give up and become increasingly belligerent.

These examples indicate the potency of the peer group and of successful individuation in the expression of cognitive development. They also suggest that schools need to be flexible enough to recognize different rates of progress within supportive and nurturing environments that appreciate and respect difference.

Problems and disorders

Within adolescent culture there are a number of disorders and temptations that take individuals into not only the illegal but also the dangerous. These are:

1   extreme antisocial behavior;
2   feelings of inadequacy;
3   self-consciousness;
4   shyness;
5   delinquency;
6   drug and alcohol abuse;
7   eating disorders;
8   depression; and
9   suicidal tendencies.

Adolescence and risk-taking

The teenage peer group provides a context in which it is common, and even expected, that the status quo should be challenged and, consequently, the ability of adolescents to make sensible decisions is threatened by several factors. Adolescents are attracted to risk-taking, pushing the boundaries, experimentation, and recklessness. At the same time they also tend to believe they are invincible. As a group they are in a process of separation from the adults in their lives and are therefore likely to reject many of the values that they associate with adulthood, such as caution and reason.

Adolescence is a transitional period between childhood and adulthood. It is when young people develop the social and intellectual skills that prepare them for their roles in the adult world. They develop their expectations of how they will fit into this world, and set their educational, lifestyle, and occupational goals at the same time that their biological, cognitive, and psychosocial clocks are developing at a fast and sometimes seemingly out-of-control rate.

Adolescents move from being dependent to being self-reliant and to making their own decisions. This means making choices in relation to career, family, friendships, health, morality, peer pressure, politics, and schooling. It is a time of exploration, discovery, and pushing the boundaries, which opens teenagers up to vulnerability in many areas of their lives. Some of the decisions they make are likely to be risky or poor, and some place them in grave danger.

Examples of risk-taking are failing to use contraception during intercourse, sexual promiscuity, carrying or using weapons, experimenting with alcohol and drugs, speeding in cars, associating with peripheral and criminally motivated individuals, and doing physically dangerous activities like skateboarding on busy roads and swimming in unpatrolled and unknown waters.

In a supportive and healthy environment adolescents are able to learn from their mistakes, pull back from extreme risk-taking, adjust their positions, and move ahead. If this does not happen, they may suffer from ongoing problems and the consequences of their choices, and find it hard to pass unscathed into adulthood. In addition, personal, psychological, and social difficulties and disorders may become more apparent as individuals struggle to cope with the changes and pressures of adolescence. Whereas in childhood peer approval is important, it is not as crucial as it is in adolescence or as toxic when it turns to disapproval.

Suicidal tendencies

In New Zealand, after car accidents, suicide is the most common cause of death for young males aged 15 to 24 (males make up 80 percent of these suicide statistics). These statistics are similar to those in other OECD[4] countries. In the US, suicide is now the third leading cause of death in 15–24 year olds (Santrock, 2001: 480).

Feeling out of control, hopeless, and useless causes some adolescents to take extreme actions. The emotions young men and women experience (such as depression and despair) and the external events that intrude on their lives and cause distress (such as bullying, relationship breakup, and sexual identity confusion) can push some of them toward suicide (whether they think seriously about it, attempt it, or succeed in it).

Talk of suicide by an adolescent or any other signs of suicidal tendencies (such as talking about feeling desperate and hopeless, giving away prized possessions, visiting favorite places and friends for a final time, stockpiling potentially lethal medication, obtaining a weapon, and appearing calm after a traumatic event) should always be taken seriously.

Some people treat unsuccessful attempts at suicide as melodramatic, manipulative, immature, and attention-seeking. Adolescence is full of "acting out," experimenting with roles, being melodramatic, and making poor decisions. Attempts at suicide should never be ignored, and this is certainly an area in which the adolescent should not be blamed, dismissed, and judged. An attempt at suicide is an indication of crisis, and just another step along the path to self-destruction. While sometimes suicide may be the result of volatility, an impulse gone wrong, poor decision-making, or the effects of alcohol or drugs, it is final and devastating in its impact. No amount of guilt, regret, reinterpretation, or soul-searching on the part of those left behind will reverse what has happened.

The tragedy of suicide is not only the obvious desperation and despair that must have led up to it, but also the fact that in all likelihood even a day later the events or feelings which drive the individual to suicide may have changed, abated, or have lost their extreme potency. It is essential that any indications of suicidal feelings are taken very seriously (Haugaard, 2001).

The end of the adventure

All adolescents take risks but some take more than others. When this happens to an extreme, they place themselves in danger. Of the six students in our case study, Simon and Celeste were the most scarred by their problems and disorders. Simon is a prime candidate for depression, with suicide being increasingly likely. His inability to form satisfactory relationships and his violent temper will make him difficult to employ. He has not formed his own identity, and this also makes him much more likely to be involved in peripheral and at-risk cultures. By the age of 22, in fact, he has already served one term of imprisonment for repeated drink-driving offenses, has had several abusive relationships with women, has fathered two children with different women, and has been the subject of several nonmolestation orders. At 21, stoned and driving to the strip joint with yet another drunken boyfriend, Celeste suffers a broken jaw and two broken ribs. She is destined for a life of abuse, multiple partners, poverty, and unhappiness. By 21, Sylvia's anorexia is no longer a problem and she is studying at university. Saul is not a professional athlete, but is at university doing a criminology degree. Marianna and Jon are both beginning professional careers.

These six individuals have passed with varying success through the turbulent sea of adolescence. One has almost drowned in the process, and another is finding it hard to stay afloat. Two have had liferafts thrown to them at crucial periods and are now successfully moving ahead with their lives, and two were always adept at plain sailing. Those who are not sinking are typical of the vast majority of the human population who have emerged from adolescence, damaged or undamaged, having charted a way through all the shifts, swings, surprises, and challenges that are part of human development.

Notes

1 When we refer to "secondary school," we are using the wider American understanding which includes both the junior (intermediate and middle schools) and senior high school sectors. We use the term "primary school" to refer to what Americans and Canadians call elementary school.
2 Hackysack is a game in which the players stand in a circle and kick a small, sand-filled ball from person to person. The aim of the game is to keep the ball from touching the ground using only leg kicks.
3 Attention deficit hyperactivity disorder.
4 Organization for Economic Cooperation and Development.

3

The Social Climate of the Secondary School

Arriving at secondary school

First-year students arriving at secondary school enter a totally new culture. The differences between primary and secondary schools are so great that it is less a process of transition than of sudden culture change. These differences include the following:

- Primary schools tend to be small and secondary schools to be large. Even where a secondary school is comparatively small, it is most likely to be much bigger than the school a student previously attended.
- Secondary schools tend to be more rule bound, curriculum driven, and impersonal than primary schools.
- At primary school, students have a single teacher with whom they spend most of their time. In secondary schools, students have several individual-subject teachers. Their home-room or form teacher is usually someone they see only once a day.
- Whereas primary school teachers principally focus on teaching their class, secondary school teachers focus first on teaching their subject area.
- First-year students experience the loss of a significant adult in that they no longer have only one teacher.
- At primary school, students tend to stay together with the same social group throughout each day over the school year. At secondary school, they are part of several class groups as they move from subject to subject throughout the day.
- In the secondary school much more emphasis is placed on the curriculum, achievement, and assessment, so that a clearer distinction is made between those who are seen as able and those seen as failures or at risk. These

academic differentiations present themselves in all kinds of ways that create subcultures and microcultures within schools.

- Primary school students tend to live locally and to have many of their school peers living nearby. At secondary school, students are likely to come from a wider area and to have fewer of their school peers in their immediate neighborhoods.
- Student populations in secondary schools come from a variety of socio-economic and ethnic communities, often creating complex social relations which carry over the problems that affect the wider society in which the school is located.
- Students at secondary school are more likely to be anonymous unless they are academically and socially successful.

In addition to having to adjust to these abrupt changes in culture, students at this time in their lives are also coming into adolescence and are simultaneously struggling with physical, psychic, and emotional turmoil. There is tension between their perceptions of themselves as children or adults, between the sexes, and in relation to physical and developmental changes.

In yet another difficult conjunction, it is also a time when they *have* to form new relationships. At best, they may be self-confident, attractive, and outgoing, finding it is easy to adapt to change and to make new friends. They may have come to secondary school with a few friends from primary school with whom they can maintain links. Sometimes these friendships last, but more often they give way as new friendships and pathways are found in the different social milieu of the secondary school. At worst, they may arrive at school knowing nobody, find it hard to adjust, fail to fit in, and become socially isolated.

The culture of the secondary school

In the first six years of school, from the beginning of the school year each child has an opportunity of developing a sustainable relationship with one significant teacher. While the quality of this relationship depends greatly on the skills and empathy of this adult, it is irrefutable that each student has one person who knows him or her and to whom the child and family can look for support. In primary schools, the class teacher has an enormous influence over all the students in the class. He or she is crucial in establishing a safe emotional and physical learning environment and the ethos of the group. This relationship allows the emergence of individual, child-centered teaching and learning to take place.

Secondary schools are complex, have more rules, lack the sense of integration that exists in primary schools, and deliver their curricula very differently.

A small primary school tends to offer greater security, whereas secondary schools breed anonymity and are more likely to feel unsafe. There is no longer a cohesive and reliable peer group, and validation more typically occurs through academic and athletic success than through simple social appraisal.

At the same time that teenagers are entering the secondary school, they are undergoing physical changes and being confronted by dynamic and unpredictable social expectations and behavior. They are dominated by a need to belong and are constantly checking their normalcy with the peer group. For many the need to be accepted takes on epic proportions. It is ironic that as these forces are gathering, young people are moving into a school system that is larger, more complex, and more impersonal.

There is less flexibility in the secondary school system than in the primary school. At the time when adolescents begin to broaden their horizons, the type of school they attend is generally more restrictive. Students are confronted with less integrated and more discrete curriculum and assessment regimes. For many it is at this stage of their schooling that they are faced with absolute differentiation, often in the form of streaming and also as the assessment system takes over and they choose (or are chosen for) subject specializations. It is a time when it becomes apparent that some students are failing when this was not as apparent before. Such failure can cause poor self-esteem and confidence, and can end up defining the person. Students who do not receive validation in this system and those who are looking for trouble or are dissatisfied may become disruptive or rebellious to gain identity.

In secondary schools, there are two separate cultures, of teenagers and adults. In primary school, adults are present as nurturers and significant others. In secondary school, this dependent and symbiotic relationship is challenged by the developmental dynamics of adolescence. While teenagers expend enormous amounts of energy pulling away from the controls and restrictions of the adult world, they also tend to dam up huge reservoirs of anxiety about who they are, how they look, their sexuality, whether they are accepted, and where they belong. Neither parents nor teachers can provide this reference point, and are in fact more likely than not to be rejected as arbiters of appearance, behavior, beliefs, manners, morals, opinion, and taste. Teachers are first of all adults, with different attitudes, interests, relationships, and values. They are part of the establishment and are characterized as "others," like parents.

While the world of the adolescent is exciting and "buzzy," a time of growing independence, it is also a time of uncertainty, insecurity, and lack of identity. Although teenagers are entering the adult world, they are also aware that they largely oppose the adult world. They are less likely to stand on their own two feet than to seek identity and approval from the peer group. In school, they find it difficult to operate as individuals and to demonstrate that they want and need approval. They sometimes act out confusing signals that teachers see as negative.

The duality between adults and students in secondary schools means that the peer group becomes more and more important. For many students the loss of a significant adult may open up their exposure to negative role models that can attract the more aggressive of them to challenge the hierarchies and oppose the norms. The life of being a rebel can seem glamorous and attractive, and at least provides an identity. Similarly, developing or taking on the role of a bully can also give someone an identity, with the apparent concomitant rewards of power and manipulation within the social group. The secondary school is therefore naturally a site of duality in which subcultures and anticultures may develop unchecked, and by which there is a greater chance of antisocial behavior becoming a hallmark of the school and of seedbeds that germinate bullying and other dangerous dynamics being laid down and sustained.

As our society becomes increasingly fractionalized, there are fewer community and family opportunities to normalize the process of puberty and to mark puberty as a rite of passage. More and more young people are left to come to their own understanding of what is going on. The traditional approach of celebrating puberty is largely gone from the postindustrial society of the twenty-first century, apart from the exceptions of bar mitzvah and bat mitzvah, and other specific cultural celebrations. The school is for many the only institution that has the capacity to help emerging adolescents navigate this change.

Often, secondary teachers do not feel that it is their job to oversee peer activities, but regard their job as being classroom focused. Teachers have all the problems of assessment, the requirements of the curriculum, the balancing act of teaching multiple classes, and the stresses of overfull timetables to deal with. They are not generally trained in pastoral skills and are driven by the need to cover the curriculum and get the job done. Teachers also have their own personal and philosophical reactions to social and bullying issues. They may see these as being a discipline problem or something that the professionals, such as the guidance counselors, should handle. Secondary teachers are not available to students as they are in the primary school.

Peer relations at secondary school

There are three main groups of students in the secondary school population (Figure 3.1):

1 the first-year students;
2 the middle students; and
3 the finishing students.

In coeducational schools, significant and separate groups are also formed by girls and boys.

First-year students

When children first start secondary school, they bring with them their social knowledge from primary school. At the beginning of the school year, they jockey for position and the social situation is fluid and chaotic. However, a closer examination would soon reveal the emergence of a variety of roles: dominant individuals (prosocial leaders and bullies), neutral individuals (followers and bystanders), and those on the periphery (outsiders and potential victims of bullying). When students who have been bullies at primary school arrive at secondary school, they assume that they will carry on as before.

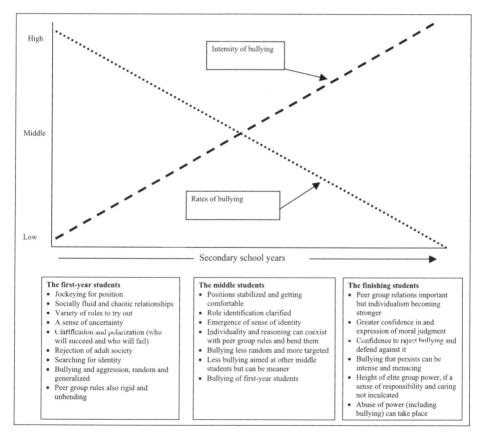

Figure 3.1 *The changing nature of peer groups and individualization during secondary school years*

In this new setting they have new levers because everyone is uncertain about their roles, relationships and hierarchies are unclear, and the social rules are indecipherable. A sexual lever is added to this arsenal, and isolation becomes an even more important and devastating tool than it was previously at primary school.

For some students, school becomes boring and the peer group exciting, and in gravitating toward excitement and rejecting school norms and values, such students take on a mantle of identity which may give them only a side-line position but one by which they gain at least a modicum of acceptability. For others, commitment to rebellion and risk-taking behavior may become a *raison d'être* and escalate throughout the first year.

Students who are potential victims of bullying are often unsure of themselves and do not know how and whether they fit into the peer group. They are unsure how to be successful and what is successful. In this setting, classrooms become havens from bullying or adjunct sites of bullying, as dangerous as the school yard, depending on the teachers' stance and the safety of the school.

This establishment of dominance among first-year students is assisted by several factors. The physical changes occurring during puberty force teenagers to seek reassurance that what is happening to them is normal. Parental support for many is not enough and validation is sought from peers. Consequently, peer pressure becomes a powerful force and is a potential weapon for those who seek to maintain or establish a negative leadership role. Coercion and manipulation and the need for strong group identification all combine to make a powerful cocktail for bullying behavior.

Those who have been socially aggressive in the past now have these new weapons at their disposal and in a departure from previous practice abandon random acts of bullying in favor of sustained and targeted attacks. This new approach is even more successful as these bullies assume a powerful leadership role when the peer group naturally moves away from parent and adult authority figures. Alienation from parents and society is a feature of juvenile behavior: they seek independence from authority figures as part of the development of their adult individualism. During emerging adolescence, teenagers desert parents at the same time as they are seeking reassurance from their peer group. For the leaders this is an ideal vacuum to fill. For those who have developed antisocial skills, it ensures a powerful following, and plenty of potential victims.

Whereas dominant behavior can seek to inflict pain and to ostracize some students while drawing others into a web of influence, it can also be affiliative, where positive ties are made between people and the peer group dynamics are kept open and healthy. It is not the characteristic of dominance that is therefore problematic, but its expression.

Middle students

In the middle years, students as a whole feel comfortable with the social norms of their peers. The desperate jockeying for position of the first year has dramatically reduced and, depending on the nature of the school, the culture will have settled into a self-examining, restorative whole whose main aim is to sustain and include all the individuals within it, or it will have fragmented into a series of subgroups that will form and re-form into varying hierarchies.

While students will continue to challenge identity and allegiance, they generally have attained some degree of self-awareness and identity that is their own and does not only belong to the group. Some will stand out, for extremely prosocial or antisocial behavior and values. The rest will continue to align themselves primarily one way or another, but the beginnings of a more stable culture have been laid down.

Bullies use the first year of secondary school to establish their dominance, which is the peak of bullying behavior in adolescence. Their aggression is often random as they seek out victims, evaluate support, and estimate what the school culture will let them get away with. By the middle years, the aggression decreases overall, but it becomes more targeted and the victims are more clearly defined.

When bullying does continue in the middle years, it may be extended and harmful, and sometimes takes on a menacing and precriminal complexion. The bullies (who tend to be active and dominant) carry over their victims from the previous year, target new arrivals who are perceived as weak, and proceed to demonstrate their power wherever they can. They do not pick on strong students and rely on their allies for support. These dynamics show a degree of social intelligence.

At the same time, various other dynamics begin to erode their power and they tend to gravitate toward each other, often causing another power struggle to occur in which some of the bullying behavior may self-destruct. Uncertainty is a breeding ground for bullies, and if uncertainty evaporates for various cultural, developmental, or temporal reasons, then the hold that bullies have over their sidekicks and the passive reinforcers (see Chapter 8) may loosen and fall away at this time.

But the main reasons why bullying decreases in the middle years are the developmental factors of adolescence that, in a safe school, may be sustained and reinforced by the school culture and philosophy. By about age 15, the peer group is both more influential and simultaneously able to allow a degree of individuality to assert itself. At this age, adolescents are beginning to develop a values system, whereas in early adolescence they are torn apart by confusion, uncertainty, and mortification at being "different." Most students by year 11 will have started to reject antisocial behavior and thus have the confidence to support victims of bullying.

Physical development is also important in the general decrease in aggression during middle adolescence. By then, most cases of boy bullying will have stopped. Boys develop more slowly than girls, but by about 14 they tend to get bigger and are thus less likely to be picked on than when they are small and puny. They may become taller and bigger than the bullies and develop the confidence to get angry, to get even or to move gracefully out of the bullying dynamic altogether. At the same time, the pecking order will have started to wear itself out, and girls will to some extent have sorted out who they are, who their friends are, and where they fit in. This will reduce the levels of aggression, isolation, and ostracization.

In some schools, students are mercilessly confined within in- and out-groups, and in these settings bullying will continue for longer and reach new depths of virulence. The powerful peer group bully will still be able to bully and may pick on year 9 students, but not on his peers. The diehard bully will continue with the behavior against all odds.

Finishing students

By the time students reach their final years at secondary school, most will have become individualized. Clever bullies are likely to have grown out of being bullies, and not-so-clever bullies are likely to have left school. Older students are more confident and independent unless the school they attend has a conforming and rigid culture.

Under normal circumstances, finishing students are less reliant on the peer group and have started to make more thoughtful moral judgments: in other words, they have become individuals. Because of this, the rate of bullying decreases in later adolescence. Finishing students are the oldest and most mature group of students in the secondary school, and their qualities make them ideal positive leaders and peer mentors.

A dangerous exception to this is where elite groups exist. If an elite is allowed to lord it over other students and to bully them, then it is likely that bullying will become endemic in the school. Because the school approves of members of the elite, the message is also that their abusive, tough, and bullying behavior is condoned. Bullying thus becomes institutionalized. A gang culture has a similar dynamic, and when the behavior of such groups is approved of, institutionally or because of the closed nature and power of the group, it is difficult to challenge and change the culture.

In these settings, students have to be in the elite to have status and kudos, and rituals and traditions usually support a secret and exclusive culture. Exclusivity gives power to someone over another person, which is just like the bullying dynamic. Secondary schools are exclusive enough without this added burden. They are often structured by streaming, clubs, and houses;

and the enforcement of year, age, and gender hierarchies. In this system, students who have power are protected. It is a two-faced system. It says "We have no bullying here" while in fact condoning it through promotion of division and exclusivity, and the recasting of bullying behavior as "character-building."

In safe schools, everyone will have been encouraged to individualize and achievement will be rewarded and recognized but not to the detriment of an anti-bullying ethos. By the time students reach their last two years of school, they will be learning to think for themselves and to see themselves both as individuals and as part of a mutually responsible society.

PART II

WHY "BAD" THINGS HAPPEN TO "GOOD" SCHOOLS

4

Let's be Honest about What Schools Do

The whole-school approach

Schools have found that, even with the best of intentions, problems such as bullying are very difficult to solve. The idea of involving not only teachers and administrators, but also students, parents, and knowledgeable community members in creating a foundation of mutual understanding, support, and problem-solving from which schools can address fundamental issues has come to be known as the whole-school approach. The *whole-school approach* merely means that everyone involved is consulted and their experience used to deal with that issue. This is as much an attitudinal as a systemic change.

Schools that believe they have put a whole-school approach in place tend to be led by principals who have read the literature, know the statistics, and seek success for their schools. However, the adoption of a whole-school philosophy is not a guarantee for success, nor is it a guarantee of safety. It does not automatically create a healthy community in which academic and social learning will flourish. A whole-school philosophy is easily written into school charters, policies, and vision statements, or expressed in the rousing words of school assembly addresses, prize-giving speeches, or market-driven advertisements for a school that are issued in the months leading up to a new school year. The philosophy can become a blind, and a dangerous one at that. A whole-school philosophy must not exist only on paper or in words.

It can be as much of a barrier between words and actions as it can be a beacon that illuminates the realization of policy into a holistic, endemic, and totally supported safe school culture.

In the British Sheffield project that focused particularly on the application of a whole-school approach to the problem of bullying (see Sharp and Smith, 1994; Smith and Sharp, 1994), the research team led by Peter Smith found that a deep and thorough application of a whole-school approach to bullying worked. It is clear that the schools in the Sheffield project interpreted the approach in a variety of ways.

> What came through, however, was that schools that had gone through this whole process properly and thoroughly, and then maintained it, had much better results in stopping bullying as compared with schools that had only partially applied a whole-school approach.

As with most issues, theory is very different from practice. Most institutions are conservative and highly complex. When real changes need to be made, there may be some compliance on the surface, but mechanisms and processes at a deeper level can stop these changes from taking place. We have termed this the blocked drain syndrome (Figure 4.1). If this concept is applied to a school, on the surface there may be support for an anti-bullying initiative, a well-intended school philosophy, and policies and programs whose workings have evolved organically over a long period. They may be applied but they will not work because inside the drain is blocked. As with blocked drains, you cannot necessarily see what is causing the blockage.

In this part of the book we discuss the types of blockages that can stop an anti-bullying initiative from working. We also suggest ways of identifying the blockage and then how to remove it. In doing so, it might sometimes feel that the beacon of hope has dimmed, but it is necessary to go into the darker places of the school system in order to cast light on what really happens: to be really effective it is important to be honest about the way schools often work (or not, as is sometimes the case).

What we know/what we do

Schools throughout the last decade have had access to:

- the whole-school approach;
- anti-bullying tools;
- strategic planning statements; and
- national anti-bullying policies and priorities.

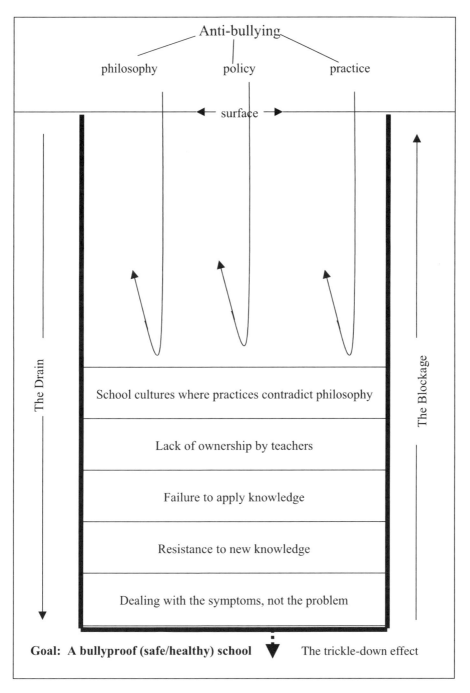

Figure 4.1 *The blocked drain syndrome*

While a lot of school personnel are familiar with knowledge that researchers have generated around the world, such as what Smith and his team found out in the Sheffield project (see Sharp and Smith, 1994; Smith and Sharp, 1994), this has not drastically changed what happens in schools. There has not been a paradigm shift that enables teachers to know what to do about bullying. While teachers and schools are under pressure to deal with bullying, they constantly have to prioritize what they do and how they do it. Anti-bullying programs have been bought and brought in, and teachers know that exemplary teaching practice is inclusive and results in bully-free classrooms. They examine good quality practice and educational packages to help them in the turmoil of classroom teaching. They may know from experience that anti-bullying programs will deal with 80 percent of antisocial behaviors that disrupt learning, and are therefore likely to want to find out about such programs and the whole-school approach in which they are often embedded.

But schools are very busy places and may rest uncritically on the laurels of their philosophy, stance, and academic success. It may seem that because they appear to be doing well and to have adopted a whole-school approach they are bully-free and problem-free.

Within a whole-school approach, a school may have various anti-bullying responses, including:

1 that bullying issues are discussed in the health curriculum;
2 that the school has an avowed anti-bullying policy;
3 that the school has anti-bullying rules;
4 that the school has a zero tolerance policy towards bullying;
5 that students are always encouraged to report cases of bullying;
6 that the guidance counselor regularly uses the No Blame Approach; and
7 that other anti-bullying strategies are periodically purchased and implemented by the school.

Even in the face of this anti-bullying arsenal, bad things still happen. This is because it is easier to *say* something is being done about bullying than to *do* something that is fully effective. A whole-school approach can create a glass ceiling between words and actions, untruth and truth, passivity and proactivity, denial and responsibility, a hierarchical system and a nonhierarchical system, and authoritarianism and authority.

How some schools respond to bullying

Schools react variously to the issue of bullying. Some carefully adopt and maintain a whole-school approach that sets up safe strategies for staff and students and is always vigilant about bullying. But cradled in the espousal of a whole-school approach, there are many responses to bullying that indicate only a partial adoption of the approach, a lack of honesty about the school's position and effectiveness in relation to bullying, a power structure that condones and promotes bullying and exclusivity, a cynical disregard for the harmfulness of bullying, and a denial of its presence in the school in question.

Many school personnel take refuge in the attitude towards bullying, "We know about it, therefore it's not a problem," believing that because they know about the problem it will somehow go away. However, their response is both passive and anti-intellectual. By being uncritical and unreflective, they abdicate their responsibility as educators and human beings.

> A safe school provides an active and "engaged" environment. It encourages and supports diversity in staff and students, and aims to create a culture based on affective intelligence, intellectual activity rather than intellectual passivity, and cooperation and respect. In this sort of setting, social as well as academic learning can flourish.

Unsafe schools tend not to deal well with problems, diversity, or nonconformist behavior. They are likely to be permissive and out of control, or hierarchical and authoritarian. In the first, bullying is not seen for what it is and is ignored or dealt with haphazardly or not at all. In the second, a lot of time is spent running around "putting out fires," and bullying is not dealt with well. In authoritarian schools, there is a hierarchy with the principal at the top and the teachers with all their various seniorities vying for position below in a top-down structure that ultimately rests upon a "Do as I say" approach to discipline and rule enforcement. Teachers generally wield unreasonable power, and rule by fear and intimidation. Students in such settings are not encouraged to challenge ideas or to think for themselves. Their passivity is institutional and behavioral, and affects all aspects of how they act, in the classroom and outside it.

This one-size-fits-all approach supports teachers who condone and even take part in bullying, and hides behind its assertion that it is dealing with bullying. If any problems persist, and a student maintains, for instance, that she is being bullied even though the school has supposedly "handled the problem," then the school will say it has done everything it can to support her, gone out on a limb, and bent over backwards. The problem, of course, is the student's: she is a drama queen, dishonest, attention-seeking, socially inept, or has psychological problems. But, in fact, this type of school actually only bends over backwards to defend itself.

The only way forward here is to pull the school apart, to unblock its drains, and then to let it run more smoothly. However many things are put in place to deal with a problem like bullying in this sort of school, the problem remains and the strategies do not work.

There are other responses that are commonly heard from various types of schools. These include:

1 the "we don't have it here [because we don't condone it]" response;
2 the "we're too busy to deal with it" response;
3 the "too much emphasis is put on bullying" response;
4 the "yes, it's a good idea, but we're already dealing with it" response; and
5 the "zero tolerance" response.

The "we don't have it here [because we don't condone it]" response

The first of these responses rests on the myopic belief that what is not seen does not exist. It is unwise in its smugness and dangerous in its lack of responsibility. Many schools are unwilling to admit that they have a bullying problem, because it is too hard to deal with, or reduces the attractiveness of the school to potential "customers." But still others insist that because they do not condone bullying they therefore inevitably do not have it. This is a little like saying, "I do not approve of cancer, therefore I will not get it," or, "I am never going to get sick because I don't like being sick." This could be called the Pollyanna response to bullying.

The "we're too busy to deal with it" response

The "we're too busy to deal with it" response is likely to arise in a disorganized, overloaded, underresourced, and poorly functioning school. All schools are very busy and all teachers are overloaded, but some schools remain healthy and safe while others do not. This response hides behind excuses and also, arguably, tries to gain indemnity and/or immunity by appealing to the understanding of would-be critics. These excuses may include the following:

1 It is too hard to get the staff behind a new initiative.
2 Our staff are teachers, not counselors and therapists. They need to do what they were trained to do—control their classrooms.
3 It's up to parents to make sure their children behave well at school. It's a family issue!
4 A lot of bullying problems are caused by the home life of students.
5 We don't have time to deal with this. We have the new qualification structure to introduce.
6 If I did everything using a whole-school approach (such as literacy, bullying, professional development programs), we'd be having meetings every night.
7 We're just too busy to deal with everything that happens during the school day.

The "too much emphasis is put on bullying" response

The "too much emphasis is put on bullying" response is also likely to be the catchcry of a school that is not coping. It aims to reduce criticism by deflecting attention from one problem onto myriad others. It attempts to downplay the seriousness of bullying by suggesting that there are far more pressing issues that the school must deal with and that bullying is, by implication, a hotbed of imaginary harm and a site of hysteria, attention-seeking, and self-seeking behavior. This is an evasive and dishonest response.

The "yes, it's a good idea, but we're already dealing with it" response

This response also uses a certain degree of deflection, but makes some attempt to face up to the issue of bullying as well. The excuses in this case are usually many, for example:

1 There is too much call on other resources.
2 We're playing this anti-bullying game, but if the truth be known, you're not going to change this behavior. Boys will be boys. We've had various experts in, but in the end, that's the way of the world, and the students have to learn how to cope with it.
3 The health teachers/guidance counselors deal with this in our school. Everyone knows that and it frees the rest of us to get on with our real job, which is teaching.
4 We've done bullying. We have other priorities at the moment, and we don't need to rehash everything.
5 The government education assessors have been and they felt all our students were on task.
6 Let's be really honest here. We don't have lots of bullying at our school. I make it clear that we don't tolerate bullying, and I've kicked out several students in the last year who've been chronic bullies.
7 We have a very clear discipline structure that deals with bullying. Students get detentions, get suspended, or get expelled.
8 Since I talked about bullying in assembly, there doesn't seem to have been a problem.
9 We can't waste our time with the sort of kids who bully. The school is a better place without them, and I make that clear from the start.

The "zero tolerance" response

The final response is the "zero tolerance" response. This is often advocated by authoritarian schools that believe behavior can be contained and controlled by discipline and rules. While zero tolerance confronts the reality of bullying and does not try to reframe it as nonexistent, minimal, or normal, it usually rests its power in rhetoric that is impressive linguistically but ineffective in reality. No amount of huffing and puffing about the intolerability of bullying and its total unacceptability to the school will make it go away. It is never possible to legislate for good behavior, to force morality on the amoral, and to grandstand for social responsibility. Slogans are not a substitute for holistic and thoroughly applied policy and process.

Facing up to bullying

Students in the face of these sorts of messages are very confused. They hear that there is no bullying in the school, while they know there is. They are told that there are more important things that need attention, but can scarcely function at school if they are being bullied. They are told that it is being dealt with (and by implication is not a problem), when they know that they cannot safely tell teachers about it. They hear that it is not tolerated by the school, but know that it is lurking, waiting to jump out whenever the opportunity arises. When students are constantly informed that the school neither tolerates nor *has* bullying, they think it must be their fault when it occurs or that what they are experiencing is in fact *not* bullying. If they complain, they might be told, "You can always go elsewhere. We didn't force you to come here. We have a waiting list, you know."

What does all this say about the culture of a school? While the school may espouse an anti-bullying philosophy, and claim to have a whole-school approach, it actually has a culture of blame and fear. At best, the intentions may be good, but the practice is almost inevitably ineffective.

Teachers need ways to deal with every type of event, from an authoritative rather than authoritarian position, fully supported by the school within a safe anti-bullying school system.

The case studies

What follows are case studies of events that happened in several different schools that exemplify the statement that introduces this part of the book, "Why 'bad' things happen to 'good' schools," and that confront the issue that is brought into focus by the title of this chapter, "Let's be honest about what schools do."

The class that went nowhere

We often underestimate the impact a bullying culture has on the students in a class and how well this culture is hidden. During some research into a particularly bad case of bullying in a school in the Wellington area, a number of students were interviewed about their experiences of being in the same class as an identified bully. In the course of these interviews, it became apparent that this case of bullying was not isolated, but that in fact the class was a hotbcd of bullying and all the members of the class were affected by the behavior to a significant extent.

Despite this school's proactive anti-bullying focus, the class had developed and sustained a hidden bullying culture. Of concern was the fact that this abuse had gone undetected for some time, and came to light only by accident.

Attendance and discipline records for the class were checked and they failed to indicate anything unusual. In fact, there were few obvious indicators that there was a serious problem. The class was a mixed ability group with a similar make-up to the four other classes at their year level. When the academic record of the group was compared with the rest of the cohort, however, it became clear they had performed well below the others. Also glaringly obvious was the high numbers of pupils who left the class during their first two years at secondary school. Nine of the original group of 27 had left before the end of two years, 14 students joined the class during this time, and only two of them were still attending school by the end of year 10. Only seven of the original pupils lasted five years at secondary school while the rest of the cohort had an 80 percent retention rate, and only three of the original members of the class sat the University Bursary examination when at least seven would have been expected to do so.

It was initially unclear why individual pupils left the school; in only two cases could it be established that a pupil had left because of bullying. However, in the interviews a sinister picture started to emerge: the students stated that many who left had been targets of bullying. What also emerged was that the secret and hidden nature of the behavior obscured the causes at the time, and for unknown reasons many of the victims had given other plausible reasons for their departure.

During the interviews, it became apparent that the bullying was almost exclusively perpetrated by a boy named Darren and a handful of others, and directed toward anyone who was perceived as being physically weak, who was new to the school and therefore had not yet established a support network, or who was diligent about their schoolwork. Despite the fact that most of the class recognized the destructive nature of the behavior, the bullying of newcomers was accepted and, from comments made, was almost a source of pride: "We made heaps of people leave," "The other people in the class didn't care," "They just sort of laughed and [made] you feel good about it."

One of the most blatant incidents of bullying involved a boy who was tormented during a brief stay at the school. New and vulnerable, he was publicly humiliated (by verbal taunts) by Darren on his first day. On day two he left the classroom in tears after Darren, who earlier had unnoticed slipped a tampon into the outside pocket of the boy's backpack, then called attention to it in front of the whole class who erupted into laughter. The victim, like the other transients, did not report the incident and left the school soon afterwards, citing family reasons.

The majority of the students went along with the bullying, either because they were too frightened to act, felt safer being part of the action, or simply did not care. While some students had the power to challenge, for a variety of reasons they lacked the resilience, energy, or leadership to galvanize the rest into rejecting the bullying. The three physically strongest boys in the class never challenged Darren and were content to be passive onlookers. The only student who confronted him was Annabel, but because she was not supported, her protests had no impact. Without anyone to challenge Darren's leadership, the class fell more and more under his influence and domination, and they all became trapped in the abusive culture of the group.

What is clear from this investigation is that, despite this school putting a lot of effort into dealing with bullying, a pervasive bullying culture was able to develop and remain hidden over a two-year period. While members of the group were aware that the school was active in its opposition to bullying, they believed themselves to be individually powerless. Taking action, or talking to teachers or a parent, were seen as being too risky. Instead, they sought refuge in compliance with their peer abusers, hoping that this would provide protection.

Unfortunately, this passive response to the abuse had the effect of strengthening the power of the bully. It looked as if the rest of the class was not concerned about what was going on. Little or no real communication took place and what did was often on the level of miscommunication. Motivated by self-protection, the bystanders allowed the abuse to continue and, because of the departures, a steady stream of potential victims (new pupils) was presented to the bullies.

The impact of the bullying on the class is surprising. The victims suffered most, but as a whole the class performed very poorly academically as compared to the rest of the cohort.

What this case study shows is how dangerous bullying is, how well it can be hidden, and how it can infiltrate and dominate an entire class even in a school that espouses a whole-school anti-bullying approach. The school's response may be typified as falling between the proactive honest stance that recognizes the pervasiveness of bullying and the belief that so much anti-bullying work has been done that there simply cannot be a major bullying problem. In this instance, the rules of the young adolescent peer group (noninterventionist, undifferentiated, nonreporting) held sway over a sense of morality, a willingness to stand up for the weak, and courage in individuality. It was only because an incident of bullying occurred that could not be hidden, and because the school took the responsible step of examining the incident, that the extent of the bullying came to light. And it was then only because not only attendance and behavior records, but also records of academic achievement were gathered and examined that indicators of a potential problem were identified. The use of such records is thus a crucial weapon in the anti-bullying arsenal.

The Taradale incident

The following case study describes a bullying event that highlights in tragic detail some of the extreme impacts of bullying.

Hawkes Bay lies on the east coast of the North Island of New Zealand and is regarded as a beautiful area that enjoys long hours of sunshine, a bounteous viticulture, and a stunning coastline. The entire country was shocked when in October 2001 a group of seven Taradale High School 17- and 18-year-old male students were arrested after a fellow student was assaulted at a party. Recognized school leaders and popular with their peers and teachers, the seven boys were charged, tried, and jailed for sexually violating their classmate with a broomstick after an unsupervised drinking session at the home of another student whose parents were overseas. The main perpetrator chose to plead guilty and gave evidence against the other six who denied the charges.

As the court case developed, a very sad story unfolded. The victim was new to the school, having been home schooled for a period prior to coming to the school for his last year before university. He had previously been traumatized by bullying at another school (in another town) several years earlier.

Possibly as a result of the earlier events, he was very keen to fit in and actively sought the friendship of those who eventually turned on him. He was often the butt of jokes and reportedly received more than his share of teasing and put-downs from the group. Despite this, he reported that he was enjoying school and got on well with his peers.

On the night in question he had gone with others to the party, had consumed a lot of alcohol, and had gone to sleep on a bed. Twice he was dragged out of bed by the assailants. On the first occasion they failed to get his trousers down, and the second time they regrouped, planned their assault, and held him down while one of the boys inserted a broomstick smeared with liniment into his anus.

Despite the defense the boys and their lawyers put up, a clear picture emerged in court of a culture of bullying operating within the group. They often punched each other when they made mistakes, and there were constant put-downs, jockeying, and rivalry among them. In an incident publicized during the trial, a junior student had his collarbone broken when he was tackled and knocked unconscious by the same older students. They then dragged him to the toilets and flushed his head several times. There were also suggestions that in one class pupils were encouraged to punch those who were disruptive during lessons.

The victim was an easy target and his keenness to be part of the group made him very vulnerable. His so-called "friends" escalated their conduct until it became violent and criminal. The school was ineffective in addressing the behavior despite having clear evidence that it was going on (the collarbone incident), and the rest of the students in the same grade appear to have had little sympathy for the victim of the broomstick assault.

The pupils involved represented the school leaders. That they failed to recognize that their behavior was abusive suggests that the school had not adequately educated them on the nature of leadership and the impact of bullying.

In fact, this event polarized the community. While many vociferous supporters of the perpetrators excused their behavior as a "prank," "drunken tomfoolery," and "fun that went a bit too far," the victim and his family were silent. The media response reflected the opinions of the wider society, in which the perpetrators were seen as youngsters making, at worst, a silly mistake, while the victim generally received little public support.

The judge, in sentencing the boys who pleaded guilty to the criminal charges, said that an incident earlier in the evening when the victim was manhandled and had one of his eyebrows shaved off was "part of the overall narrative of a developing seriousness of bullying and violent behaviour" (Judge Glendall, cited in Hay-Mackenzie, 2002: 88). The judge reported that another boy had told the victim he had suffered a similar attack to the sexual violation, and described it as "a rugby prank." The judge continued:

> it was no prank ... It was the commission of a cowardly crime involving serious violence and degrading, humiliating violation of a young man. Let me make it quite clear that if young men, through what is euphemistically known as peer pressure, but is really group thuggery, believe or regard such acts as acceptable behavior within the culture of sporting social activities ... then the time has come for all to be disabused of that idea. It is not within the scope of civilized behavior in a civilized community for young men to believe that such is permissible. (Ibid.)

A recent audit of the school showed that it had extensive pastoral programs and qualified and experienced counseling staff. The school had taken the issue of bullying seriously and had devoted a significant part of its recent in-service training to strengthening its knowledge of the behavior and had adopted a whole-school approach several years earlier. It believed it was proactive in addressing bullying and was able to point to policy to prove this.

Comment: This is a salutary story for all schools. The school's well-thought-out and documented anti-bullying approach clearly failed to work. The abusive culture that was able to take hold and flourish among the elite senior students survived despite the school's policy on and approach toward bullying.

The school believed that it provided a safe environment, and that it had taken all necessary precautions to protect the weak and vulnerable. The initial reaction of the school to the charges was that the victim must have been at fault and must take some of the blame.

However, it is clear that there was an abusive and bullying culture present in the senior school. Largely hidden and ignored by the majority of the students, it was allowed to grow and develop almost as a secret society. The failure of the school to address this culture and its dominance over other students permitted the abuse to escalate.

As in the case of the class that went nowhere, schools have a duty to work actively to detect incidents before they become full blown and to break down such cultures when they do. Programs need to be put in place that force the bystanders to step in and report the abuse and environments need to be developed where victims of abuse will be supported so the choice is not either to be abused or to be isolated.

The Columbine High School tragedy and its legacy

At about 11:20 A.M. on Tuesday, April 20, 1999, at the start of the first lunch period, two teenage boys, Eric Harris, 18, and Dylan Klebold, 17, entered Columbine High School, a suburban high school of 1,945 pupils located just south of Denver, Colorado, where they were students. They were laden with guns, ammunition, and bombs and were intent on mass destruction.[1] Part of their original plan was to set off two homemade propane pipe bombs in the school's cafeteria. The bombs failed to explode, but if they had exploded, 488 people could have been killed. Within 16 minutes of their entry, however, Eric and Dylan had killed 13 and wounded 21, and had then turned their guns upon themselves. Why would two young men with their lives ahead of them murder their schoolmates and a teacher in cold blood and take their own lives as well?

A number of characteristics of the incident were identified:

1 *Eric and Dylan were considered "outsiders."* Eric and Dylan were identified as "members" but not leaders of the Trench Coat Mafia, a loose, social affiliation of former and current Columbine High School students. Members of this group were regarded as "outcasts" and, both individually and as a group, they were often harassed by the "jocks"[2] of the school.
2 *Eric was the leader and Dylan the follower.* The police evidence suggested that Eric was the leader and Dylan the follower. Their relationship seems to have involved co-dependency, lack of differentiation and an us-and-them mentality.
3 *The easy availability of guns.* These middle-class teenagers had easy access to the weapons they used. At least three people were involved in providing them with their guns and ammunition.
4 *Evidence from their journals, yearbooks, and videos showed long-term planning*

and extensive preparations. The police report indicates that the two boys were antisocial and very troubled. The hatred they both felt was documented at least from 1997 and they started their planning at least a year prior to the event.

5 *Eric glorified violence and had a lack of empathy for others; the pair of them lived in a world of fantasy and were out of touch with reality.* In 1998, Eric wrote, "God I can't wait till they die. I can taste the blood now—NBK [Natural Born Killer]," alluding to the cult film that glorified the type of anarchic and violent behavior Eric and Dylan acted out. The following statement indicates his state of mind: "You know what I hate? ... MANKIND!!!! ... kill everything ... kill everything ...." He also drew a picture of a gunman amidst a pile of dead bodies with a caption, "The only reason your [*sic*] still alive is because someone has decided to let you live."

Eric and Dylan seemed to have little concern for their friends and the siblings of their friends, many of whom were killed or injured on April 20. In fact, they mentioned casually in their writings that some of their friends might die and that their families would be devastated. They justified their sentiments by saying, "War is war."

6 *A major motivation for Eric and Dylan was revenge.* The report on the Columbine incident states that they plotted against those they found offensive—jocks, girls who said no, other outcasts, and anybody they thought did not accept them or had ever harmed them. The report says that most were unaware they had ever offended Eric or Dylan. Eric wrote on another occasion, "I hate you people for leaving me out of so many fun things."

In his diary, Eric said how much he hated the world and that he and V (Dylan) were different as they had self-awareness. Eric wrote, "I will sooner die than betray my own thoughts, but before I leave this worthless place, I will kill whoever I deem unfit ...."

In October 1998, Eric wrote that someone was bound to ask, "What were they thinking?". He answered, "I want to burn the world, I want to kill everyone except about 5 people ... if we get busted any time, we start killing then and there ... I ain't going out without a fight."

He went on to say, "It's my fault! Not my parents, not my brothers, not my friends, not my favorite bands, not computer games, not the media, it's mine." In another entry he stated, "I'm full of hate and I love it."

7 *They described themselves as having low self-esteem, not fitting in, and being rejected.* The Trench Coat Mafia to which they belonged gave them a presence outside of the establishment, and their isolation and growing hatred and rejection of most people allowed them to distance themselves from human society in general.

Barbara Coloroso (2002: 26–28) describes the culture of Columbine as one where there was a hierarchical structure, with those showing athletic prowess given special status and taking on the right to tease and humiliate those who were seen as different (for having unusual hair-dos or for being "homos"). She identifies that cliques are formed along interest lines and that where some cliques are valued more than others by the school authorities, discrimination and bullying are sure to follow. She also describes two humiliating incidents involving Eric and Dylan: firstly, when they were falsely accused of bringing marijuana to school and subjected to a search of their property; and, secondly, when they were surrounded by a group of students who squirted them all over with tomato ketchup that they then had to "wear" all day. They did not fight back and a teacher was in attendance.

The events of April 20, 1999 at Columbine High School were tragic and frightening, and the incident is not only the worst school shooting in US history, it is also a symbol of what can go wrong in schools in the extreme. What was particularly chilling for Americans was that Columbine was not a poor inner city school with a raft of social problems, but a suburban school typical of middle America and therefore apparently a safe haven:

> While this report establishes a record of the events of April 20, it cannot answer the most fundamental question—WHY? That is, why would two young men, in the spring of their lives, choose to murder faculty members and class mates? The evidence provides no definitive explanation, and the question continues to haunt us[3].

Nothing can justify the killing and maiming Eric and Dylan carried out, or ameliorate the devastation they wreaked on their community and themselves, but it seems that there were a number of alarm bells ringing in the background and nobody was listening.

On March 19, 2001, an issue of *Time* magazine featured what it called "the Columbine Effect." It told the now well-known story of 14-year-old Charles Andrew Williams (Andy) who, as a result of chronic bullying, decided to turn on his tormentors. Two years prior to the event, Andy had moved with his father from Maryland, where by all accounts he had been happy at school, to Southern California where he attended Santana High School in Santee. He was slight of build, unable to defend himself, and was picked on by various students. The incidents of bullying were relentless and extreme: some students heated up a metal lighter and pressed it against, and burnt, his neck; on other occasions, for no apparent reason, students walked right up to him and punched him in the face; his head was dunked in a toilet containing human waste; students tried to set fire to him after spraying him with hairspray; he was called names and taunted constantly.

He told at least 12 people that he was going "to do a Columbine." He was not taken seriously and nobody did anything either to stop him or to warn the police or the school authorities. One day he took his father's 22-calibre revolver to school and fired over 30 shots in a toilet and the adjoining court-yard, killing two students and wounding 13 people.

Another article in *Time* (January 7, 2002) stated that, "When he appeared in court Wednesday, he was alone—neither his mother, who lives in South Carolina, nor his father attended the hearing. This kid, it is clear, is operating utterly without the safety net called family". Could this claim also be made in terms of Andy's school, and the safety net called community?

> ... four students who reportedly heard Williams talking about his planned rampage and who dismissed his plans as "a joke" were barred from returning to school for the rest of the year. And while school officials insisted the suspension was for these students' own safety, there is an indisputable air of retribution about the action. Why didn't you tell anyone? You could have saved two lives and incalculable pain.
>
> Today, the walls of Santana High School in Santee, Calif., are pocked with hastily covered bullet holes. And while the halls are once again filled with students, there are some absences. This weekend, the community will gather to say good-bye to its dead and attempt to collect its shattered illusions of safety. And the rest of the country will watch, feeling guiltily grateful that the latest shooting happened there—and not here.
> (http://www.time.com/time/pow/article/0,8599,101847,00.html)

Andy was the subject of a recent "20/20" documentary on television, interviewed by Diane Sawyer. What we saw was a young, slightly built boy who was hardly able to string a sentence together. With no evidence of his academic record or skills, he seemed either like a special needs student or someone who had severely damaged himself through substance abuse. Yet earlier videos of him showed a happy, articulate child. What was clear was that this young man, who had been mercilessly bullied at secondary school, had extremely low self-esteem, was very confused in his thinking, and was full of remorse for what he had done.

Could Columbine or Santana High School have prevented the murders that occurred there and the devastation and loss to families with ricocheting effects throughout the communities involved, and indeed the whole country and even further afield? In the face of tragedy, it is easy and human to blame, but it is also fruitless and a perpetuation of the sort of mentality that allows bullying to take flight. It is more important to examine how the schools in question might have instituted and safeguarded a culture that would have been inclusive of *all* its students.

The extreme tragedy of murder, as occurred at Columbine and Santana, and the desperate sadness of self-destruction as has occurred far too frequently among adolescents who leave suicide notes telling how they can no longer bear their constant persecution, are the most final, hopeless, and desperate responses to bullying. At Columbine and Santana, there were clear indications of isolation and ostracization, and at Santana specifically of bullying in various forms. We can only surmise that at these schools the violence remained hidden until it was too late and that the schools were dominated by blame cultures (the Santana response to Andy Williams's confidants), where an elite may have been allowed to go unchecked (the jocks at Columbine, and those in the Taradale incident), and the isolation of individual students was not noticed or dealt with.

It is of life-giving importance, therefore, that the beacon of hope that is offered by a properly adopted and carefully maintained whole-school approach is held up bravely enough to see into the deepest recesses of school systems so that everyone is kept safe and nurtured within a safe school environment.

Notes

1 The factual information here has been taken from the official report of the Columbine High School incident produced by the Jefferson County Sheriff's Office of Boulder, Colorado, released on May 15, 2000. A copy of the full report can be found at the following website:
   http://www.cnn.com/SPECIALS/2000/columbine.cd/frameset.exclude.html
2 "Jock" is a derogatory term for male students who are good at sport. They also tend to be stereotyped as chauvinistic and unintelligent.
3 This is an excerpt from the letter from the Sheriff's Office of Jefferson County introducing the report, dated May 15, 2000.

5

How Teachers Contribute to a Bullying Culture

Introduction

As with parenting, teaching styles can be categorized into three types:

1 authoritarian;
2 permissive; and
3 authoritative.

An analysis of the literature on good teaching practice and styles reveals universal support for an authoritative style. The authoritative teacher is demonstrably in control of the classroom environment, and has a clear agenda and purpose, while encouraging the individual members of the class to develop their self-determination and independence within reasonable boundaries.

The competence and motivation of most teachers means that the majority of our classrooms are safe places. Most class settings do not naturally develop a bullying culture. However, all teachers need to be aware of the correlation between their style of classroom management and the development of an unsafe environment that can lead to a bullying culture.

There are various types of teacher responses to bullying. In a safe school, which has proper management, policy, and procedural structures in place, no teacher will find himself or herself struggling to respond to bullying from their personal philosophy and experience, and acting in a piecemeal and haphazard fashion. Instead, they will be supported by clear procedures within a network of systematic responses that are part of a whole-school approach. But there are other situations in which teachers actually contribute to a bullying culture. That is what this chapter is about.

Teachers who contribute to a bullying culture

The types of teacher behavior that are most likely to coexist with and even encourage bullying are:

1 the authoritarian teacher ("In my class ...");
2 the narcissistic, queen bee teacher whose goal is to be adored by some at the expense of others;
3 the active bully teacher;
4 the disinterested teacher ("Tell someone who cares");
5 the wishy-washy, liberal, permissive teacher, who is all talk and no action, and lets everything wash over him or her.

The authoritarian teacher

The authoritarian teacher models bullying behavior by establishing and running a classroom based on an autocracy. At this extreme, the teacher expects on the one hand to *control* behavior that threatens classroom efficiency and, on the other, *displays* behavior that is domineering and based on the same sort of power model as bullying. The authoritarian teacher relies on slogans like, "In my class, we don't behave like that," when in fact "we" clearly do. He or she appears to believe that aggression, anger, intimidation, rules, threats, and often ridicule will stamp out behavior that makes classroom management and teaching difficult. This pedagogic approach is akin to a parent smacking a child for hitting another. The extreme espousal of hierarchy and domination is a mirror image of the bullying relationship in which power is wielded by the one (the bully) over the other (the victim).

The narcissistic, queen bee teacher

The narcissistic, queen bee teacher illustrates many of the issues that arise in secondary schools in relation to teachers and bullying. It is a more subtle syndrome than either of those at the extremes of the continuum. In our first teacher case study, we are going to examine this type of teacher.

Julie is a 12-year-old student who, for all her primary schooling, attended a small rural school that serviced a village and its surrounding settlements. Now, ready for secondary school, she finds she is the only student from her area who has to bus in to the nearest suitable urban, coeducational school. Julie is pretty and has blond hair. She was very successful and the only girl in her class at her last school, and she expects to enjoy secondary school.

Her female peer group at her new school are urban sophisticates, who are competitive about their clothing and aware of the relative cost and status-value of what they wear. There are 14 girls in Julie's new class and 14 boys. She knows no one because all the boys from her junior school have gone to a boys' school.

Her form teacher, Holly Thorn, is 38, confident, has been teaching for 16 years, is a department head (English), and thinks she is a really good teacher.

On the first day of school, Julie arrives late. The bus arrangements did not work, and Julie comes into the classroom hot, sweaty, unsure of herself, and embarrassed. However, she composes herself quite quickly.

Julie: I'm sorry I'm late, the bus from Springwood didn't come on time.
Holly Thorn: Well, thank you for gracing us with your presence at last (a pause and a smile at the rest of the class sitting quietly in rows while she perches on the edge of her desk, slim legs crossed). This school starts at 8.30, not whenever you decide to arrive.

> *Comment*: The teacher and the class are in collusion against Julie within the first hour of the first day of the new school year. The teacher uses the laughter to gain support from the class and to allow the "cool" students to identify themselves. She captures the class by creating a scapegoat.

The class titters. Julie looks embarrassed, and goes red-faced to her seat.

Later that day when the home class meets again for English, someone takes Julie's pen from her desk. She tells the teacher, who says, "Oh, for goodness sake, can't you even look after your own gear? You're at secondary school now. I'm far too busy to deal with this sort of thing."

> *Comment*: The teacher makes it clear to Julie that she has no significant adult present, and gives her the message for a second time that day that she is failing in the popularity, OK-ness stakes.

On the third day, the first-year students are allowed to try out for sports teams and clubs. Julie proves to be a good tennis player. Holly Thorn walking by asks her, "Are you trying to be another Anna Kournikova," and glances with a slight smirk at some of Julie's classmates who are standing nearby. They laugh, and Julie decides not to try out for the tennis club.

On the fourth day, it rains, and the form class is allowed to have lunch in their home-room. One of the girls picks up Julie's lunchbox and says how cute it is. She looks slyly at the other girls and they laugh. One says, "Oh Julie, I wish my mum would buy me a lunchbox just like yours." Again they laugh. Julie quickly sees that they don't have lunchboxes, but buy their lunch or bring junk food in packages.

Comment: She learns that what she does and what she has are not OK.

By the end of the second week, everything about her—her clothing, her hair, her lunches, how she writes, how she talks, her opinions, her taste in music—has been commented on and denigrated. Soon she is isolated and unhappy.

She becomes reluctant to go to school and eventually tells her mother what is going on. Her mother rings Holly Thorn. Ms Thorn says she has not noticed anything wrong. She says to Julie's mother, "She's mixing with bright girls now. We have very high standards here. Secondary school is much more demanding than primary school. These sorts of thing happen. Don't worry, they invariably settle down. She can always come to me, I'm there to listen."

Comment: In this way the teacher neutralizes Julie's support from her parents.

Julie's mother starts to think Julie must be exaggerating. Julie ends up feeling that the events were indeed trivial and that she should not have made a fuss. After Julie's mother confronts her, Ms Thorn decides to investigate and calls a group of girls together to ask what has been happening to Julie. They laugh and say, "We've only been joking," "We've only been having a bit of fun," "She's making it up," "She's exaggerating," and "What a load of rubbish" in a cacophony of denial. Holly Thorn feels that she has done the right thing, has followed up the parental complaint, and is now in a position to demonstrate her handling of this to Julie's mother. She rings Julie's mother and says, "I've spoken with the girls, and Julie's exaggerating. It was nothing more than harmless fun."

Comment: In the process several things happen. First of all, Ms Thorn believes that she has operated with professional responsibility and has "done all she can." She has questioned a group of purportedly dispassionate eyewitnesses who can give her a "true" account of what actually happened. She has informed Julie's mother of the outcome of her investigations and thus continues to undermine Julie's support from her mother. She reidentifies the behavior in question as Julie's fault, rather than seeing it for what it is—bullying. The redefinition takes place within a context of blame and shame, and results in the victim being dismissed and held accountable for what happened and the other girls having their credibility confirmed while Julie does not.

In this situation, the victim is also often accused of seeking attention, being a drama queen, being malicious, or being a liar.

At the same time, the teacher will have presented her story in the staffroom and got the other teachers on side. Once Julie's general reputation in the school is damaged, she will be seen as Holly Thorn presents her. Because of her isolation and unhappiness she will not be able to withstand the further ostracization and denudation of her character. She is now seen as an irritant.

The bullying escalates. There is open intimidation and antagonism, Julie gets hit, has her bag thrown around, and goes home unable to hide her tears. Her mother rings the school again and asks for another meeting with Holly Thorn.

Mother: Julie's a mess. She's being bullied by girls in your class and you've done nothing about it.
Holly Thorn: I've talked to the girls, I've done everything possible and, frankly, Julie doesn't do anything to help herself.
Mother: I'm taking Julie home until you get this dealt with. She's incredibly upset and just isn't coping with what's happening.
Holly Thorn: I've been teaching for a long time now and it'll go away. We don't support bullying here. We have a very strong anti-bullying policy. Julie's a highly strung girl and this is just a phase that girls go through. It's just a part of growing up. But look, I'll work with the class to get this sorted, don't you worry.
Mother: Well, I hope you do. I just don't know what to do to help Julie.
Holly Thorn: Trust me, I'll keep my eye on this. I've been teaching for 16 years and I've dealt with lots of these cases. Let Julie stay home tomorrow and we'll sort it out.

During her absence, Holly Thorn takes aside a group of popular and pretty girls from her class and tells them, "You've got to be nicer to Julie. She's from the country and doesn't have any friends. She's really struggling to come to grips with her work. The school she's come from wasn't really up to our standard, and she's falling behind. You've got to try to be nice to her and make her feel welcome. See if you can give her some tips about how to fit in better."

The teacher then informs Julie's mother that Julie should return to school and that the problem really does seem to have been resolved.

When Julie arrives the next day, the girls in her class are obsequiously nice to her, especially the subgroup chosen by Holly Thorn to "deal" with the problem. They tell her how she can become popular and more accepted. They refer to her clothes and her hairstyle. The momentary attention does nothing to assuage Julie's anguish, and their patronizing appraisal of her causes her to become even more withdrawn. She feels isolated and desperately unhappy and is embarrassed to know that her form teacher has talked about her in her absence.

The elements at play in this scenario are the following:
- The teacher is the queen bee. She tries to be one of the girls and in fact she makes sure she is the Number 1 girl, and vies for popularity by manipulating the social dynamics of the class.
- She nominates and isolates a victim.
- She abuses her power on the first day.
- Her behavior is repetitive.
- She encourages group participation.
- She colludes with the bullies, and takes away and undermines any support or potential support that Julie may have attracted on her own.
- She has favorites.
- She controls the class.
- She actively humiliates the victim and highlights her weaknesses and differences while pretending to be supportive. Her actions contradict her espoused position.
- She blames the victim for what happens.
- She does not believe bullying is occurring.
- She does not believe the victim. She thinks the victim is exaggerating, causes it, asks for it, is unattractive/provocative, and could help herself.
- She does not see and/or overlooks acts of bullying in the classroom.
- She appeals to a subgroup of popular girls to "help" Julie, not Julie's more natural potential peers.
- She enlists the support of the other teachers: "I've tried this and I've tried that and I just don't see what else I can do unless she helps herself …".
- She undermines parental support by throwing doubt on how truthful Julie is. She questions whether Julie has exaggerated what has happened, and uses her authority to undermine Julie's story.

Comment: Holly Thorn hides behind her years of experience, her confidence in her teaching, and her avowed understanding of adolescents. Her attitude is like that of the café owner who serves up inferior coffee and, when challenged by a new customer, says, "We've been in this business for 300 years and we've never had a complaint before." She minimizes and dismisses the complaints and thus denies the existence of the bullying events. In these dynamics, Holly Thorn's position is supported by the class, the other teachers, and the school administration. Their response to criticism or queries is likely to be, "She's done all she can. Julie has a problem." The end result is a denial that there is bullying going on and the problem is placed firmly at Julie's feet.

This scenario highlights one of a range of teacher behaviors that sometimes occur in a school that does not have a safety culture.

The active bully teacher

The active bully teacher exists in the center of this continuum and takes the coercive and colluding behavior of the narcissistic teacher to the extreme where a student is constantly and regularly hounded, belittled, and bullied by the teacher. The emphasis is less on creating a scapegoat than on making someone a victim, less on ineffectually "dealing with" a parent's concerns by reassurance, redefinition, and rallying other teachers against the student than on continuing and being allowed to continue a campaign of cruelty towards a student within the structures of the school. In the following case study, the active bullying by the teacher is very apparent.

Merrill is a 14-year-old girl in her second year of high school. Her form teacher is a young science major who is only in his third year of teaching, but who is highly qualified and well thought of by the school. His name is Rod Crossley. Merrill completed her first year of high school with good marks in all subjects, a few friends, and no major problems. She is slightly shy and introverted, but reasonably well adjusted. She does not become part of any of the dominant girls' cliques in year 10, but shows no signs of unhappiness or isolation. With Mr Crossley as her form teacher she develops a particular interest in science that leads her to question many things in the world around her. By the second term her parents notice a change in her behavior. She becomes listless, morose, and monosyllabic when asked about school, and has stomach pains most school mornings. Her mother is unsure whether they are genuine and takes her to her doctor who says they may be related to stress. She tries to talk to Merrill about how she is feeling but gets little response. One day she sees an acquaintance in the supermarket whose daughter Jo is in Merrill's form class. Jo's mother tells her that Merrill is being picked on by Mr Crossley in class.

Merrill's mother then gently tells Merrill what she has heard, and Merrill says that Mr Crossley has been yelling at her in class, humiliating her, and has twice sent her out of the room. Her mother asks her what she has done to make Mr Crossley so upset with her. Merrill does not know and can only think it is because she asks a lot of questions.

When Merrill's mother speaks to Rod Crossley, he denies that he yelled at Merrill, says that she was put outside the classroom only once "for being silly," and that Merrill tends to ask a lot of questions that are ill thought through and badly timed. He says he encourages his students to question everything but does expect them to have some sense about when it is appropriate to ask questions. He feels that she acts as if she were the only student in the class. Merrill's mother describes Merrill's changed behavior at home and Rod Crossley says she has no problems at school, apart from needing to learn how to fit in better with what is going on in the lesson.

A week later Merrill is found crying in her bedroom after school. She tells her mother that she asked a question in class about the process of photosynthesis and was yelled at by Mr Crossley "for asking stupid questions." She felt totally embarrassed and belittled when the class laughed at her.

In the next week, Rod Crossley sarcastically challenges Merrill when she does *not* ask a question when questions are invited after a lesson on plant reproduction. He looks to the class for approval and is rewarded with a titter. Merrill's friends start to fall away from her and she begins to feel totally isolated.

Her mother decides to go to the school principal, who assures her that Rod Crossley came to the school with the highest recommendations and the best qualifications. He also says that good science teachers are very hard to get, but that he will nevertheless speak to Mr Crossley himself. He makes it clear to Merrill's mother that he does not want her to take any more action herself.

Within days, the same thing happens again, and Merrill is humiliated in class. Her mother rings the principal. He says he is surprised at her story but will check it out with Mr Crossley. A week later Merrill comes home in tears, and tells her mother what happened in science that afternoon. When Merrill bravely tried to fill a gap in her understanding of transpiration and repeated a question, Mr Crossley yelled at her.

Her mother decides to return to the school and confront the principal once and for all. He says that Mr Crossley has explained that Merrill is a pedantic, slow thinker who constantly interrupts his lessons with questions. While he encourages curiosity, he does not appreciate idle inattention and mindless questions. Merrill appears to be not concentrating in class and then expecting a lot of one-to-one input when there are 28 students to attend to. The principal suggests that she may need some remedial help and some counseling.

Merrill's mother asks if the principal approves of yelling and sending students into the corridor as classroom management strategies. He says his staff do a sterling job in very difficult circumstances, catering to all levels of needs, and that he totally supports his team. Merrill's mother asks him again if he approves of Rod Crossley's teaching strategies, and he says he has had no other complaints and that Mr Crossley has the highest credentials. He tells Merrill's mother that she can write a letter outlining her concerns if she wishes.

She does so cogently and thoroughly, and lists the incidents about which she knows. In reply she receives the following response from the principal:

> We would like to express the fact that we do take all complaints seriously, and we have acted on your complaints appropriately.
>
> When a complaint against a staff member is received, we investigate the complaint and consider an appropriate course of action.

We have high expectations of teachers' conduct in the classroom. To ensure that, each teacher has a sponsor teacher to whom they can go with any problems and stresses. Sponsors meet weekly. In addition, we carry out an annual appraisal process that was described very positively by the Education Review Office[1] as "rigorous."

You can be fully assured that we have seriously considered your complaints and taken appropriate action. Although we are not in a position to debate these matters because of our obligations under the teachers' employment contract, we will continue to monitor the issues raised.

A month later, Merrill was still reporting acts of bullying and intimidation by Rod Crossley and her parents, in despair, removed her from the school. She went on to excel in science at her new school.

Apart from Rod Crossley's bullying of Merrill itself, one of the saddest dimensions of this story is the fact that the school at which he worked closed ranks against a reasonable concern from a parent, and hid behind a bandstanding of support for its teachers, ignoring evidence of gross misconduct, bullying, and poor classroom management.

The disinterested teacher

The fourth type of teacher who contributes to a culture of bullying is the disinterested teacher, the one whose message when a student comes with a problem is, "Tell someone who cares." This sort of teacher has often been dissatisfied in the job for too long, uses ridicule as a major control device, and resorts to cynicism both in classroom interactions and outside the classroom. While the school may have a policy which says that it encourages students to talk to teachers when there is a problem, not all the teachers subscribe to this policy and they are allowed to go their own ways and to maintain their own idiosyncrasies. This sort of teacher basically cannot be bothered and probably thinks that students should sort out their own problems anyway.

The permissive teacher

Finally, at the furthest end of the continuum is the permissive teacher. This type of teacher allows bullying to happen through disinterest, lack of observation, nonreflective responses to student behavior, not finding out why people are sad, and overlooking graffiti and other indications of an unsafe culture. Whereas the disinterested teacher hides behind cynicism, the permissive teacher runs an "anything goes" classroom, opts for compromise rather than taking a moral stand, gives unclear messages that allow students to justify bullying and other antisocial behavior as "ragging," "a bit of fun," or "a lesson in survival," and prefers popularity to responsibility. Permissiveness and liberality are regarded as morally good and politically correct, and a *laissez-faire*, dog-eat-dog culture is allowed to develop in the classroom.

Conclusion

In safe schools, teachers with a range of beliefs, adequacies, and skills are supported to follow school policy and develop professional expertise and excellence. Accountability does not become an excuse for witch-hunts but a vehicle of ongoing learning and development. When a principal or school board closes ranks against parental or student complaints, in the belief that they are thus supporting their staff, they are in fact creating a citadel against complaints, queries, and uncertainty, and allowing an unsafe culture to develop. The point of paying appropriate attention to such complaints is not to denigrate the teacher in question, but to honor the complaint and to keep an open culture. If there is a problem, then the teacher needs to be supported through it in a nonblaming way.

While teaching styles vary and beliefs about discipline are multitudinous, when a school has a policy about bullying and harassment, and a complaints procedure, then these need to be "owned" by all school staff and to be easily applicable and actioned by any staff member faced with a difficult situation. Only in these ways can schools become safe places, not only for students but also for teachers.

Note

1 The Education Review Office is a government-funded and endorsed body that assesses the performance of schools throughout New Zealand, using a system of school visits and quantitative appraisals.

6

Parents, the Other Victims

Silence and marginalization

In this part we have looked at the inner workings of schools that are unsafe and analyzed how they respond to bullying. We have also described the types of teachers who in some way give support to a bullying culture. It is important also to examine what happens outside the school when bullying comes to light and how this outside component is dealt with in schools. This chapter therefore looks at the parents, principally of the victims of bullying.

Parents are secondary victims of bullying and can be marginalized by both the adolescents involved and the school. When their child is being bullied, parents want it to stop. Whereas the child feels powerless, parents often get angry and will take steps such as going to the school to try to solve the problem. When they do this, schools sometimes treat them as if they are part of the problem, but they need to be part of the solution.

Bullying thrives in a culture of secrecy, disproportionate power, and constant intimidation, and those who are victimized generally do not tell. If they inform a teacher that they are being bullied, they are sometimes told to deal with it themselves, not to be a sissy, or to go away and not tell tales.

Even more than younger children, adolescents tend not to disclose to parents what is going on in their lives and what troubles them most. They do not tell for a number of reasons:

- They do not want to appear to be inadequate.
- They want to sort out their problems themselves.
- They are scared the bullies will find out they have talked to an adult.
- They do not want their parents to worry.

- They are afraid that parents will overreact and make things worse.
- They are ashamed that it is happening to them.
- They may feel it is their fault.
- They may be inarticulate, lacking in confidence, unfocused, and unclear about what they should do.

Consequently, bullying usually comes to the attention of parents further down the track, at some sort of crisis point: for example, when their child comes home distraught or with ripped clothing. At this point the parents' protective energy will be activated and they are most likely to ask what the school's response has been and what their son or daughter has done about it.

When parents decide to contact the school, they do not make such approaches lightly. Most do so thoughtfully and out of a sense of concern, duty and, sometimes, despair. While it is true that there are parents who are habitually litigious, hypercritical, overprotective, and paranoid in their dealings with others, such parents are rare. Most parents care very deeply about what happens to their children and appreciate all the efforts that school staff make for their benefit.

Parents sometimes find it hard to approach the school when bullying occurs because they:

- lack confidence;
- do not feel they have any rights;
- are illiterate or inarticulate;
- feel intimidated by the school;
- come from another culture; or
- speak a different first language.

In approaching a school staff member, parents often have to deal with their own feelings of apprehension, fear, and sense of unfairness.

When parents report a problem of suspected peer abuse, they expect the school to take a genuine problem-solving approach. If the school is in denial that it has a bullying problem, or feels threatened by a parent's approach for some other reason, obstacles will be put in the parent's way and a process of filibustering will occur. At the same time, the teacher or principal involved may say, "Leave it to us, we'll deal with it." If this is the case, that is fine, but what if these words of reassurance are nothing more than words?

One of the responses teenagers have to being questioned by parents about bullying is to feel confused and to cover their embarrassment by lying. They often deny that they are being bullied when questioned. Once the crisis point occurs they can deny it no longer, but as they have already lied they may have to dig an even deeper hole. They might admit that something has happened, but they will not be completely truthful about detail, extent, sequence, and/or consequences. When their parents ask them what they did about the bullying, at this point they might feel inadequate and think that they should have acted more effectively ("I should have stood up for myself"). They might embellish their efforts to deal with the situation, and say they told a teacher. This will set up a conflict when the parent approaches the teacher and the teacher does not know what they are talking about. This will cloud both the parent's trust of their child *and* the teacher; and the teacher's view of the student.

After speaking to the teacher, the parent is likely to think, "My child has exaggerated," or "The teacher is lying," or "This is a slack school, nothing has been done even though my child complained."

> By saying that they have told the teacher, the victim is trying to shed their feeling of helplessness and passivity. What it does in fact is to open them up to being blamed where they are actually blameless, so that attention is paid to their dishonesty rather than to the bullying that preceded it. In handling this situation poorly, and by default colluding in their own victimization, the victim may be demonstrating the lack of confidence which set them up to be bullied in the first place.

When parents complain to schools, there is a tendency in many schools to see them as irritants that get in the way. In the complex event just described, schools stall for time, find the victim dishonest and a troublemaker, and are then able to dismiss the complaint. In this sort of situation, a teacher might approach a group of students implicated in the initial complaint and say, "I want to get to the bottom of this. What happened the other day?". This group probably includes the bully and the bystanders, who will plead ignorance, misinterpretation, or complete innocence. All that happens here is that the bullying is pushed further underground and a gap widens between the school's position and that of the parents. Or the principal might stand up in an assembly and say, "I've heard that some students have been bullying Jones. Leave him alone or you will be in trouble." Such a response is not only ineffective, it sets the victim up as "a rat" and puts him in further danger. In neither case is the school addressing the bullying or responding appropriately to the parents' claims.

Faced with inertia or misunderstanding on the part of the school, parents often become angry, angry because their child has been bullied and they have not protected them, angry because they have not been protected by the school, angry because someone is lying and they are not sure who, angry with the child, and angry with the school. At this point, they are more likely to take matters into their own hands and perhaps to seek out parent-to-parent solutions that in fact can complicate matters.

If parents do not get angry, they are likely to give up. It takes a lot of commitment, determination, energy, and resilience to take on a school that is in denial or is acting irresponsibly. They might jump through all the hoops the school puts up for them; go to meetings, make telephone calls, produce written reports, go back for even more meetings, and yet still be unable to solve the bullying problem. They may eventually give up in despair because they themselves are ostracized and written off by the school and sometimes by the wider community if they pursue their case vigorously.

When parents come up against brick walls, get blocked, and have barriers put in their way when they approach school staff with complaints or difficult issues, this is a sure sign that things are wrong and not working healthily in the school. Because parents are secondary victims, they need to be involved, and schools by ignoring them only make things worse and do them and the school a disservice.

Case study: a real "worst case" scenario

The following is a case study about a boy's courageous parents who insisted that a school deal with a prolonged and dangerous case of bullying. This case study[1] illustrates the nature of parental involvement; the repeated attempts by the school to deflect, minimize, and deny their concerns; the role they had to take to try to make the school deal with their issues; and the toll this long process had on them and their family.

The parents, Gary and Rebecca, noticed during the first year of Sam's attendance at secondary school that he changed from being easygoing and friendly to being volatile and withdrawn. At first they put it down to adolescence and were not overly concerned. They went to see his form teacher just to reassure themselves, however. She told them Sam was not adjusting well to high school, that he needed to try to fit in better, and that she herself was not "qualified" to deal with these kinds of difficulties. She said the best thing they could do was "to take a tough stand" with Sam.

By halfway through the year, he was frequently losing items of his uniform, getting poor reports, and showing little interest in the world around him. Although his parents checked with him frequently, he constantly denied that anything was wrong and insisted he was happy at school.

During the third term he was given a detention for truanting, and his parents were called to the principal's office. They heard how Sam seldom completed homework and was seen as a poor student with an "attitude." They heard that he was a troublemaker and a bully, often picking angrily on other students and starting fights.

That night they talked to Sam. He continued to assert that school was OK—that he just got a bit bored. He appeared nonchalant in the face of their concerns, was vague about his truanting, and rejected the principal's descriptions of his behavior. The next day he came home without his school jersey and Rebecca was upset when he said he had lost it. She felt angry with him for his apparent carelessness, especially in the face of the negative comments made about him by the school principal.

Later that night, when Sam was watching a video, she asked him to do his homework and he insisted he did not have any. She decided to take a step she would not normally have taken and to check his schoolbag. Inside it, she found his jersey, covered in mud and ripped apart at the shoulder seams. When she showed it to Sam, he was angry at first and then started to cry.

For the next two hours, she and her husband heard about Sam's first year at high school. They heard how he was constantly kicked and punched by a group of boys in his form class, he was called names, girls in his class made lewd remarks about his sexuality, and random students took his things and threw them around the classroom.

Sam begged his parents to do nothing, but the next morning Rebecca rang the principal, Andrew Royd, and made an appointment for her and Gary to see him later that day. The parents wrote their own account of this and subsequent meetings:

> We were grateful at that time that Mr Royd consented to see us, at such short notice. We presented him with a full account of all the instances of bullying Sam had told us about and described how he was being "ganged up on," isolated, and excluded, both in and out of school. When we mentioned that Stevie Biggs was the main instigator and ringleader of the bullying. Mr Royd said, "I don't think Stevie would behave like that." Repeatedly, throughout the meeting, we pointed out that we were there to meet Mr Royd in a spirit of cooperation—we were not there to get a "head on a plate." At one point, Mr Royd looked up and said, "But we don't have a bullying problem here. And you have to remember that boys will be boys."
>
> Mr Royd then went on to suggest that Sam should be referred to a psychologist to establish if he was "*a problem child.*" However, he promised to "spend the whole day looking into it." We took what he said in good faith. We expressly asked him not to interview Sam as we felt that he had been traumatized enough.
>
> We heard nothing from Mr Royd until a week later when we received a letter asking us to attend a meeting with himself, Sam's form teacher, the Deputy Principal and another teacher whom we did not know on the following Monday morning at 9:30.
>
> On Monday morning, we arrived at the school to discover that only the principal and another teacher, Mrs Vested, were attending the meeting. We were told that she was there representing the

staff. Mr Royd then opened the meeting by stating that he was "there as an observer only," and that he had discussed the matter with the staff and that they *"all agree that Sam is the bully,"* and that the other boy is "a good all-rounder." We were given no explanation, or supporting evidence. We wondered why, if the school could so categorically state that Sam was a bully, this had never been brought to our attention before. We were astonished that Mr Royd, who clearly demonstrated his ignorance of bullying at our previous meeting, should diagnose our son as a bully.

During the course of a two-hour long discussion we could not get any evidence from Mr Royd that he had fully investigated our complaint. He told us that we had given him no proof that our son was in fact being bullied, despite, at this stage, having discussed the matter with him for over two hours and having provided him with numerous incidents which we perceived as bullying. He proposed the following solution to the problem: he was going to give a blank sheet of paper to each of Sam's teachers, so that they could "observe" him for a week. This prospect horrified us. We could not get over the fact that for several months the bullying had taken place, in secret, and that now Mr Royd was proposing to put Sam in a "goldfish bowl" environment. Where is this procedure outlined in the school's Policy on Bullying, which, we note, was "lifted" from the national educational guidelines on countering bullying? We were also very conscious of the fact that Mr Royd did not propose to give each teacher a blank sheet of paper to record Stevie Biggs' actions or the actions of any of the other students in Sam's class.

We told Mr Royd again about what Sam had told us. We explained that we felt that the bullying behavior had been conducted in secret. Mrs Vested appeared to support Mr Royd's stance. She said, "Sam had behavior problems before he came to the school." To support this "theory," she said, "Sam was willful." Our initial response was: since when does a personality trait become a personality problem? The more we thought about Mrs Vested's remarks, on behalf of all the teachers, the more we wondered how she could have made such a value judgment about Sam. At one point Rebecca asked Mr Royd, "Are you, or are you not, going to interview this other student?" Mr Royd vacillated. Rebecca asked again. Mr Royd replied, "The more you ask me to interview him, the less I am inclined to do so." When pressed further, he eventually agreed to interview Stevie Biggs. Our meeting concluded shortly thereafter. Mr Royd took obvious pride in photocopying the school's Policy on Bullying for us.

Once Sam realized how seriously his parents were taking the matter, he began to describe other incidents of bullying that had occurred during his first year at secondary school. Gary rang the principal later that evening and gave him full details of the seven additional types of bullying behavior that Sam had been subjected to:

---

1 Stevie and some of the other boys sometimes drag Sam into the toilet to verbally and/or physically assault him.
2 Sam described how somebody in class ruled out his name on the list for the computer. Because of this Sam never gets adequate time on the computer. They make fun of him for not getting his work done and call him names ("Dummy," "Dickhead," "Nerd").
3 Sam described how a boy told the girls in class that he, Sam, was gay and was a sexual pervert. They constantly jeer at him.
4 Stevie punches and kicks Sam frequently, "accidentally" crashing into him whenever he can.
5 Stevie has made it clear Sam is not "cool" and no one should associate with him, and because of this Sam has lost his few friends.
6 The boys in an older class sometimes take Sam's things and make a huge joke of it with Stevie and his sidekicks.
7 Sometimes Sam has tried to hit back or to reclaim his possessions, and every time he gets reported to a teacher as the instigator of the fracas.

The principal muttered something about wanting to reach a resolution over the issue.

The next morning, Rebecca telephoned the school, as she felt it vital to talk to Sam's form teacher. She told Rebecca she would "keep a close on eye on things."

Mr Royd finally interviewed Stevie Biggs that morning, but naturally enough he did not confess to any of the bullying. After the meeting Stevie waited for Sam with four other boys in the classroom at break time and threatened him and pushed him around, saying, "I'm going to smash every bone in your stupid body, and then I'm going to kill you." When Sam came home with a bruised cheekbone and a ripped collar, Rebecca and Gary were upset. The principal had assured them that he would "deal with" the problem by speaking to Sam's main tormentor, and his form teacher had said she would be vigilant. The school still took the line, when challenged, that Sam had started most of the fights, that "boys will be boys" and that the school did not have a bullying problem.

Gary and Rebecca were unsure where to turn. They were already familiar with the school's anti-bullying policy and now checked the school's Handbook for Parents. It stated: "Pupils will be encouraged to report bullying and harassment to the school and their parents ... Various forms of intimidation are unacceptable behavior and therefore need to be taken very seriously ... Complaints ... of harassment will be written down and investigated and reported to the Bullying Group and the Board." The Handbook also stated, "Pupils alerting adults to acts of harassment ... will be protected from victimization."

They spoke to the chairman of the school board and were told that verbal complaints were "given little weight and generally not acted on." He also said that there were no witnesses to the events, and the school could not be expected to take their version of what supposedly had happened as gospel.

They prepared a comprehensive written case for the school management, documenting the history of events and all of their concerns, listing their unanswered questions, and providing supporting documentation from the school's own anti-bullying policy, the Handbook for Parents, and anti-bullying scholarship. They concluded their case with the following paragraphs:

> It is our belief that Sam learned to respond in a physical way to the violence, verbal taunts, isolation, and name calling, particularly as he felt that he got no assistance from his teachers ... We do not condone the behavior exhibited by Sam in reaction to bullying, but we can certainly understand how it came about. We cannot help but feel that the principal and teachers chose to "see" only this aspect of Sam, and that either through ignorance or bias or both, they chose not to investigate the underlying causes of Sam's apparent bad behaviour, i.e. it is our belief that the teachers treated the symptoms and not the underlying cause.
>
> Despite the obligation placed on the management of the school by the Department of Education to cooperate with parents and pupils in drawing up the school's Policy on Bullying, neither Sam nor we have ever been consulted. We showed him the school's Policy on Bullying and, as we had suspected, he confirmed that this was the first time that he had ever seen the document. It seems evident therefore that the school's Policy on Bullying was merely copied from the government anti-bullying guidelines, and *promptly shelved*. We find that the principal and many of his staff do not fully comprehend bullying behavior, much less how to prevent this type of behavior.

They listed the following questions:

- Why was Sam allowed to be bullied continuously in school?
- What specific steps did the school take to stress to students, teaching staff, and ancillary staff that bullying needed to be prevented at the school?

- What provisions exist to carefully monitor and supervise the behavior of students in classrooms and toilets at break times, at lunchtimes, and on rainy days?
- We note that *all* incidents of bullying are to be recorded, no matter how trivial. Please let us see the written reports of bullying against Sam. Equally, please let us have the written reports of bullying, purportedly conducted by Sam.
- We note that *all* incidents of bullying are to be investigated and then dealt with by teachers. Please let us have the details of how the teachers "dealt with" the incidents of bullying behavior which both Sam and we reported.
- We note the following statement in the Policy on Bullying: "parents of victims *and* bullies to be informed by Principal or Deputy Principal earlier rather than later." If Mr Royd and the teachers "*all agree that Sam is the bully,*" why were we not informed?
- We do not accept that Sam is a bully. However, the following statement appears in the school's Policy on Bullying: "Bullies may need counseling." What specific counseling was provided to Sam?
- We note the following statement in the school's Policy on Bullying: "Victims may need to have their self-esteem raised." What specific steps does the school take to raise self-esteem, in the case of the bully or the victim? What specific steps were taken in relation to Sam to raise his self-esteem?
- Why were our allegations of bullying not investigated in a fair and equitable manner?
- What procedures has the school put in place to ensure that teaching staff do not engage in and condone bullying behavior?
- Why did the principal and staff not operate the school's Policy on Bullying?
- Please let us have copies of the incident reports in relation to the serious physical assaults on our son Sam.
- Where does it say in the school's Policy on Bullying that each teacher is to be given a "blank sheet of paper" and then to be told to observe a student for a period of a week?
- Why were Sam's falling grades not brought to our attention?
- Where is the spirit of openness as described in the guidelines?
- Mr Royd stated at our second meeting that he was there as an observer. Why did he not manage the situation, as he was obligated to do under the guidelines?

In their conclusion, they wrote:

> The writing of this document has severely traumatized us both. We believe that we have uncovered consistent and unchecked abusive, bullying, and threatening behavior directed towards Sam. We do

not make this statement lightly and we have had to try and put aside the idea that we feel this way simply because Sam is our son. It has proven immensely difficult to have delved deeply, to have analyzed both our role and the role of teachers in this whole sorry debacle. We had to do *your job*. We had to do the research, to source, as much as possible, independent verification, and to try to piece together what actually happened in your school and how it could have gone unnoticed by the principal and the teaching staff alike. We have talked to Sam over and over. You cannot possibly comprehend how painstakingly difficult and draining it has become to try to elicit the information from him. In all of our investigations we have done our level best not to let our adult perceptions color the telling of Sam's sad and sorry tale.

Not heard, not resolved

Ultimately, the parents were regarded as enemies of the school and as troublemakers. People seeing them in the street started to say things like, "Your name comes up a lot," or "What is it you want? Do you want blood?" They were written off as overprotective and stirrers. As they explained:

> These responses only act to intimidate and demonstrate that despite all our communications we have not yet been listened to, let alone understood. The more persistent we have become in pushing for a resolution (the first step being acknowledgment that there is a problem), the more we have met with defensiveness and denial … The school's reaction is to blame the child, blame the parents, and close ranks … There is an environment of fear at the school. Many parents (and staff) are afraid to speak out for fear of themselves (and sometimes their children) being blamed, labeled as troublemakers and ostracized.

Although other parents told them they knew Sam was being bullied, they did not want to speak on their behalf or to be involved. They felt that if they did so, their children could be singled out and they would also be branded as agitators.

In this example, the parent is intended to be silenced by the attitude, "You're the only person who has ever complained about this and I'm not going to act on a single complaint." The school is in denial: "We don't have bullying here;" the victim is dismissed and redefined as causing it ("he brought it on himself"), or for not telling the truth ("We have no proof"); and the main bully is upheld as a victim of misidentification and misjudgment ("Stevie would not behave like that").

While lip service was paid to some sort of resolution, this had as much meaning as a riddle written backwards in a foreign language, and scratched on sand in the face of an incoming tide. The parents wrote:

> The closure you keep referring to is not possible without a comprehensive response, a clear understanding that the issues have been recognized and addressed, and how they have been addressed ... Closure requires resolution, resolution cannot be achieved until the issues are acknowledged. Healing begins with recognition that there is a problem and addressing it.

All these parents wanted was for the school first of all to listen to them and then to act, to *do* what it stated in its anti-bullying policies that it would do. All they got were accusations, avoidance, blame, deflection, denial, gainsaying, and intimidation. They were treated carelessly and disrespectfully. While they were repeatedly reassured that the problem was being "looked into," "handled", or "dealt with," nothing was done, no policies were applied, and no responsibility was taken by the school.

Where does this sort of treatment leave the parent? Angry, confused, vigilante, taking the law into their own hands, and looking for their own solutions. They might become bullies themselves, threatening the bullies or their parents, causing chaos and bad feeling. They might make threats about the victim's father or big brother (or mother) sorting out the bullies, muddying the channels of reconciliation that could exist in the school community. Unresolved parental bullying complaints can have further impacts on the family, with siblings at school, and when intergenerational bullying (feuding) moves unchecked into a community. Ultimately, they may remove the child from the school, thus taking the onus off the school to own and deal with the problem. This also means that the bullied adolescent is taken out into the community where the cycle can continue. This is a lose–lose situation.

Parents, like schools, want the best for their children, and because they present the school with a problem, they should not be kept outside the solution. The love they feel for their children can be reflected in the care and consideration that the school gives them when it listens. Instead of turning out the light when parents come with reports of bullying and keeping the lines of communication blocked by accusation, denial, and defensiveness, it is better for schools to include parents in their problem-solving processes as they follow their procedures that attend to parental complaints and concerns.

Note

1 This is a real (though composite) case study.

PART III

MAKING THE WHOLE SCHOOL SAFE

7

Developing a Whole-School Approach

What is a whole-school approach?

If there is one thing that anti-bullying scholars agree on, it is that the most effective way for a school to address bullying is for it to adopt a whole-school approach. This approach is the foundation work upon which an anti-bullying ethos can be built. As we have seen in the previous part, unless a school is committed not only to the whole-school process, but also to the adoption of the values and beliefs that underpin it, the exercise provides little protection. While the approach does not guarantee success, it is an essential part of combating bullying behavior.

The strategy's success hinges on the involvement of *all* members of the school community in reaching an agreed definition of the behavior, and their participation in the development and implementation of an approach to dealing with it. In other words, the whole school works together to arrive at a common understanding of bullying and then, using this shared knowledge, develops strategies to counter the behavior. It is essentially a simple methodology and, as many anti-bullying research projects have discovered, one that works. This approach to countering bullying was developed in Scandinavia by Dan Olweus (1993a) and further refined in the UK (Sharp and Smith, 1994; Smith and Sharp, 1994). Interestingly, it was one of very few youth and educational interventions given the thumbs up by a US Congressional Enquiry during the late 1990s (Sherman et al., 1997).

The six stages in the whole-school approach

The approach involves a number of active processes and is action based and reflective in that, at every stage, what works and what does not work is taken into account in order to create the best possible initiative:

1 *Gaining knowledge and expertise*
   (a) Read available anti-bullying literature.
   (b) Become familiar with accepted definitions and available programmes.
2 *Convincing key groups that an anti-bullying initiative is vital, including:*
   (a) principal/head teacher;
   (b) school board (trustees);
   (c) senior management team (SMT);
   (d) teaching staff; and
   (e) senior students.
3 *Forming a planning group to develop a genuine whole-school approach*
   This must be small (6–10), influential (one SMT member, one trustee), motivated, and familiar with the management of change.
4 *Developing an action plan*
   The action plan is developed by the planning group so that the whole-school approach can be implemented.
5 *Implementation—putting the plan into action*
   (a) Research: undertake in-school research, using student surveys and observations.
   (b) Raise awareness/consult: use this information to raise awareness of bullying within the school community. Begin a consultation process.
   (c) Develop an agreed definition of bullying.
   (d) Develop a policy.
   (e) Interventions: put in place a carefully thought-out intervention program, including anti-bullying processes and strategies that will support the aims of the policy.
6 *Evaluation*
   A process of evaluation provides a check on program success and, where necessary, refocuses the initiative.

Making the approach work

The whole-school approach is a simple strategy but it demands careful and precise implementation. The success of the approach depends largely on the enthusiasm and influence of the one or two key, school-based individuals who need to be behind the initiative. The reality is that most schools are very busy and awash with competing demands. Unless the intervention is well planned and resourced, and fully supported, it will fail in the face of other initiatives that vie for attention. In the large-scale research conducted in

Sheffield in the early 1990s, a direct correlation was found between the time and quality of commitment spent in the development of the initiative and the success of subsequent interventions.

Stage 1: gaining knowledge and expertise

Gaining knowledge and expertise is relatively easy (see References for a list of useful resources, and Appendix 1 for information on useful websites), and is an essential first step. The aim of this preliminary work is to understand what constitutes bullying and what programs and strategies are available.

The leaders of the intervention need to be clear about how the whole-school approach works and why it is a good choice. Once this understanding has been gained among the leaders, they must explain to key participants why the approach is essential and how to go about introducing it.

Stage 2: convincing key groups that an anti-bullying initiative is vital

The first step in this stage is to spend time identifying the key groups and people who need to be involved in the anti-bullying initiative. These will include the school's governing body, the principal, the senior management team, and individual staff members who are known opinion-holders and often influence decisions and policy.

Gaining the support of the school's governing body is essential, and a sound grasp of the issues by the school's principal will make this easier.

When approaching the governing body, be it an individual school's local board or the district or area board, the initiators should come armed with their strategic goals and statements that support an anti-bullying initiative.

Most educational authorities have broad and inclusive educational goals that are likely to echo the purposes of any anti-bullying initiative. It is very helpful to point this out to them.

The principal/head teacher

Any successful change in school culture requires almost universal support. The identification of key players is therefore crucial. Experience (backed up by extensive research) suggests that the involvement of the head teacher/principal is pivotal. An anti-bullying culture demands effective and collaborative leadership, and without the commitment of this key individual a holistic (schoolwide) approach is unlikely to succeed. The absence of such leadership will pose significant problems. However, there are few school leaders who are able to resist the compelling attractions of an anti-bullying strategy that aims to increase academic success while building the resilience of students, especially when the initiative has much in common with national and local educational goals.

School board

The school board usually includes more parents than school staff and is therefore a very valuable bridge between school and community. In order for a whole-school approach to be fully implemented and supported, it is essential for it to become part of the understanding and vocabulary of the whole school population. Almost all parents put the welfare of their children to the fore, and it is important therefore to involve them (through their representatives on the board) in an anti-bullying initiative.

Senior management team

The strategy must gain the support of the school's senior management team, and particularly one or two key members to be the public face of the project. All members of the SMT will need to give a firm commitment to the project.

Gaining the support of the teaching staff

Once the school's management supports the initiative, the next key event will be the first full staff meeting.

The presentation to the staff of the anti-bullying philosophy is of huge importance. A carefully planned introductory session should be designed primarily to give teachers time to reflect on the issue of bullying. The presentation should aim to build on teachers' knowledge and to add pieces of information that will, when combined with reflection time, give teachers a chance to make sense of behavior that they commonly encounter every day.

The aims of the initial staff meeting are:

- to raise awareness and knowledge of the issue;
- to allow staff to reflect on their personal experience (at their school, for their own children, in their own classrooms) and probable failure to counter bullying effectively in the past;
- to use research findings to show the pervasiveness of bullying and the effects of certain interventions;
- to discuss safety issues and examine the misery caused by bullying—depression, isolation, criminality, suicide;
- to emphasize teachers' social obligation to empower students to reject intimidation;
- to reflect on the social consequences of not developing compassion and tolerance;
- to discuss the right of every member of the school community to feel safe;
- to discuss the concept of social inclusion and teachers' responsibility to facilitate it;
- to discuss the damage done to onlookers who are "wounded" by their choice not to support victims;
- to discuss ways of empowering "good" students to modify the behavior of others;

- to outline the steps of the whole-school approach.

It can be useful to have an outside expert who supports the philosophical intentions of the school to present this information.

> Care should be taken to ensure that the educational benefits of an anti-bullying project are spelt out. Nothing is more likely to gain teacher, student, and parent support than the promise of improved academic outputs.

In anticipation of gaining faculty support, subsequent events need to be carefully prepared:

- The method of data collection to gain information on the amount and frequency of bullying in the school.
- What outside agencies are able to support the school's initiative.
- What curriculum interventions are available.
- How the curriculum information will be delivered (staffing and timetable issues).
- How the senior students could be mobilized to support the initiative.
- When the parent community will be asked to participate in the development of the strategy.
- A realistic time line (it is likely to take 12–18 months for the innovation to be planned and implemented, and it should be durable and long-standing).

Senior students
Senior students can be very useful in an anti-bullying initiative, and gaining the support of a small group who can play a key role is important.

Schools have successfully involved senior students in a wide variety of roles and each school needs to look at how best they can involve their own students.

- The interest of senior students in the issue can be activated through informal class discussion, existing forums, or as special projects.
- At least one student representative should be included in the planning group.

Stage 3: forming a planning group

By now, a huge amount of resource material has been gathered together, and aspects of the school's own charter or mission statement as well as provincial, state and/or national government educational policy that supports an anti-bullying stance have been presented to all the key groups. From meetings with the principal, school governors, board, SMT, teaching staff, and senior students, the initial small group of committed individuals has expanded to include others who have volunteered or been co-opted. The ideal planning group includes the principal and/or a member of the SMT, a board member, a senior student, and other teaching staff or parents.

Once this group is formed, the full process of developing, custom-building, introducing, applying, revising, maintaining, and monitoring a whole-school approach can begin.

Stage 4: developing an action plan

Developing a plan of action involves discussion, consultation, and review within the planning group but also with reference to other community and school members and anti-bullying practitioners.

As important as the action plan is, it will only be as successful as its acceptance, application, completion, inclusivity, and review/evaluation are. It can be adapted to meet the needs of any school community, and changed because of new input or circumstances. The only thing that should not change is commitment to the initiative, and its completion. Leaving it half done is as dangerous as not doing it at all, and arguably more so.

Stage 5: implementation—putting the plan into action

Research
- A carefully constructed survey of bullying behaviour in the school may provide valuable primary information and will also establish benchmarks for later evaluation and historical comparisons (see Appendix 2 for a school bullying questionnaire).
- Any student survey places an ethical responsibility on the school to report back and to act on findings reasonably soon after the survey has been done. Failure to do this will dash the raised expectations of the victims of bullying.

Raise awareness/consult
- Hold a series of awareness-raising meetings with parents and students in order to develop an understanding of the nature of the behavior and the consequences and impact of bullying.
- The aim is to establish confidence that there are strategies to help victims and bullies.
- Underpinning all these strategies is the need to gain the trust of students so that, when intimidated, they will act with knowledge that there are support structures available to help them.
- An environment in which individuals feel safe to tell if bullying occurs is a desired outcome.

Develop an agreed definition
A major job of the planning group is to develop a commonly agreed definition of bullying. To do so, they need to be clear what it is (see Chapter 1) and then

hold a series of discussions and meetings with teachers, students, and parents so that they can arrive at a mutually agreed and understood definition.

Develop a policy

A policy that identifies what bullying is and the school's policy on it can now be written. This can include:

- a clear definition of bullying;
- how staff, students and parents should respond if they see or become aware of bullying;
- encouragement to speak up, with suggestions of who to approach when bullying occurs;
- procedures for contacting parents;
- ways of making sure the policy is working.

Possible themes within the policy may be:

- a belief that bullying can be stopped;
- a culture in which students feel able to tell if they are being bullied;
- the fact that everyone needs to share responsibility to help stop bullying behavior;
- the fact that the problem is the bullying behavior rather the victim's behavior.

The policy also needs to list points of contact for students:

- use of e-mail alerts and anonymous concern boxes;
- senior students who are part of the anti-bullying team;
- staff who are also part of the anti-bullying team.

The policy should be based on the two following procedural principles:

- All staff need to be committed to a common response to bullying when it does happen. Their immediate intervention is crucial.
- Clear procedures must be used when a case of bullying is discovered.

Interventions

The school needs to select a series of interventions that can be used when bullying occurs. These should be supported by a clear list of procedures with which all school staff must be familiar, and should range from classroom and curriculum interventions to specific programs and activities (see Part IV).

Stage 6: evaluation

The initial school surveys and other more subjective methods should be used to test the effectiveness of the program on an annual basis. Accurate record keeping will also provide the opportunity to review procedures and to help target the hot spots around the school. Regular evaluation allows the program to continue to be fully functioning and also precludes a need to "reinvent the wheel" in three or four years' time.

Case study: implementing the whole-school approach at Pounamu High School

As a result of some university study, two teachers at Pounamu High School[1] in New Zealand, Tumoana and Judy, were keen to launch a whole-school approach anti-bullying initiative in their school. Pounamu is a large inner-city school with a student population of 812, and a decile rating of 5.[2] The school principal is lukewarm, but agrees to let them make a short presentation to the school's board of trustees' next meeting. Before the meeting they carefully read the school's charter, mission statement, and strategic plan, identifying points that could be linked to their initiative. They also use the Ministry of Education's website and identify national strategic goals that are supportive of their intentions.

From the school's charter:

This school undertakes to serve its community in a partnership that encourages and supports *mutual responsibility, cultural safety, and personal integrity.*

From the mission statement:

We will provide students with an academic coeducational learning experience that promotes knowledge, *self-understanding, and mutual respect.*
In all activities *encourage the personal growth*, adaptability, and attainment of each student's full potential.

From the school's strategic plan:

Goal 1: Students will leave as independent thinkers equipped to make *socially responsible choices.*
Goal 4: The school will provide a *student-focused environment.*

Specific objectives that are part of the school's strategic plan:

Objective 4.3: To provide *a caring supportive environment* for all individuals and groups within the school.

> From the Ministry of Education:

The New Zealand Ministry of Education has recently developed eight education priorities. The second priority perfectly supports an anti-bullying initiative:

Priority two—a safe learning environment
Schools will provide a *safe physical and emotional environment* for all students.

Armed with these statements, Tumoana and Judy met with the board and, using current research information, linked the school and Ministry goals to their anti-bullying project. The board was enthusiastic and supportive, with one representative volunteering to be part of the planning project. They also met with the SMT, with the response from each meeting shoring up and giving strength and credibility to the next.

They then planned an initial meeting with the entire school staff, and worked out a careful program for it. They decided to give staff some brief precourse reading. This included a short article on school bullying from an educational research journal and a recent newspaper article.

The primary purpose of this meeting was to get staff on board, to enthuse them about the potential of the whole-school approach, and to convince them of the detrimental effects of bullying on academic and social achievement, as well as on personal happiness and stability which are, in turn, prerequisites for successful learning.

The aims and objectives of the meeting were presented as follows:

Aims and Objectives for Initial Full Staff Meeting

Aim:
To gain the support and commitment of the school staff for a schoolwide anti-bullying approach.

Objectives:
1 To explain what a whole-school approach to bullying is.
2 To provide an opportunity for staff to reflect on what school bullying is.
3 To make available up-to-date information on the incidence and frequency of bullying.
4 To support them in developing an agreed definition of the behavior.
5 To use the definition to extend understanding of the behavior.
6 To establish that bullying damages and undermines the teaching and learning environment.
7 To explore strategies that will support the development of an anti-bullying culture.

The program was outlined as follows:

Introduction: Aims and Objectives

Task Sheet 1: Is this Bullying?
Discussion: Up-to-date information about bullying
Discussion: Myths about bullying
Task Sheet 2: Myths about Bullying
Discussion: What is bullying 1?
Discussion: Confronting adult passivity about bullying
Debate: If adults get involved, they make it worse
Discussion: What is bullying 2?
Resource Sheet: Bullying Scenarios—Yes or No?
Situation Cards: Bullying Scenarios—Yes or No?
Definition: What is bullying?

Task Sheet 1 was handed out to all participants and they were given 5 minutes to fill it in.

Task Sheet 1: Is this Bullying?

Which of these statements do you agree with?

It's only a bit of harmless fun	Yes ☐	No ☐
It's often the fault of the person bullied	Yes ☐	No ☐
It's a problem in my school	Yes ☐	No ☐
Children just have to put up with it	Yes ☐	No ☐
It is all part of growing up	Yes ☐	No ☐
Children can usually sort it out themselves	Yes ☐	No ☐
Victims eventually toughen up	Yes ☐	No ☐
It is mainly physical	Yes ☐	No ☐
Adults getting involved makes it worse	Yes ☐	No ☐
It is inevitable	Yes ☐	No ☐
Bullies need to be hurt	Yes ☐	No ☐
Bullying is part of human nature	Yes ☐	No ☐
Children need to learn to "fight their own battles"	Yes ☐	No ☐
There is more bullying than there used to be	Yes ☐	No ☐

Participants were then asked to compare their views with those of a neighbor and to discuss any differences.

After a short time, the resulting questions and comments were used as a springboard for Tumoana and Judy to begin to introduce up-to-date information about bullying. This information detailed recent and local research into the nature and extent of the problem.

> In our experience this activity is one of the most crucial in the whole process. It will provoke a compelling discussion and is a key stage in the workshop as it quickly and clearly establishes and reframes the prior knowledge and experience everyone has of the behavior. This allows teachers time to reflect and to discover that they are very familiar with bullying, yet in reality know very little about it. They become aware that they have not yet made sense of the behavior. The facilitator needs to be conscious of the importance of this discussion and to be fully prepared for it.
>
> The discussion will bring to the surface a number of widely held views that already shape the school's and the community's view of bullying. In our experience in working with thousands of teachers and students involved with bullying, there are a number of commonly held views, assumptions, and assertions that need to be explored in the quest to uncover why bullying is often condoned or ignored.

At this point, Judy introduced a well-known anti-bullying researcher to comment about her findings in a large metropolitan area of New Zealand where she had conducted a survey with 1,500 students. She led a discussion on myths about bullying, having already pinpointed some that had arisen in the discussion about Task Sheet 1 and the forum afterwards.

Participants were asked to fill in Task Sheet 2, Myths about Bullying and to address further and related issues.

> *Task Sheet 2: Myths about Bullying*
> People hold beliefs about what is bullying, who gets bullied, who bullies, and how to handle it. These beliefs need to be identified and challenged. Note down on this sheet any myths about bullying that you hear, become aware of, or have yourself.

Tumoana recited a list of responses to bullying that could be called the "Rite of passage" myth:

- *"It's only a bit of harmless fun"* or
- *"Children just have to put up with it"* or
- *"It is all part of growing up"* or
- *"Children need to learn to fight their own battles"* or
- *"Victims eventually toughen up"*.

> A strong belief abounds that bullying is inevitable and therefore acceptable. This view contends that bullying is a normal part of human nature and happens as part of the growing-up process.

He invited comments about these responses, which led to a clearer understanding among the participants of how people can hide behind myths about bullying.

> These types of responses provide a value-ridden and dismissive view that has the potential to marginalize victims and others affected by the behavior. If this view is not powerfully challenged, talked through and rejected, the whole-school approach will not work. The facilitator must use the collective knowledge present in the workshop to tackle it head on.

Tumoana was well prepared and used evidence to show that victims of bullying suffer lifelong consequences and that the behavior can have equally devastating impacts on the others involved, both abuser and onlooker. He cited the following:

- Researchers have established a clear link between future criminal activity and school bullying for both the victim and the bully (Marcus, 1999; Miller-Johnson et al., 1999).
- Other studies have suggested that a class that has a bullying culture will make significantly less academic progress than a comparable bully-free group (Cleary, 2001).
- Strong links between school bullying behavior and future domestic abuse have been established (Cullingford and Morrison, 1997).
- Investigations into school shootings such as Columbine have shown that the perpetrators had been bullied by their peer group (Coloroso, 2002).

The key aim of this part of the workshop was for all members of the school staff to reject the myths about bullying. The *"it is going to happen and there is nothing we can do about it and it's not all that bad anyway"* stance was confronted and completely rejected. It was clear that all involved needed to adopt a much more assertive and proactive approach.

The main ideas that should be established at this stage are:

- Bullying is going to happen; it is inevitable and potentially very damaging.
- We have an absolute duty to take every possible precaution to make sure that students are equipped to tackle bullying when it happens.
- We have an absolute duty to deal unequivocally with all reports of bullying and to be vigilant about signs of its presence.

At this point, the SMT participant introduced the topic of adult passivity about bullying. He set up a half-hour debate on the issue, "If adults get involved, they make it worse." Two teams of three volunteered to take negative and affirmative sides, while he took the chair.

The "*adults getting involved makes it worse*" view is used often by adults and almost always by young people as an excuse to avoid intervention. It is an important debate that needs to be addressed, as there are apparently compelling arguments in support of it. The focus of this debate should be on the style of adult intervention and how careful and thoughtful adults and peers need to be when intervening in a bullying situation. During the debate, it is likely that examples of inappropriate and damaging adult interventions will be given. It is important in the subsequent discussion to look at these examples as they will help participants to understand the complexity of the behavior and highlight the pitfalls of various approaches.

At the end of the debate, the bullying expert wrote the following points on a whiteboard:

Some Key Understandings

- Victims of bullying need support, understanding, and advice.
- Changing the behavior of the bullies will not come about through adults threatening or challenging the perpetrators.
- Adults who get inappropriately involved can make it worse.
- Adults who do not get involved can also make it worse.
- Adults need to be part of the solution.

> Like so many things to do with education and parenting, getting the balance right is crucial. We must avoid the extremes of either an authoritarian or a permissive approach to bullying (see Chapters 4 and 5).
>
> The authoritarian approach decrees that bullying will not happen and outlaws the behavior. No effort is made to include those being protected and harsh penalties are imposed on those caught bullying. This will inevitably drive the behavior underground where it will flourish despite the oppressive climate on the surface. The authors in their research have unfortunately become only too aware of the prevalence of this approach. Teachers in authoritarian schools believe they are taking decisive action and that they are being successful. This self-belief is fueled by the lack of reporting of bullying in these schools, "There is no bullying in my school" being the mantra here, followed closely by the assertion that any bullying behavior will be stamped out!

The participants now broke into small groups of five or six whose task it was to clarify what they meant by the term "bullying."

> An effective approach developed by the Strathclyde Local Area Authority in Scotland (McLean, 1994) is to provide each group with up to 20 situation cards and ask them to sort them into three categories: Definitely bullying, Could be bullying, and Definitely not bullying. The small groups discuss each scenario and work out where to place the card.
>
> The facilitator asks each group to explain why they have placed particular cards in each category. The groups are then asked what extra information would be needed about the scenario to move it into a different category. This helps explore the key elements that help ascertain if a particular incident is bullying.

All the participants were given the Resource Sheet: Bullying Scenarios—Yes or No?

Resource Sheet: Bullying Scenarios—Yes or No?

A group of senior boys "wolf whistles" as Helen walks past them in the corridor.
Carol is teased by her friend about a boy liking her.
A group of boys continually puts each other down.
Katrina decides that no one is to speak to Tracey.
Brian's friends mark his birthday with the usual "put downs".
The teacher uses sarcasm to manage the class.
At interval, the others will not let Donny join in, claiming that he always spoils everything.

Two boys have a fight in the grounds.

Jean-Paul, a natural leader, criticizes anyone who spoils the game.

Caleb forces his way to the front of the canteen queue every day, shoving aside anyone who is in his way.

The others constantly hassle Fiona to tidy up quickly so that the group will get more points.

A group of senior students makes fun of the student teacher.

They were then given situation cards (one for each of these scenarios) and asked to place them into one of the three categories, discussing their decisions with others in the group. For example, with the scenario, "A group of senior boys 'wolf whistles' as Helen walks past them in the corridor," one group decided that this was definitely bullying, though they admitted that they were not too sure why. Another decided that if Helen smiled and said "Hi" to the boys, this was not bullying. Yet another said that if she went red and scurried away, and if it happened more than once, then she *was* being bullied. In the joint discussion afterwards, it became clear that it was not the event itself that made it bullying or not bullying, but the intentions of the "perpetrators" and the reactions of the "victim." Someone pointed out that a common anti-bullying deflection device is to *pretend* that one is unaffected by taunts and potentially bullying behavior. If Helen does not show she minds, she may be immune to further attention as the wolf-whistlers most probably want a reaction more than anything. Thus, she steps out of the bullying dynamic. But she may have an involuntary reaction such as blushing that makes her open to further attention. It became clear that the issue is a complex one and depends as much on perceptions as on actual events, on reactions as well as intentions.

The group now felt ready to devise together a definition of bullying. Here is what they wrote:

Bullying is an act of intentional cruelty, physical or psychological, that is repetitive, that victimizes someone, and is based on an unequal power relationship. It includes physical aggression and violence such as hitting, spitting, pinching, punching, kicking, biting, and cutting; using threats, criticism, ridicule, verbal insults, name-calling, telling tales, making up stories; using graffiti, the Internet, and other media and methods to spread untruths and/or unpleasant and embarrassing information about someone; stealing and destroying property; ostracizing, excluding, controlling the responses of other students toward the "victim"; and using body language and gesture to put another down.

After the initial awareness-raising sessions with the school's trustees and staff, the planning group (with expanded membership) ensured the various components of the initiative were put in place. The information gained from the various definition exercises and ongoing discussions was used to develop a draft policy on bullying that was sent to all the homes and discussed by the staff and student groups.

Three fundamental issues were addressed in the policy:

1 the nature of bullying;
2 the preventative measures the school will take to stop it occurring; and
3 the response of the school to the behavior.

Pounamu High School developed a clear set of strategies to bullying so that each staff member would know what to do when bullying occurred. It focused on finding ways to make its policy become practice and to monitor levels of prosocial and antisocial student behavior. It decided to set up several curriculum-based anti-bullying workshops for each cohort of students (see Chapter 11), a comprehensive leadership program (see Chapter 12), and a peer mentoring scheme (see Chapter 14). It chose to train staff in the No Blame Approach (see Chapter 15), which in itself reflected the philosophical stance the school community decided to take in relation to bullying.

At Pounamu High School, the whole-school approach was holistically adopted, rigorously put in place, thoroughly supported by school policy and practice, and evaluated and revised regularly and as need arose.

Notes

1 Pounamu is the Maori word for greenstone, a type of jade.
2 In New Zealand, schools are ranked using a decile rating—1 (poorest) to 10 (most affluent).

8

The Power of the Bystanders

Introduction

We argue that in most bullying situations the real power lies with the peer group. Bullying is usually a group activity. Although it sometimes exists one on one, it only really flourishes with an audience. If the peer group rejects bullying, then the wind will be taken out of its sails, and it will be direction-less. Once there is no direction—no leader—then there is no bully. The bystanders are therefore the untapped resource that can stop bullying from happening. All they have to do is to move away from the sidelines, become active, and withdraw their apparent support of the bullying. Once they do this, the theater for bullying disappears, the bully ceases to be a bully, and the victim is no longer a victim. The bystanders have the power to redefine all the roles in the bullying dynamic.

However, it is hard for this sort of shift to occur unless it is strongly encour-aged and supported. Society often teaches us that much of what goes on around us is not our business. It breeds and harbors a cycle of fear and a cycle of blame. Taking responsibility and acting with compassion and a social con-science do not come easily. Instead, people learn anonymity, alienation, dis-engagement, and invisibility. Adolescents learn bystanding in life—in their families, in society at large, and all too often at school. Like most of us, they learn very quickly the social convention that it is better not to get involved. How can empowering national educational goals, school values, and even cooperative group learning occur if individuals cannot cooperate in their day-to-day social groups?

Adolescent culture reflects this sort of attitude too readily anyway—gener-ally, the code of adolescents is that they should not tell on their friends and they should not confide in adults. In the school setting, this detachment is often reinforced by both authoritarian and laissez-faire style teachers, whose response to student intervention or requests for teacher involvement is often comments such as "I don't like tell-tales," "You're not involved," "Keep out of this," "Go and tell someone who cares," or "They need to sort it out themselves." An authoritarian approach does not seek to change the motivation for behavior but issues rules and proclamations that tend to drive antisocial behavior underground. A laissez-faire attitude rests on the belief that children and young people need to be able to sort things out for themselves and intuitively know how to act.

Although the bystanders from an analytical point of view form an organic group, they are unaware of their identity and are shapeless and directionless. As individuals, they are desperately keen to fit in and are busy looking for status and role. They are not conscious of the dynamic of which they are part, and are usually open to direction from any source.

When power vacuums form, they are like a vortex to potential bullies. They appear as short-lived windows of opportunity for active students and opportunists to fill, first, because they exist outside a controlled situation and, secondly, because they are the means by which such students create an identity. But it is not only the bullies who are drawn into this vortex, but also all of the peer groupings and relationships around the bully, that are reconstituted within a new power structure dominated and controlled by the bully.

In the bullying system, bullies may take or seize power, indulging in behavior such as teasing, name-calling, physical violence, ridicule, and exclusion. The bystanders are sucked in by the bullies to be complicit. They feel powerless, and know unconsciously and unreflectively that if they are not complicit they could become victims. Once the bully begins to operate, each student in the group (whether it is a small group or an entire class) is in effect marked and tagged as a victim or a bystander. It becomes a situation of divide and rule, in which no one dares to get singled out.

The role of the bystander changes and develops as the bullying dynamic takes hold. They soon become distant from the victims, and are able to depersonalize them. At the same time, they are beholden to the bully for being bystanders rather than victims themselves, and thus they succumb to coercion and collude in the bullying. By this time, a functioning bully culture has been established.

Once the group has no bond with the students selected as victims by the bullies, the bystanders are unlikely to move out of their passivity and breach the code of silence and complicity. However, while the bullies *take* their power, they are also *given* it by the bystanders.

If the bullying goes unchecked, the roles become hardened and more difficult to shrug off. It is like a system of psychological blackmail. The threats and controls are:

1 If you support me, I won't bully you.
2 You've watched what I do, don't pretend you're not part of it.
3 You see how useless he is, he deserves everything he gets.
4 He can't even fight back, he doesn't deserve to live.
5 You know I'm right, the victim is a loser anyway.
6 If you support her, then you're a loser too.

However, while this appears an indomitable system, it is permeable and there are ways in and out of it. It is clear from research on the bystanders (such as Adair et al., 2000) that in most cases they feel uncomfortable about being party to the bullying. When they witness bullying, their fear of being the next victim makes them connive at what they see, but in another context, perhaps with a caring adult or a concerned peer, the fear that freezes their prosocial responses can be thawed so they can act with more concern and responsibility.

The bystanders can be helped to develop their decision-making skills and to stand up for each other. With proper guidance and leadership, they can be helped to empathize and to become active, concerned, and responsible, as they would be in an ideal society. This is more difficult in the case of provocative victims, who are adept at destroying connections. However, the bystanders need to be motivated to be able to extend concern even to the most difficult and provocative of their classmates.

Participant roles in bullying

What happens in schools reflects what happens in society. In the face of domestic violence, people try hard not to get involved, and even the police when called sometimes assume that they "should not get involved in domestic incidents." When a dying man crawls bleeding to a doorway to beg for help after a violent mugging, as happened recently in Auckland when a man was robbed of the pizzas he was delivering and less than $20, the person inside ignores his cries because they "don't want to get involved." When a government decides to exterminate an entire population because they are of the "wrong" ethnicity, people turn the other way and pretend it is not happening. They are also afraid that the violence may rain down on them and their families. And if *they* are forced to be the exterminators, they plead later that they were "only obeying orders."

While it may seem overdramatic to compare witnessing genocide to witnessing bullying, the same issues of care, concern, morality, and responsibility are relevant. These are the altruistic characteristics that make us truly human, but all too often they fall into abeyance, disappear, or lose out to fear, greed, and self-preservation. While bullying is not genocide, it *sometimes* involves murder or leads to suicide, and it *always* causes damage, incites terror, and does harm, often for a whole lifetime, to its victims. For the bystanders, it involves them in an unhealthy culture and morality that is based on fear rather than compassion, on apathy rather than action, and on manipulation rather than integrity. Bystanders lose access to their conscience.

Bullying research gives us a series of snapshots into bullying behavior. The passivity and helplessness of the bystanders is indicated in a lot of research. While students may intervene if the victim is a friend or has some status, those without friends or status are isolated and alone (and become nonpersons) and an intervention will not occur (Adair et al., 2000). The recurrent wildlife documentary image of a weaker, slower wildebeest being cut off from the herd, surrounded, and then killed by predatory lions, comes to mind.

Who are the bystanders?

Christina Salmivalli identifies the following participants in adolescent bullying. The main actors are:

1 victims "who are repeatedly and systematically harassed"; and
2 bullies who are "active, initiative-taking perpetrators" (Salmivalli, 1999: 453).

Those who witness the bullying take on various roles:

1 assistants to the bully who "eagerly join in";
2 reinforcers who may not actively attack but give positive feedback to the bully through coming to observe (providing an audience), making encouraging gestures, or laughing (inciting);
3 outsiders, who stay away and do not take sides but in doing so silently condone the bullying;
4 defenders, who provide comfort to the victim, take the victim's side, and try to make the others stop; and
5 those who have no clear role (ibid.: 453–4).

In the Finnish study, the roles are adopted in the percentages that are shown in Table 8.1. Clearly, the bullies, assistants, and reinforcers are a dominant force in the dynamic illustrated in this table, outnumbering the defenders by approximately two to one. They outnumber the victims by between three to one and seven to one;[1] and the outsiders form a group that is about as large as the assistants and reinforcers together.

Table 8.1 *The percentages of children and adolescents in different participant roles among sixth (n=573) and eighth (n=316) graders*

Participant role	Grade	
	Sixth	Eight
Victim	11.7	5.7
Bully	8.2	8.5
Assistant	6.8	10.8
Reinforcer	19.5	15.2
Outsider	23.7	32
Defender	17.3	19.6
No clear role	12.7	8.2
Total	100.0	100.0

It is possible to analyze the bystanders a little differently. What Salmivalli calls the assistant, we call the sidekick; and although in her empirical research there was a significant group that had no clear role, we find instead that this lack of clarity may well be a reflection of changing roles, apathy, some of the hidden dynamics of peer relations, and moral and personal ambivalence. The dynamic remains the same in this breakdown of bystander behavior. We have called our bystanders by the following names:

1 the sidekicks;
2 the reinforcers;
3 the outsiders; and
4 the defenders.

The sidekicks
In the bullying literature, there is a group of bystanders who are variously called the assistants, helpers, henchmen, lieutenants, or sidekicks. We think sidekicks is the best term, as it suggests a person who has been manipulated, someone who has been captured by the bully and used by them. Despite its derogatory connotations, it adequately describes how the role played by this person is subservient to and at the beck and call of the bully. Often these children have been victimized by the group and then plucked from obscurity to this role. Grateful for this elevation, they happily do the bully's bidding. However, because they lack high levels of sophistication and innate social skills, they are often caught by the school authorities. If they get caught, they are given status for their incursions into bullying behavior by the larger group and the bullies.

The sidekicks are the ones who throw the bag around, hold the victim down, and join in the fighting. They stand on the sidelines and call names to the victim and encouragement to the bully. They sometimes initiate bullying behavior, and in the absence of the main bully maintain the abuse of the victim. They are mostly grateful to be "in."

In the sidekick–bully relationship, there is an element of apprenticeship. But some research confuses sidekicks with bullies. Bullies never let sidekicks get too powerful and sidekicks are habitually ingratiating. In the power relationship, sidekicks are always below the bullies and a threat always hangs over them. The process involves their being drawn in, pushed away, drawn in, and pushed away. They are controlled by bribes and threats like, "You can come to my party," "You can't come to my party. I was only joking." They are manipulated unceasingly by the bullies, given approval, and then have the approval taken away.

The reinforcers

The reinforcers laugh along with the bullying and, most of all, they stay there. They are part of the audience and give feedback. They will join in with the name-calling once it has been started. They need leading. While they may have reservations and feel discomfort at the very beginning, they may also benefit from the inclusion that comes from being part of the action, and also be attracted to the thrill and excitement. They may take pleasure in the negative activity and feel they are pushing the boundaries along with the bullies and the sidekicks.

They lack the confidence and certainty to initiate action and are conflicted in their responses. If they start to feel uncomfortable, they are likely to go with the bully and dehumanize the victim.

The outsiders

The outsiders do not participate in the laughter and jibes on the sidelines but at the same time they take no action. They distance themselves from what is happening but do nothing to support the victim or to stop the bullies. They tend to be the biggest group (see Table 8.1), reflecting the power dynamic of inaction, apathy, and secrecy that sustains the bullying culture. While they are witnesses to the bullying and are party to it simply by being present, they metaphorically close the blinds and do nothing about it. For them, their safety lies in being on the periphery and not challenging the prevailing power structure. At least there they feel that they are part of the group.

The defenders

The defenders are more active, and have more highly developed empathy skills. They are prepared to comfort and support the victim, and may even challenge the bully and sidekick groups. Unfortunately in many schools the defenders are nowhere to be seen.

A case study: entrenched roles in a bully culture

The following case study illustrates the way a bullying culture sustains itself, traps people in roles, and operates below the surface.

Terence's story

The insidious nature and power of bullying behavior was strongly brought home when we interviewed an ex-student of Mark's whom he knew had been bullied at school when Mark was Deputy Principal (and in charge of disciplinary matters) a few years ago. Shannon, enrolled in a university course, surprised us when during the interview he admitted to being a bully himself when he was in year 9. He reminded Mark about Terence. Everyone thought Shannon and Terence were "friends." Here is a brief history of Terence's journey through secondary school.

About halfway through his first year at secondary school, Terence was sent to Mark because he had punched a classmate, Ian, in the face in class. This was the first time Terence had come to Mark's notice for physical aggression.

Mark contacted Ian's mother to tell her what had happened and she came to see him the next day. She said that Ian had initially been reluctant to talk to her, but had then opened up and informed her that he and a group of other boys had been bullied by Terence since school started, but this was the first time Terence had hit him.

Ian's mother was a secondary teacher who was aware that the school was proactive about bullying and was keen that it be dealt with. Ian was anxious about her reaction because although he had told her about the bullying, he did not want anything done about it.

Terence was immediately punished by being placed on a three-day internal suspension and his father was called in for an interview with Mark. The punishment did not change the dynamics and, rather than being supportive of Ian, the other boys (who had also been bullied by Terence) continued to hang around Terence. They acted as sidekicks and reinforcers—anything to avoid being the butt of the attacks themselves. Ian was unhappy and isolated. Both the school and his parents were concerned, even though Ian did not complain. He refused to discuss the situation with either his mother or his form teacher.

Because this bullying incident had come out in the open, the extent of Terence's bullying now became apparent. Careful observation by the form teacher and other parental complaints confirmed that Terence was continuing to manipulate the group of boys.

During a discussion between the Dean, Deputy Principal, and the form teacher it was decided that the best way to support the boys would be to move Terence into another form class where they hoped he would be unable to harass Ian and the other boys further.

The move aggrieved Terence and, rather than lessen his power, it appeared to give him greater exposure within the year group. In fact, it increased his audience. He felt he had been harshly treated and certainly did not accept any blame for the incidents that precipitated the move. During the next two years, despite being a capable pupil, he became increasingly difficult and alienated. He continued to come to the attention of the Guidance Department and was frequently punished for being disruptive, for general disobedience, and for failure to complete his work. Despite all this he remained popular with his peer group, who sought him out as someone it was fun to be with; he was clearly a natural leader. He was articulate and, while not a physically dominant boy, he always seemed to be able to gather two or three other pupils around him who were physically imposing.

Terence remained at school until halfway through year 12 when, with attendance problems and facing academic failure, he left school and joined a work scheme. He appeared to have been slowly left behind by his companions and during his last months at school it was clear from observations that he was no longer the "leader" of the pack.

The bystanders' subtext

At the beginning of any school year, the bullying is random, and the roles of the peer group are in a state of flux, especially for first-year students. At this school, there is a power vacuum and Terence steps into it, unbeknownst to the teachers. Although they may be aware of what is going on at the surface, peer relations have a deep structure, with a hidden power base and a hidden set of rules.

Terence clearly emerges as the bully leader. He is central to the peer group and he controls through bullying and manipulation. We would classify him as a not-so-clever bully. Around him the bystanders take up their various roles as sidekicks, reinforcers, and observers. The sidekicks are bigger boys who do Terence's bidding and align themselves with him; the reinforcers are boys and girls who do not like Terence's behavior but see their support of it as their means of survival; the observers are outside this and do not get involved. Further away from the center of the action are students whose roles are not yet defined but who could become defenders. At this stage there are three victims, including Ian, Halmona, and Shannon.

We know from the research that a number of people are victimized by those who bully in the process of establishing a pecking order. We are also aware that when roles become established, victims become identified and the breadth of victimization drops off. Some of those who were victimized stand up to the bullying and act in ways that make them harder to victimize. What is apparent to us through our observations is that it also means that some students who know they are potential victims choose to be sidekicks or reinforcers because they are safer here than in the victim role. They choose these roles almost by default. It is also true that some become sidekicks because they like being close to the power generated by the bully.

Ian, Haimona, and Shannon are initially bullied by Terence and his sidekicks. While Ian remains a primary target and Haimona less so as the peer group sorts itself out, Shannon eventually wins favor (at least temporarily) with Terence and he deflects attention from himself onto weaker victims. He migrates from being a victim to being a sidekick.

Shannon has mixed feelings about being drawn into this group. He enjoys the adrenalin rush of being part of a bullying culture. Although it is negative, it is "buzzy;" besides which, he does not want to be a victim of bullying. He is quick on the uptake and is able to make light of the bullying, and has the social skills to avoid being bullied once he gains confidence in the first term of secondary school.

In the interview seven years later, Shannon expressed guilt for having participated in the bullying of the other two boys. Such was Terence's power that he was able to include and exclude at will. Shannon talked about how, in the first term of secondary school, Terence would one day call him over to look at something, such as a magazine, and then when he approached, Terence would deliberately prevent him from looking. The others, feeling included, did not want to jeopardize their inclusion and did nothing to challenge this manipulation. This no doubt left them uncomfortable with their lack of support for the victim but still not prepared to act. They behaved this way despite the fact that they knew that the next day it could be them who was on the outer. Shannon soon learnt how to deal with this push-me-pull-me manipulation and moved out of the victim group into the bystanders group.

Clearly, the whole process was very demeaning for those who were witnesses, but the manipulative skills of Terence allowed his bullying to go largely undetected and unchecked. While the school had developed a firm anti-bullying ethos, when confronted with a case of ongoing manipulation and bullying, teachers found it very difficult to act in an effective manner. The students involved were loath to complain and felt (correctly) that there was little the school could do to stop Terence's bullying tactics. Terence was a very popular and charismatic member of the class, and his energetic personality made him fun to be with if you were not the target of his manipulation.

The school's actions in moving him merely extended the number of pupils who fell into his orbit. At no stage was the school able to make him accept the consequences of his actions effectively or to provide any reason for him to change. The message he was receiving from the peer group was almost always positive. His "relationship style" was to produce friends and supporters. The attempts to punish him were ineffective and were seen by other students as unhelpful or unfair.

The school's inability to act effectively in this case, either to support those boys who were being manipulated by Terence or to help Terence avoid eventual academic and social failure, was felt strongly by those staff who had helped develop the school's anti-bullying initiative. It is an important illustration of the power of the bully leader, and the huge waste in potential to the whole group involved, when the behavior cannot be changed.

In light of recent experience in dealing with bullies and in particular the use of more inclusive approaches, it was clearly a mistake to move Terence from the class; indeed, for everyone's sake it was most important that the issues surrounding the bullying were explored and better solutions found. The No Blame Approach would have been a safe and effective way of allowing the members of the peer group successfully to challenge Terence's behavior. This would have relieved them of the burden of being bystanders who were at the mercy of Terence's manipulations and perhaps have given them the power to become defenders and for the bullying dynamic to have dissipated altogether.

What was happening here?

In a school with a very strong anti-bullying program, Terence was known for his disruptive behavior but it had not been picked up that he was systematically manipulating, controlling, and bullying others in the class.

Terence was small but powerful. He controlled physically stronger boys through manipulation and had the support of others because they feared him. As is common in bullying, his victims did not tell for a variety of reasons. The bullying never came to the surface until the tip of the iceberg appeared when he punched Ian in the face in class.

In order to try to change the dynamic, the school moved Terence to another class. Unexpectedly, rather than decreasing Terence's locus of control, he was able to increase it across his year. Because the bullying was dealt with in a punitive fashion, it largely went underground, and Terence maintained his control and kept up his bullying behavior but made sure that the school was unaware of it.

During the next few years, Terence's negative behavior continued and it was manifested in his increasing number of run-ins with the authorities. Bullying was just one symptom of his anti-school behavior. Although academically potentially able, he lacked structures and an ability to organize himself. His academic performance declined and he increasingly started missing more and more school.

For the bystanders, the bullying was an uncomfortable and sometimes destructive indication of the nature of peer group relations. It left them variously uneasy and guilty. If they had been mobilized by a prosocial leader or supported by the school to participate actively in healthier peer relations, they would have been able to support the victim, stop the bullying, and redefine the peer group roles.

Understanding the bullying dynamic

Once an individual has adopted or (in the case of a victim) been forced into a role, it is hard to shed the role and all it implies. The group rewards behavior in accordance with the role and punishes behavior that is contrary to it. When adolescents define themselves in terms of these roles, they end up believing themselves incapable of other behavior.

In the case study, Shannon is able to stop being a victim and to become a sidekick, and he carries the guilt of seeing himself as a bully into adulthood. His guilt comes from his knowledge that he acted to protect himself and was unable in this dynamic to become a defender.

It is usually hard for children to lose their victim status even in new situations with none of their former classmates. Entering a new group is very difficult, and the insecurity and fearfulness that result from the trauma of recent bullying goes with them, giving a message to the new group that they are a suitable target (Salmivalli, Kaukiainen and Lagerspetz, 1998). Similarly, bullies (such as Terence) take their role into a new situation. For the bystanders their entire identity within the peer group rests on their various roles in the bullying dynamic. If the sidekicks or reinforcers feel so uncomfortable about the violence of a particular bullying event that they decide to defend the victim, they risk becoming victims themselves. In doing so they shift out of the safe reaches of the group. This is a peculiarly dangerous and vulnerable position to take, and most individuals are loath to risk it. Even where perhaps two or three of the reinforcers agree in private that an act of exclusion is so cruel that it is abhorrent to them, their solidarity with each other may waver in face of the opinion and collusion of the whole group. If one of them "sticks their neck out," they may find themselves metaphorically decapitated, with their two "allies" suddenly returning to the reinforcers' fold.

If there are no defenders at all, the reinforcers are likely to get pulled into the negativity of the dynamic even more. This is what can happen when "good" students go "bad". The role of the sidekick becomes less important as an abusive culture becomes more established. Every member of the group in the Taradale incident (see Chapter 4) was powerful, suggesting that an abusive culture had firmly taken root.

And when the sidekicks are also victims, seemingly at random, as they are in Terence's story, the system is harder to shake to its foundations.

Over time, bullying decreases throughout the secondary school years. Although the number of bullies tends to stay constant, they become more and more selective in their targeting. As they grow older, victims become more assertive, get bigger, or grow out of being victims; and the bystanders individualize and have less need to be drawn into the bullying dynamic. Vulnerable students at the beginning of secondary school become more active, less passive, and move out of their state of vulnerability. By 16 or 17, the students in the reinforcer group are likely to have smelt the radium of bullying on the breath of the bully, to have read the signs, and to have become able to defend themselves better. The reinforcers by this stage can become defenders.

It is crucial to treat bullying as a dynamic that involves not just the bully and victim but also the wider peer group. Changing the group dynamics is the surest way to undermine the dynamic (see Coloroso, 2002; Salmivalli, 1999; Sutton and Smith, 1999). Specific strategies such as peer mentoring and peer support are formalized methods of harnessing the prosocial abilities and inclinations of the group (see Chapter 14, and Boulton et al., 1999; Cowie and Sharp, 1996; Naylor and Cowie, 1999).

> But at a more basic level, it is crucial that the bystanders are released from their roles in the bullying dynamic through every device in the prosocial arsenal that families, schools, and society at large has to offer. This means that they do not have to change from being victims to being sidekicks as Shannon had to, but can become members of a healthy peer group that is based on prosocial inter-actions and can handle conflict in fair ways.

An excellent means of analysis and action to bring about this change in the bystanders' group and the bullying dynamic at large can be developed through the use of the Strathclyde approach.

The sociometric triangle model (McLean, 1994) maps the social dynamic in a clear way and shows the parts played by each individual in any social group. The triangle is made up of two continuums:

1 the passive–active line; and
2 the rejecting–accepting line.

The passive–active continuum (Figure 8.1) forms the base of the triangle.

Figure 8.1 *The passive–active continuum*

The more passive a person is, the greater the isolation, withdrawal, unsureness, and self-consciousness they display. Conversely, the more active the person, the more influential, involved, confident, and self-assured they are. As students grow in confidence, they are able to move along the passive–active continuum.

The children at the passive end of the continuum often lack many of the prosocial skills needed to sustain and maintain friendships, while those at the active end typically have good networks among peers.

In a bullying situation, those at the passive end of the continuum are much more likely to be victimized. They will typically lack the skills to combat their victimization, and often take refuge in being more passive in an effort to deflect or hide from the attention that will come their way. Children who are new to a social group are vulnerable and therefore they are more likely to hover near the passive end.

Students who are active are much more likely to instigate bullying or to intervene when they see it occurring. The further they are along the active line, the more power individuals have to influence what happens.

The individual's position on the continuum can change

- over time;
- in location; and
- in reaction to events.

At any given *time*, the position will suggest the individual's:

1 *self-perception*: endorsement gained from the peer group (Figure 8.2);

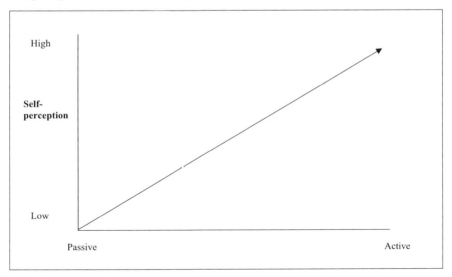

Note: The individual's self-perception increases in relation to how active they are.

Figure 8.2 *Self-perception*

2 *influence*: associated with number and frequency of contacts and peers (Figure 8.3);

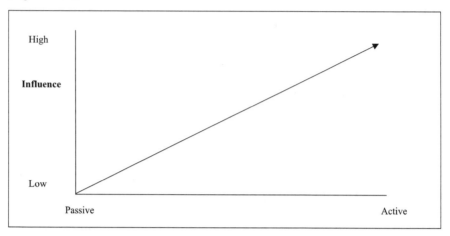

Note: The amount of influence an individual has increases in relation to how active they are.

Figure 8.3 *Influence*

3 *leadership*: directly related to self-confidence and influence (Figure 8.4);

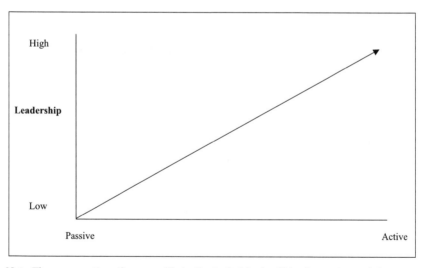

Note: The more active, the more likely the individual will lead members of the group.

Figure 8.4 *Leadership*

4 *involvement/inclusion*: ability to integrate with and participate in the group, which increases the activeness of the individual (Figure 8.5).

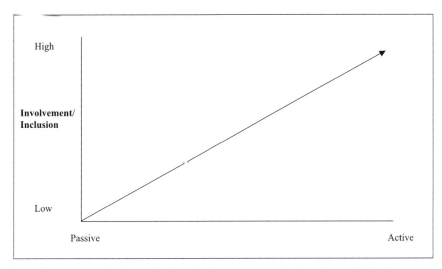

Note: The more active the individual is, the more involved and included in the group.

Figure 8.5 *Involvement/Inclusion*

The *level of submission*, on the other hand, is typified by high levels of passivity (Figure 8.6).

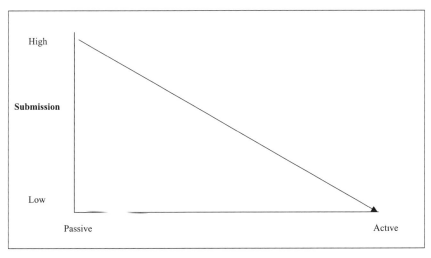

Note: The more active the individual the less likely they are to submit to another member of the group.

Figure 8.6 *Submission*

The second continuum relates to the *relationship style* of each individual. The more active the individual is, the more impact they have on the peer group dynamic and relationships. The extremes of this vertical continuum are reject-ing and accepting, while the baseline continuum goes from low to high.

High levels of empathy (Figure 8.7) and developed prosocial skills (Figure 8.8) result in an acceptance and awareness of others. *But* high levels of selfish-ness (Figure 8.9) and manipulation (Figure 8.10) with poorly developed or used prosocial skills are the result of a lack of acceptance of the needs of others.

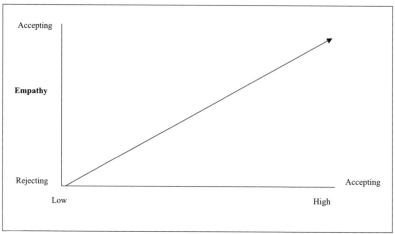

Note: An individual's empathy increases in direct relation to their ability to accept difference in others.

Figure 8.7 *Empathy*

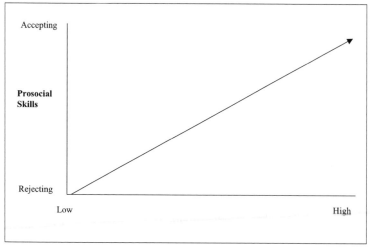

Note: An individual's prosocial skills increase in direct relation to their ability to accept difference in others.

Figure 8.8 *Prosocial skills*

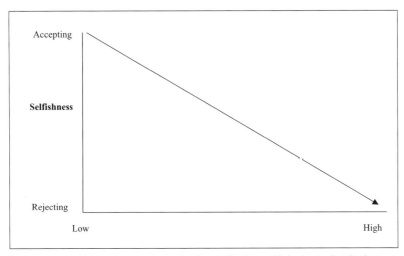

Note: The more accepting of others, the less selfish the individual.

Figure 8.9 *Selfishness*

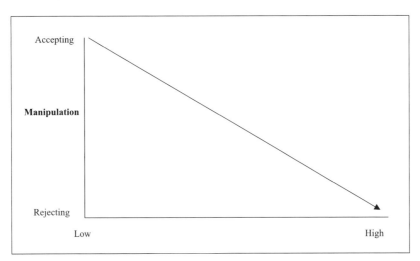

Note: The more accepting of others, the less likely the individual will manipulate others.

Figure 8.10 *Manipulation*

The *culture* of the group will be determined by the leadership of students who are at the active end of the continuum. It is important that leadership roles are assumed by the prosocial students and role-modeled by them so that no one remains passive and the bystanders take action and become involved.

Combining the continuums results in the Strathclyde triangle (Figure 8.11).

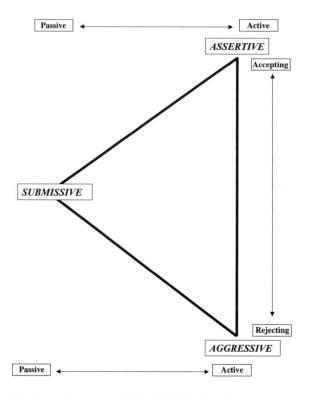

Figure 8.11 *Combined continuum and Strathclyde triangle*

Individuals who are both active and accepting will have an *assertive* relationship style. *Assertive students* will typically:

- be grounded;
- be popular;
- have genuine friends;
- be busy and involved in lots of extra activities;
- be secure and confident;
- have achievements recognized and publicly acknowledged.

On the other hand, those who are both active and rejecting will have an *aggressive* relationship style. *Aggressive students* will typically:

- be surrounded by followers;
- be involved in risky and extreme activities;
- seek and need reinforcement;
- seek acknowledgment;
- not be involved in demanding extra activities;

• be physically successful;
• constantly seek audiences and opportunities to assert their power;
• be determined to maintain status.

Individuals who are active will lead in the establishment of the group culture.

  Bullying occurs when aggressive students capture the group's culture. The shape of the group will form early (Figure 8.12):

1 Aggressive student *A* seeks an opportunity to demonstrate "power" and thus gain support and influence.
2 *A* will instinctively target a weaker/more vulnerable student *S*. *A* knows not to target *Z* or well-supported student as this will lead to "conflict," a showdown and potentially a loss of power (six to ten years of schooling have taught *A* well).
3 *A* will humiliate *S* in one of a thousand different ways. The others in the middle of the triangle will instinctively react to:
   (a) protect themselves (self-preservation);
   (b) be "one of the group."
4 If *Z* does not intervene, they will slowly side with *A*, isolating *S*.
5 The more active ones will join in with *A* and support and endorse their actions:
   (a) because *Z* chooses not to act, *U, V, O, N, M, L,* and *K* take no action.
   (b) *B, P, T,* and *Q* see an opportunity to raise their status and move toward *A*.
   (c) *G, F, J, E, I, H, R, C,* and *W* are all well aware of their vulnerability and desert *S* by moving to support (uncomfortably) *A*.
6 The vulnerable, unable to counter *A*'s attacks, seek refuge by "pulling their heads in," hoping that by hiding they will become anonymous and *A* will leave them alone.

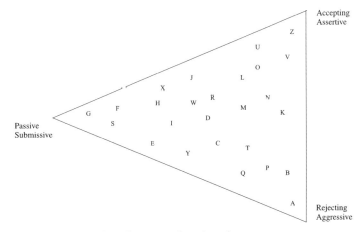

Figure 8.12 *Distribution of students on the triangle*

An abusive individualized community has now evolved. Everyone feels vulnerable but *A* will carefully target a number of the more vulnerable and perhaps even manipulate and draw *S* into his support group.

To *alter the culture*, then, *A* must stop his targeting. This will not happen until his supporters reject his actions. While they continue to endorse his aggression, the style remains successful. However, if deserted, he will continually look for ways to be affirmed and acknowledged as he is active by nature. (See Figure 8.13.)

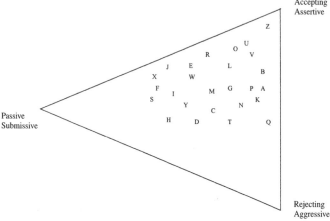

Figure 8.13 *Changing positions on the triangle*

Analysis

1 *A* needs to become more empathic and accepting of others' needs/rights if they are to become positive contributors. *This should be easy.*
2 The middle group needs to be given opportunities to voice empathy and acceptance. The bullying dynamic stifles these feelings.
3 *Z* needs to be connected to and lead the group, recognizing their skills and their duty to lead.
4 *S* needs to be given a safe enabling and supportive environment to develop prosocial skills.

Conclusions

It is important to teach students how to take charge, how to be part of things, how to fit in, and how to participate in what is going on around them. This will help them move from being bystanders to being participants. Teachers need to set up safe environments where all students feel able to be participants, moving from passivity to action, from standing back to taking part, from inactivity to activity.

Interventions such as the No Blame Approach and curriculum-based strategies (see Part IV) need to be available in all schools, because even when an ecological approach is taken to make a school healthy and safe, in which bullying incursions are quickly identified and weeded out, and students have the confidence and morality to tell, bullying will still occur. When interventions are put in place, children can fall out of role. The point of paying attention to and empowering the bystanders is to change the roles within the bystanders' group and to take the power away from the bully who, without an audience, sidekicks, or reinforcers, is unable to operate.

Note

1 This finding corroborates our argument that while bullying has fewer targets as children reach middle adolescence, the bullies maintain a high level of antisocial behavior.

9

Authoritative Teaching Practice

Introduction

Authoritative teachers maintain and support a healthy learning community. Although teachers are a huge and diverse group, with different temperaments, teaching styles, and philosophies, almost all of them enter their profession because they want to make a difference to society, they relate well to children, and they love learning.

Secondary teaching is a very complex job. Whereas primary teachers are able to establish classroom atmosphere and routines very easily, secondary teachers are less able to do this because of the conditions under which they work. It is also harder for them to form sustainable relationships with their students because of the relative brevity of their contact.

Adolescents need to be told what they are doing and why. In order to teach them effectively, teachers have to be able to create stability for them, to be organized, and to put their lessons into meaningful contexts.

Many aspects of the work are outside of the teacher's control:

- the changing landscape of teachers' and students' daily routines;
- the number of classes;
- the variable levels of maturity and ability of the students in any one class;
- the different times of day students are seen, when they are sleepy, hungry, or tired; and
- the vagaries of timetabling, for example, sometimes students arrive in a calm and receptive state, perhaps after a well-structured class, but at other times they arrive hyped up, lacking in concentration, and provocative, perhaps immediately after lunch or a physical education lesson.

In addition, because of assessment and curriculum requirements:

- each subject is more prescribed;
- teachers have to concentrate first on knowledge acquisition rather than on teaching their students how to think; and
- the emphasis is on teaching the subject, not the child.

Some teaching styles are more effective than others and are more likely to contribute to a positive and safe learning environment. When a teacher is authoritative, they lead by example, they are clear about what is acceptable and what is not, there is consistency and follow up, they pay attention to each student, and never use ridicule or sarcasm as a classroom management device. When a teacher is authoritarian, they rule by commands and threats, they show no respect for individual students, and they are likely to resort to verbal aggression and put-downs in order to control their classes. A permissive teacher, on the other hand, tends to be inconsistent and unfair, to be unclear about what is and is not acceptable, and not to follow up when things go wrong.

These styles are illustrated in the three following teacher responses when Sean walks late into class.

The authoritative teacher says, "Sean, there's a desk over there. Could you please go and sit down. How can we get you here on time?" Later, the teacher speaks to him privately.

There is minimum disruption to the lesson, and the teacher makes sure Sean is included in the lesson as quickly as possible, and follows up with him later.

The authoritarian teacher says, "If you're late one more time, you can stay home. I'm sick of your lazy attitude. Now, don't you dare cross me again today."

This is a public and arbitrary response, and no effort is made to find out why the student is late. The teacher moves from annoyance at his lateness to a comment on his attitude. There is huge potential for escalation.

The permissive teacher says, "Well, got here finally did we? Seamus, is it? Now, let's get on with it."

The teacher does not know Sean's name, is sarcastic, and does not really care. There is no follow-up.

The foundations of authoritative teaching

Authoritative teachers recognize the need not only to be effective in their teaching but also to practise the values that underpin the school's anti-bullying approach. They should be aware of the fluctuations that occur in adolescent behavior, and be prepared to deal with each student as an individual as well as attending to the class as a whole. Authoritative teachers:

- are well-organized, have clear lesson plans, and share these objectives with the class;
- are able to teach in ways that meet the different learning abilities and styles within a class;
- are flexible and able to deal with issues and crises that arise in the course of a teaching spell;
- are interested in and knowledgeable about their subject, and communicate this with passion;
- are in control and are vigilant for antisocial behavior;
- are fair and do not have favorites;
- are always looking to give praise and support (often privately);
- are never sarcastic and never put down their students;
- do not play for attention;
- make their classrooms free from ridicule;
- have an expectation that each student can succeed, and have high expectations for all students;
- are nonconfrontational and nonjudgmental in style;
- use a good range of conflict resolution and problem-solving skills;
- are good communicators;
- give feedback that fosters enthusiasm for learning;
- encourage thinking and participation;
- strive to build connections between students;
- make sure their classroom is a sanctuary from the turbulence associated with adolescent changes;
- are aware of peer relationships in adolescence;
- are aware of cognitive, physical, psychological, and social development in adolescence;
- use discipline authoritatively and sparingly, with clear guidelines and consequences;
- role-model prosocial behavior; and
- actively support the vulnerable and consciously prop up the weak to increase their mana[1] and develop their skills.

A positive safe classroom environment is authoritative: teachers need to be fair but in control. They should have a good understanding of the stresses that beset emerging adolescents and be aware of the negative impacts of peer pressure and bullying. Authoritative teachers have routines that are not rigid, but that support the teaching of well-organized and differentiated curricula through a variety of tasks that meet the needs of the various students. They are able to relate to their students as individuals but also to encircle and uphold each class so that it forms a sense of itself as a social group, however temporarily.

An authoritative teacher will take time out to find out what is going on in the class and to talk to others who teach that class. If there are difficulties, they can use devices such as sociometry to work out the dynamics of peer relationships in any group of students. When teachers adopt a shared approach, it is likely to succeed, but since each student will have several (probably between five and seven) teachers teaching them, then they all need to take this proactive stance so that such interventions succeed. In other words, this approach should be owned by the school, not left to the responsibility of individual teachers.

Teachers need to be encouraged constantly to question their practice and effectiveness. Authoritative teachers are reflective and engage in professional discussion about teaching and learning with colleagues. They discuss issues of curriculum delivery and classroom management in order to gain a clearer understanding of processes and challenges that take place in their class-rooms. Part of this reflection should include finding out about current theo-ries and issues from educational research.

This process can be formalized and supported by the school, so that teachers are given time to focus on their reflective practice, and are also assigned a men-tor or supervisor with whom to discuss ideas, issues, and difficulties. These rela-tionships can be supported by a wider teacher discussion group in which individual students or issues are talked about with the relevant teachers.

This approach almost requires a leap of faith on the part of teachers: they need to be in a position to pay more attention to the establishment of a pos-itive teaching environment than to curriculum coverage. This faith will be rewarded as the successful classroom dynamic makes curriculum acquisition happen more quickly. Authoritative teachers will know how much time needs to be spent, and this will vary from class to class.

Effective teachers recognize that safe classrooms create better learning environments. It takes time to achieve this, and this time is an investment. Once a healthy climate is established, teaching becomes easier and learning more productive. The teacher becomes the guardian of the class, and pro-vides a framework in which it can function to its maximum ability.

Figure 9.1 shows the key characteristics of good teaching practice that will help protect, support, sustain, and ensure a safe, bullyfree, healthy learning environment. In the naturally dynamic and robust environment of the sec-ondary school in which a lot of the seemingly chaotic behavior of adolescence is played out, it is useful to have a model that summarizes the professionalism of the good teacher.

Figure 9.2 illustrates the differing emphases in classroom management throughout the year with each class. The size and significance of each of these quadrants will change throughout the year. At the beginning of the year, it is more likely that there will be a much greater emphasis on building relationships, creating connections, and establishing the classroom environment, with less emphasis on curriculum delivery. Once a stable and safe environment has been established, there will be an increasing emphasis on the teaching and learning aspect. Teaching styles and the response to classroom issues and dynamics should be the foundation upon which classroom management is built, remaining constant and consistent, as these provide the stability that is so essential for a well-managed classroom that has a primary focus on learning and teaching.

Taking the No Blame Approach into unchartered waters

In order to be consistent (as well as sensible), it is important that the idea of creating a safe culture for students is also applied to teachers. Teachers who have difficulties need to be supported by the system just as students do.

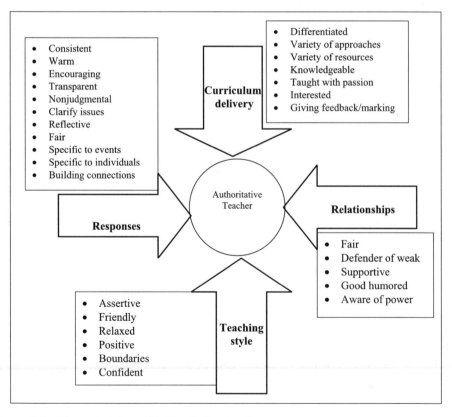

Figure 9.1 *Characteristics of authoritative teachers*

While virtually every young teacher will take time to develop their teaching skills, from time to time other teachers will have difficulties with an individual, a group, or a class. This is normal. Being a good teacher is not only an issue of innate ability or excellence of training; it is likely to be the case that teachers become "good" when they teach in a school that supports them.

In many institutions and among experienced individual teachers there can be found a culture in which, when things go wrong, a scapegoat is found (someone to blame) or the problem is swept under the carpet ("We don't have bullying here," "He's always taught that way," or "She gets very good exam results"). Just as bullies hide their dysfunctional behavior or disguise it as something else, teachers may feel they have to hide poor performance; sometimes their school hides it for them.

To avoid this, a No Blame or problem-solving approach needs to be adopted. In doing this, the school openly acknowledges that all teachers will at some stage have difficulties with an individual or a class, and the best way to address it is in an open, problem-solving, and collegial fashion. As is the case when No Blame is used with children (see Chapter 15), this will allow a significant change to occur; in this context the change will be in the way teachers deal with pedagogical issues. The main point is that teachers have to know that they are safe when they are honest about their difficulties. The following case study illustrates this process in action.

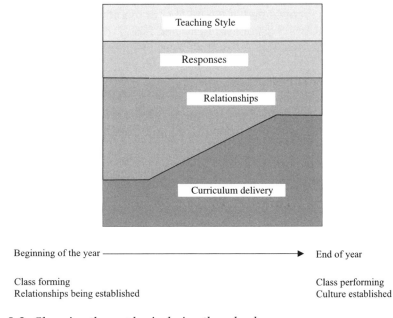

Figure 9.2 *Changing the emphasis during the school year*

A case study

A victim of bullying, Erin, is being ostracized by her form class, called names, and is regarded as an outsider. She is also having difficulties with her academic work, and as she falls further behind she becomes even more vulnerable to the name-calling of her peers. The problem is being compounded in math where her teacher, Molly Pring, is finding her exasperating and is not managing to hide her impatience. This is making matters worse, because the other students start to take Ms Pring's difficulties with Erin as corroboration of their treatment of her. Any solution to Erin's bullying must therefore involve not only her peers but also Ms Pring and Erin's other teachers.

The school has a clear anti-bullying policy and is philosophically founded on the No Blame approach. Once Erin's form teacher recognizes that the class has a bullying problem, he spends a week monitoring the class, checks Erin's academic and attendance records, and arranges a meeting with all her teachers. He knows that Molly is a source of much of the trouble with Erin.

Response Sheet for Teacher Collaboration on Bullying

Step 1 Bullying is Reported
Erin's form teacher is concerned at the number of reports he is receiving about her behavior. She is being disruptive, sulky, and failing to complete work or to attend classes regularly. He is aware that she is being bullied.

Step 2 Information gathering
He seeks written comment from all her teachers, checks schoolwide data, and discusses Erin with the dean. Erin's mother tells him that Erin is being taunted by some of her classmates and being picked on by her math teacher.

Step 3 Teacher conference
He convenes a meeting with all Erin's teachers, the dean, and guidance staff. The purpose of the meeting is to share strategies and include Molly Pring in the problem-solving process.

Step 4 Review
A review meeting is held one week after the initial conference so that the teachers can share their perceptions of the interventions and, if necessary, reevaluate the process.

If it is suspected that one or more teachers is contributing to or supporting a bullying culture, then the anti-bullying team needs to work with the student's group of teachers to problem-solve. The reason for such a meeting is to discuss the dynamics of the classes in question and to agree on strategies that can be put in place to help the situation. This will mean that there is no finger-pointing. If one teacher is contributing to the problem by singling out the victim, he or she may, through this process, recognize what he or she is doing, and learn to empathize with the student. The more these students are discussed and talked about, the greater the chance that such a teacher will be able to shift his or her behavior.

Once this has happened, and the No Blame Approach to teacher behavior has been applied, a dialogue should normally occur every six weeks or so to reinforce and maintain change and health in the system. This is a collegial and systemic approach to supporting a bullyfree culture.

Right at the start of the meeting, Molly moans about Erin. The form teacher agrees that Erin does seem to be in some difficulty as he has had eight other reports about her behavior. He summarizes these reports and adds information on detentions, bad behavior, lateness, and incomplete work.

He describes what has been happening to Erin in her peer group, and how she is being singled out and ridiculed. He especially talks about how she is feeling, and reads a poem that Erin has written:

> I cannot face your sneers any more
> I cannot haul myself into the arena
>   And be tortured again.
>
> I want to see the stars and the moonlight
> And to walk calmly through the lily fields
>   To the other side
>
> But every day it feels as if I will be wrapped in barbed wire
>   And made to confess my sins
> And have my fingernails ripped out
>
> I am nothing, no one, a waste of space
> I wish I was invisible, then, like they say I am.
>   I am nothing but a crawling bug
>   And I hate myself.

Erin is reframed as a student with difficulties, who is suffering from isolation and disapproval, and who is suffering deeply.

The form teacher tells the group that a No Blame student conference is scheduled to take place the following day. He talks about the bully, the sidekicks, and the reinforcers and how Erin has a couple of potential defenders. He again refers to her feelings of inadequacy, shame, and unhappiness.

He invites each of Erin's class teachers to talk about how they see Erin's behavior and how they might help her change. He suggests that they each share two things that went really well in one of Erin's classes and two things that did not go well, and that they identify one or two effective teaching strategies that will assist her. Each teacher then briefly outlines what they will try to do differently with Erin.

Molly needs to discover that her relationship with Erin could be better. She soon keeps quiet, listening carefully to what other people are saying. Rather than being singled out for poor teaching practice, she is given the opportunity to reflect on her performance in a dignified and supportive environment. She thinks quietly to herself about how she has in effect separated Erin from her peer group and has helped set her up to be victimized. She realizes that she can do things differently without losing face, and that she can also try some of the suggestions from Erin's other teachers to change the dynamics of her classroom.

With the meeting drawing to a close, all Erin's teachers know a lot more about her and how life is for her at school. Together they have suggested ways to make her classes safer and healthier environments. The collegial style of the meeting means that they can all learn from and be supported by each other. No one is blamed for the difficulties.

A review meeting is arranged a week later as a follow-up. Over the week, to Molly's surprise she finds Erin responsive in class and more able than she had ever imagined. She feels satisfied with her classroom management and is relieved that her uncomfortable relationship with Erin has improved. The conferencing has been helpful to all the teachers and they have all noticed that Erin has begun cautiously to participate more, to make an effort with her work, and that she looks happier.

> The review meeting can either be part of the regular class conferencing (if things are going well) or a specific meeting to focus especially on the student in question. If the initial interventions have not worked, it is essential that the school psychologist or counselor takes over the case as a special project.

The leading role of the form teacher in relation to Erin allows him to behave like the significant adult who is normally lost to students in the secondary school setting.

The form teacher needs to be a team leader and community builder for the class, helping the students learn cooperatively and collaboratively in a positive learning environment which is also bullyfree. He clearly signals to Erin and the class that the teachers as well as the students have a role to play in the maintenance of a bullyfree environment.

The teacher as team leader and community builder

An authoritative teacher has to be very conscious of status within the class, who has it and who has not. He or she needs to be aware of their powerful leadership role and use it to raise the status of each and every student in the class. The teacher consciously needs to be positive toward the nonattractive and provocative victims, and to choose them to do specialist tasks so they are not ridiculed, isolated, or set up for failure. They can be asked to take messages, help organize activities, hand out material, and make suggestions for class events. With role modeling, the teacher gives positive feedback, never unrealistically but always concretely. This is doubly beneficial because it is public praise. Any messages the teacher gives have to be clear. In any class there is likely to be a significant group of powerful students who want to dominate those with less status than they have. The teacher needs to teach these students how to treat people nicely. An authoritative teacher is never apologetic about intervening, recognizing that there is a place for role modeling. This is never dishonest or manipulative, but is clear and positive.

Authoritative teachers deliberately find time to spend with children. This shows they are interested and that they are part of what is going on. They are vigilant and pick up the first and subtle signs of bullying, so that students are confident to go to them and ask for support if they need it. If a student says, "Rewi's taken my pencil," the good teacher actively intervenes and supervises the return of the pencil. He or she deals with issues seriously and not frivolously, is explicit about what is right and wrong, and will also collaborate with the class in developing rules and procedures. He or she will also have worked out a student charter with the students (see Chapter 12, and Appendix 4).

Finally, we would like to advocate the "broken window" approach[2] as a tool for authoritative teachers. The central belief in this approach is that if minor infringements of an individual's rights (such as "borrowing" a pencil, or being insulted or excluded) are handled well, then the infringements do not escalate. In acting authoritatively, the teacher clearly sets out the boundaries between what is and what is not acceptable, and also role-models respectful behavior toward the one who has been treated disrespectfully.

The role of the teacher is to protect and maintain a positive class structure and a bullyfree environment. They will have played a leading role in building this culture and have used the teaching skills we have discussed to protect and strengthen this environment so that the class can focus on learning.

Notes

1 Mana is a Maori word meaning status, reputation, standing.
2 "Broken window" refers to a New York policing approach that gave priority to addressing minor crimes with the result that there was an overall reduction in all crime.

PART IV

THE SAFE SCHOOL IN ACTION

10

What to Do When Bullying Happens

Taking a step back

Once a school has addressed, confronted, discussed, and made policies about bullying, and has arrived at an understanding of what bullying is, the one certainty that will emerge is that bullying is a complex issue. However completely and deeply a school develops an anti-bullying policy, bullying will still occur. And when it does, schools needs to have in place structured approaches to deal with bullying that everybody knows how to use. The complex dynamics of event, response, consequences, and feelings of blame, shame, culpability, and hopelessness can all contribute to the culture of bullying. Once bullying is out in the open, the bully sometimes feels painted into a corner and unfairly singled out. They often do not regard what they are doing as wrong. Victims also feel exposed at this point, and may be vulnerable to further acts of cruelty and ostracization. In order to avoid further public exposure, bullying often goes underground and becomes hard to detect. It is therefore essential that all schools have a complete anti-bullying policy in place and that all teachers have immediate access to a one-step backwards (rather than a knee-jerk) reaction.

Although bullying is common, it is aberrant. It is both unhealthy in itself and also sustains and reinforces unhealthy systems. Teachers need to be very aware of the social dynamics in the class, the year level, and the school, and to make sure that when they hear about an incident of bullying, they rein in their reflexes and follow a calm, proactive series of steps that are fully supported by school policy and procedure, and that make sense in the short and long term.

A large part of the teacher's job is to help a healthy culture develop, to create balance in the group, to be a protector of the weak, and to give all students a degree of magnetism. It is often the student who is perceived as weak or unattractive who gets bullied. In the process such a student becomes unattractive to everyone—an antimagnet. A subtext of the teacher's job therefore involves supporting such students so as to encourage an inclusive and healthy learning environment. In secondary school this is more difficult than in primary schools because the interaction between teachers and students is for shorter periods, is less intense, and includes fewer pastoral expectations. However, in a healthy school, policy will be in place to address the problem of bullying and to give clear guidelines and support to teachers.

Applying policy

School anti-bullying policies need to be completely practical, based on common sense, logical and flexible, easy to understand, and straightforward in application. They also need to be designed to lay down a paper trail so events are not forgotten, redefined, or swept under the carpet. In addition, they must attend to all those involved, parents, students, and teachers:

1 When a parent approaches a school staff member with a complaint about bullying, they must be listened to and their complaint dealt with in a problem-solving manner, and they must be taken into the anti-bullying system, so they are part of the solution.
2 When a student tells a teacher that they are being bullied, or that they know someone else is being bullied, they must be listened to and be in no doubt that their concerns are being attended to.
3 Teachers must be fully familiar with the anti-bullying procedures of the school. The procedural steps can be printed on small laminated cards and given to all staff so they are all card-carrying supporters of the school's anti-bullying policy.

The steps provide a procedural continuum for dealing with bullying:

Bullying Incident: Immediate Response

Step 1   Become aware of a bullying incident.
Step 2   Make sure the victim is safe.
Step 3   Take no immediate action against the perpetrators. Be dispassionate and considered.
Step 4   Tell the anti-bullying coordinator about the incident.
Step 5   Put the event on record. Fill in Part One of the Bully Incident Report Form.

Teachers may find out about the bullying because they see it occur, a student tells them about it, a parent tells them about it, the victim is found upset and reluctantly reveals it, or the victim reports it. The immediate response then is to make sure that the victim is safe. This can be done by removing the victim from the line of fire: the teacher needs to deal immediately with short-term safety. The staff member involved then needs to tell the anti-bullying coordinator about the incident so that it is handed on to the team, and the first part of the incident form completed.

Once these steps have been taken, the anti-bullying team takes over. The steps they need to take are as follows:

Bullying Incident: Handover Response

Step 1   Decide who is going to work on the case (preferably two people).
Step 2   Snapshot/diagnosis: where does the incident fall on the bullying checklist (refer to Bullying Assessment Checklist form).
Step 3   Action plan: match the response to the incident.
Step 4   Fill in Part Two of the Bully Incident Report Form.

Any school that has an effective anti-bullying policy will have identified its team of bullying experts. These are people who have recognized knowledge, and who have the concrete functions of implementing procedures, supporting teachers, and helping create, develop, and uphold a safe environment. Any bullying incident should be assigned to at least two members of this team so that no one has to work alone. This is both for protection and for safety. They diagnose the bullying incident, place it along a continuum of bullying typologies so that it can be properly assessed, and then match it with an appropriate anti-bullying strategy or series of strategies.

The point of the Bullying Incident: Handover Response Steps 2 and 3 is not to provide ammunition to attribute blame but to institute a system that supports a safety culture. Once the bullying incident has been fully described and a prognosis for treatment has been made, the steps taken to handle it can be identified. The form thus embodies an incident trail. If a procedure does not work, the bullying recurs, the dynamics become more complex, and the health of the peer group or class declines, then the form gives a picture of the interventions and allows them to be reconsidered and the whole incident to be looked at again.

The second half of the Bully Incident Report Form should be filled in by the anti-bullying coordinator. On the next page is an example of such a form:

Bullying Incident Report Form

Part One

Incident Reported by: [   ]   When: [   ]

Came to my attention by:

Where did the incident happen?

When did the incident happen?

Students actively involved (circle victim):

Names of bystanders (list ALL who were present):

Brief description of incident:

Referred to: [   ]   (List of Anti-bullying Team members)

Part Two

Assessment: (*Comment on the situation. Is it one-off or part of an ongoing relationship? Have the individuals been involved in similar incidents previously? Is it atypical for this group of students?*)

The participants: (*Comment on history, background, previous incidents for perpetrator and victim. Comment on any of the bystanders.*)

Action plan: (*Identify the type of intervention that will be used, by whom, when and the type of communication that will result.*)

Diagnosis

The diagnostic process is very important. It is crucial that the reporting teacher describes the initial event as fully as possible and for the anti-bullying team to amplify this if they can. The diagnostic tool is not intended to imply that there is a relationship between something the victim did and what happened to them when they were bullied. Nor is it to attribute blame or cause, or to find extenuating circumstances. Rather, it gathers basic information and analyzes the nature and tone of the event.

Key Points for Diagnosis (Pepler and Craig, 2000)

Is the bullying and or/victimization *severe*?
(Does it involve serious physical or verbal aggression?)

Is the bullying and/or victimization *frequent*?
(Does it occur often in this child's life?)

Is the bullying and/or victimization *pervasive*?
(Does it occur in many contexts, for example, home, school, community?)

Is the bullying and/or victimization *chronic*?
(Has it been a problem for a long time, for example, since early childhood?)

It is also useful to analyze the attitude of the bully(ies), the physical and psychological condition of the victim, and the position of the bystanders/peer group in relation to the event. As a final check, this staff member should refer to a bullying incident assessment checklist, for example:

Bullying Incident Assessment Checklist

Consider each of these statements in light of this particular incident.

- Was this an instance of rough play by a boy from a family of six who is used to treating his siblings roughly (but largely in jest) and whose behavior toward a gentler child with no or few siblings is misinterpreted as deliberate, personal, and cruel?
- Or has this boy from a family of six got the taste for rough play, read the fear it invokes, and become addicted to the power it gives him?
- Is this a one-off incident between peers who normally relate well to each other? (It could be the beginning of a bullying relationship if it is allowed to develop unchecked.)

- Is it part of a pattern of ongoing harassment that is known by others in the peer group?
- The victim is not part of the protagonist's peer group.
- The victim has special needs or a disability.
- The victim is said to have provoked the abuse through his or her actions prior to the incident.
- The victim is clearly traumatized by the bullying.
- Is the victim very upset?
- Describe how the victim is feeling.
- Is the victim suicidal?
- Is this an instance of a student being shunned and ostracized?
- Was the victim depersonalized in the event?
- Does the victim have any friends and supporters?
- Are the bystanders unsympathetic to his or her plight?
- Is there anyone in the peer group who feels bad about what is happening to the victim?

In using this checklist, the reviewer is endeavoring to identify what the bullying incident tells about the relationship between the key players involved. An understanding of this is essential if follow-up action is to be appropriate. If there is any suggestion that this is more than a one-off incident, then it is important to talk to the wider peer group. Are the majority of the group colluding with the behavior or are they concerned by the bad treatment? Has the victim been objectified by the group?

Response

After making an assessment, the bully worker discusses the incident with at least one other adult. This should be the reporting teacher, the student's form teacher, the school counselor, or someone else in the anti-bullying team. The assessment should be discussed and the response identified. Should the assessment suggest that the incident involves serious and ongoing abuse, the full anti-bullying team needs to be called together. At this stage, an appropriate response is identified from the range of approved interventions.

In all cases, an action plan should be written (either by the individual bully worker or the team) that briefly details the assessment and the intervention. This will be on the back of the incident form.

The most important factor in relation to diagnosis is how the victim feels.

Choosing the interventions

Safe schools offer an environment that removes the randomness and reactivity of nonreflective responses to bullying. While such schools may still have what are identifiably "soft" and "hard" responses, it is the space between these which spreads out along a line of curriculum-based, student, experiential, and peer-driven strategies that provides the practical resource base that supports the policy of the school.

Once an assessment of the event has been made, then the team needs first to ensure the short- and long-term safety of the student in question. This will have been done initially by the teacher who first dealt with incident. It may be that some students will offer to walk home with the victim of bullying, or that the peer group is involved in some other prosocial way. The team then needs to match up strategies with the incident. The strategies available to schools with a solid anti-bullying policy are numerous, varied, and multifaceted. They are not prescriptive and rigid but are based on common sense, and can be used in various combinations and sequences. Any strategy from the resource base range may be chosen. The matching up is not a precise science but a matter of care, analysis, and intuition.

Most schools have extensive knowledge of what could be called the traditional responses to bullying. These range along a continuum from soft to hard and all schools at times will find one or other of them useful and necessary.

The Traditional Response Continuum

The "softest" response is a one-to-one request for cooperation from the key worker to the perpetrator. There is no threat and no blame, simply a request that they refrain from the behavior.

The next intervention is to ask for a discussion between the bully, the victim, and the member(s) of the anti-bullying team assigned to the case. This is still a low-level strategy that may work with simple incidents of bullying, especially when the bully sees the hurt they have caused.

Where it is clear that a one-off incident took place, and there is less a sense of imbalance of power and more a sense of conflict, then a restorative justice or conflict resolution approach may be used. For either of these approaches to work, both the perpetrator and the victim need to be willing to participate jointly in a resolution conference.

When all else has failed or the bullying is of sufficient seriousness, either because the behavior is intractable or bordering on criminality, another type of intervention is sometimes needed. This may involve behavior modification or discipline approaches that range from detention, in-school and external suspension, and ultimately to exclusion from the school community.

Exclusion should only be used if all other strategies have been tried at least once. It is an admission of defeat, and does nothing for the bully except remove them from the school and give them a new arena for their antisocial behavior.

The problem is that if a school only has these responses available, then students' empathy does not get activated, the social dynamic does not change, and they do not become part of the solution. Students in this situation float in an environment that arbitrarily allots consequences and punishments but has not developed a comprehensive way of instituting change and maintaining a safe culture.

For these reasons, we suggest that schools should first adopt a whole-school approach and add the following strategies to their anti-bullying arsenal:

1 They need curriculum-based initiatives, such as interactive classroom learning about bullying (see Chapter 11).
2 They need preventative programs, such as leadership training (see Chapter 12).
3 They need interactive strategies that provide experiential learning, such as social theater (see Chapter 13).
4 They need approaches that provide support, such as peer mentoring (see Chapter 14).
5 They need interventions that change the social dynamic, such as the No Blame Approach (see Chapter 15).

In this part of the book, therefore, we describe a curriculum-based initiative ("In the Cafeteria") and a leadership training program that are designed to prevent bullying and to create a healthy school; the use of social theater to provide experiential knowledge about bullying and victimization; peer mentoring as a safeguard and support; and the No Blame Approach which we advocate as the best anti-bullying intervention that we have, since it sets about changing the social dynamic.

Thus, the school is bolstered by strong foundations (curriculum work and the leadership program); a bulwark of mentoring; and a center that is held up by clear policy, teachers who know what to do and that they will be supported by the school when they act, and students who know they can tell adults if there are problems, who do not tolerate rejection and ridicule, and who know how it feels to be safe and to be valued.

11

Using the Curriculum to Understand and Deal With Bullying: "In the Cafeteria"

Introduction

Bullying can badly affect an individual's physical and psychological well-being, both in the short and long term. This is the case not only for victims and bullies but also for those on the side, the bystanders. Bullying is not usually a one-off event but is often long-standing. It is also a social event (albeit a negative one), and is part of a dynamic and sometimes magnetic process during which the bystanders can feel helpless and frightened or, on the other hand, excited, attracted, and drawn in. Some pretend it is not happening or that it does not affect them. Others feel compelled to go into the melee and assist the person being bullied. Bullying events are also often complex, full of undertones and suggestions (such as, "You'd better cooperate or you could be next"). It is also the case that in school with our peers, we learn how to socialize and how to survive. It is where we learn that we can act with responsibility to support and protect each other, or not, as the case may be.

In New Zealand schools, the issue of bullying is taken seriously, and both the health and social studies curricula provide places for secondary school teachers to develop lessons on the topic of bullying. In this chapter, we present several ways of teaching about the nature of bullying and how to understand and develop strategies for countering it.

The first two parts of this chapter provide a lesson plan whereby students:

1 examine possible bullying scenarios in order to determine what does and does not count as bullying; and

2 develop a definition and understanding of bullying.

The third part asks students to examine a range of realistic bullying scenarios and to select one for further discussion. They then go through a process of analysis so as to understand how the bullying dynamic works and then to develop strategies and solutions that appropriately respond to the situation.

Lesson 1: understanding bullying

Research proves that bullying is extensive throughout schools all over the world. All students will be aware of it and have experienced it in some form or another. Whenever the topic is discussed, everyone has a story to tell. As the New Zealand Commissioner for Children's report suggests (Lind and Maxwell, 1996), it is a very worrying issue for a large number of students.

When bullying is introduced for the first time in a lesson, teachers can anticipate that there will be a lot of interest in it. In order for the lesson to be meaningful, it must make sense in terms of the students' own experiences. In other words, it is not useful to lecture them about bullying; instead, it is important to use an interactive process.

The first point to convey is that bullying happens in all schools. The teacher then moves onto the next point, that students are central to dealing with it when it does occur.

The first exercise is designed to help students understand what bullying is. The teacher has six incidents written on the board. The students are asked to discuss one of these incidents in groups of three or four. If the school has teacher aides or teaching assistants, they can take part and help the students with their thinking processes.

Is this Bullying?

1 Luke says to André, "You'd better give me that $2 or else."
2 Enrico is down on the ground and Benedict is bashing him.
3 Sam is pouring a can of orange soda onto the grass while Rochelle yells, "Hey, what are you doing with my drink?"
4 Marie walks away from Joelle and Candice who call after her, "See you later at the party, Slag. Not!"
5 A group of students pelts Chelsea with snowballs while she runs away laughing.
6 Peter is walking home from school when some boys follow him and laugh at him.

These scenarios may be examples of bullying. As the events are teased out, the students learn to think about what they see, that relationships are complex, and that they can draw useful conclusions if they are careful in their assessment of what goes on around them. What is also important here is to ask them about the roles of the people who are not involved as victims or bullies.

For example, four students in the class discuss the scenario: "A group of students pelts Chelsea with snowballs while she runs away laughing." These students decide that because Chelsea is laughing, she is not being bullied. They think the people in the snow are just having fun, and that this is a snapshot that captures a moment when Chelsea is the only one having snowballs thrown at her. When they report back their findings, a girl from another group says that one of the things she does if she is being picked on is to laugh or to avoid showing that she is hurt. She says that she finds this a good way to deflect attention. She therefore argues that Chelsea may be feeling very upset but that she is laughing to try to avoid being bullied. Other students agree with this interpretation. So, instead of this being a benign picture of people having fun, it becomes a still from a missing roll of film in which Chelsea is hounded and victimized.

In relation to this example, the students discuss what they would need to know in order to decide whether this is bullying or not.

1 *They would need to know the context.* If this is one event in a history of victimization, then they can be sure it is bullying.
2 *They would need to know if Chelsea is upset.* If she is, then it is likely that this is bullying.
3 *They would need to know if she fitted into the group and had friends or supporters.* If she did not, and at least one of the other criteria was present, then they can be sure that this is bullying.

Using such ambiguous scenarios helps students differentiate between bullying and nonbullying behavior. The intention is to assist them to understand the fact that bullying involves a whole dynamic, not just an event.

Key concept: Bullying is about behavior and feelings, not just an event.

The lesson talks about bullying, who is involved, and what happens when someone is bullied. Although students are likely to have a sense of what bullying is, they may find it difficult to describe it accurately. Bullying relies on vagueness, undefinedness, and secrecy. Once it is named and dissected, it is harder for it to find life or expression: recognizing it is sometimes enough to make it melt into the shadows.

Lesson 2: defining bullying

The first exercise will have established that bullying is a relatively complex behavior that cannot be linked to specific actions or events that can be sanctioned by rules. (It can be useful to discuss futile ideas such as banning nicknames, forbidding gossip and jokes, outlawing play-fighting, or vetoeing storytelling!) It will also have been established that bullying is not simply an action or event, but is dependent on a negative social dynamic and a misuse of power.

Bullying can be looked at in the light of concepts such as abuse, cowardice, cruelty, and manipulation. It is also important to consider the opposites of these concepts: compassion, courage, kindness, and openness. These can be discussed in the contexts of philosophies and religions that have resonance for different communities and peoples.

A useful exercise in the New Zealand context is to discuss a Maori proverb that encapsulates the idea of the warrior:

> Kia kaha, kia toa, kia manawanui.

This proverb means "Be strong, be courageous and be loyal." It focuses more on the values of bravery, patience, and constancy, rather than aggression, ferocity, and rashness. It is a useful way of encouraging discussion of the issues of manliness and staunchness that are upheld by many adolescents, giving them an opportunity to examine the warrior role, which is less to do with fighting than it is to do with the values of nurturing, strength of character, and supporting others less powerful than themselves. Abusers and bullies do not display such characteristics.

The students can then talk about *what bullying is*. First, they can elaborate on the detail in lesson one, listing all *the things that people do to each other* that can be considered bullying (such as biting, hitting, punching, spreading mean stories, leaving someone out; see Chapter 1). But more importantly, they should discuss the things about the behavior that make it indisputably bullying; in other words, not just the events but *the characteristics of the behavior* that make it not an accident, not fun, not a joke, and not rough play. This discussion focuses on the *intent*. It also focuses on the *effect*:

1 It can happen to anyone.
2 It is an abuse of power.
3 Those doing it are pretty sure they will get away with it.
4 It is often hidden.
5 It tends to be repetitive.
6 It involves a victim and a bully.

7 There are usually bystanders who participate, support, or ignore it.
8 It can take various forms (physical and emotional).
9 It is hurtful.

Information can be provided about the extent of bullying in secondary schools. For example, in New Zealand, Vivienne Adair and colleagues from the University of Auckland (2000) found that for a group of 2066 secondary school students, when they were asked if they had ever been bullied at school (and given no definition), 50 percent said they had been bullied. When they were given a definition, 75 percent said they had been bullied in the last year and 44 percent that they had been a bully at some time during their schooling. Such details are readily available for many countries (see Smith et al., 1999, for example).

The lesson needs to conclude with:

1 a written summary of the class's definition of bullying;
2 a brief discussion of the school definition of bullying;
3 a description of the school's anti-bullying policy; and
4 a reminder of what students should do if they are concerned about bullying or see it occurring.

Lesson 3: developing a deeper understanding of bullying—"In the Cafeteria"

Introduction

"In the Cafeteria" uses an action-based interactive examination of a bullying scenario to explore the nature and dynamics of bullying. It is based on another curriculum approach, "On the Bus", which was developed by Mark Cleary and Keith Sullivan (Cleary and Sullivan, 1999; and Sullivan, 2000) for use in secondary schools.

"In the Cafeteria" follows on from the previous lessons, which are designed to raise awareness about how bullying works (the dynamics) and what it is (a definition). With these as a foundation, this exercise is intended to help students:

• develop a deeper understanding of how bullying works in a variety of settings;
• examine various roles that individuals take on in bullying;
• understand how certain strategies and solutions are inappropriate and do not work;
• develop strategies and solutions that fit the situation and work to stop bullying;

- dcvclop understanding, empathy, and a sense of responsibility so the students act either as individuals or as a group to stop it from occurring.

This particular strategy is best introduced once the students have had the opportunity of developing their own definition of bullying and confirming that theirs and the school's policy definition are compatible. It can also be used as an introduction to the underlying concepts of bullying for older groups of students.

"In the Cafeteria" in action

There are nine steps that can be followed.

An Organizational Template for Carrying Out "In the Cafeteria"

Step 1 Review and clarify students' understanding of what bullying is
Step 2 The teacher and students select a bullying scenario
Step 3 The scenario is discussed
Step 4 Strategies and solutions are suggested
Step 5 Feedback and extra information are provided
Step 6 Improved strategies and solutions are developed
Step 7 Steps 4 and 5 are repeated until participants are satisfied with the strategies and solutions
Step 8 Final recommendations are made
Step 9 Analysis and overview

Step 1: review and clarify students' understanding of what bullying is
The session begins with the students and their teacher discussing what counts as bullying behavior. If this is a follow-on from a previous lesson, the students can briefly revisit the definition they created.

Stcp 2: the teacher and students select a bullying scenario
The students are then given the following worksheet describing niⁿe common bullying scenarios.

The teacher reads out the nine different examples of bullying that are described on the worksheet. The students are asked to rank these examples by number along the bottom of the page. The ranking should start with the bullying that worries them the least at the extreme left and the one that worries them the most at the extreme right. The class is told to do this instinctively and quickly.

Worksheet. Typical Bullying Situations

Read the following situations and choose:

- *The ones which would concern you the least and the most.*
- *Rank all the other situations.*

1 Luana was upset when Sally and her friends constantly called her names. She felt worthless and alone.
2 Karen overheard herself being described as a "black bitch" by girls she thought were her friends. She then realized they were laughing at her and pretending to include her while they were actually making the whole class turn against her.
3 Moana and Astrid are physically very mature year 9 girls. They make on-going sexual jokes about their classmate Matt who is very small for his age.
4 Kristy was called names every morning on the school bus and felt frightened and embarrassed. She started pretending to be sick and not going to school.
5 George is sitting by himself at a table towards the back of the cafeteria. A group of boys from his year descend upon the table and noisily sit around him, "accidently" jostling him as they do. In the process he is knocked off the bench spilling his tray of food and drink all over himself and the floor. "Oh George, you're so clumsy!" one of the boys laughingly says as they all get up and leave.
6 Hilary is an attractive girl who is being sexually harassed by Charlie because she will not go out with him. He follows her around, writes notes that he sticks on her back, sends rude text messages about her to classmates' cell-phones, and rings her at home with suggestive comments and insults. The girls in her class do not have any sympathy for her.
7 Jenny is a special needs student. She has Aspergers syndrome and knows everything you could know about the history of ballet. Two girls have been taking great delight in mimicking her and laughing at her.
8 Scott was picked on constantly by Jerry, who waited round corners for him and pushed him around, always egged on by his friend Kevin. Scott was afraid that next time they might smash his glasses into his face.
9 Harry is a studious boy who walks to school. On the way to school a group of boys makes fun of him for being a swot. They take his books and throw them in the gutter. Yesterday, one of the boys punched him in the back and ran away laughing.

Least worrying   Most worrying

Write the numbers of the scenarios in the boxes above.

The teacher gathers the students' sheets, tabulates the results, and informs the students which example they have most frequently identified as the most worrying. In order to illustrate how this works, we have chosen item 5 and named it "In the Cafeteria." It is as follows:

> George is sitting by himself at a table towards the back of the cafeteria. A group of boys from his year descend upon the table and noisily sit around him, "accidently" jostling him as they do. In the process he is knocked off the bench, spilling his tray of food and drink all over himself and the floor. "Oh George, you're so clumsy!" one of the boys laughingly says as they all get up and leave.

Step 3: the scenario is discussed
To start the process off, the teacher asks the students why they think this particular scenario has been chosen over the other eight as the most worrisome. In the discussion, the following reasons are given and points are made:

1 They know people like the ones described. This type of thing happens in their school.
2 It seems that it would be hard to do anything about it. George has no power. The boys carrying out the bullying do. A very familiar set of circumstances!
3 George is probably smaller than the other boys.
4 George is alone. He has no friends with him.
5 Where are the teachers or the prefects? No one seems to be there for George.
6 Where are the cafeteria staff?
7 Who is going to clean up the mess?
8 Will George have money to buy another lunch?
9 The cafeteria is noisy and there is lots of jostling and messing around at lunchtime. That could be all that is happening, but it seems that George is being bullied.
10 If George is being victimized, this is sure to be a regular feature (in different forms) of his life at school.

Step 4: strategies and solutions are suggested
The teacher acknowledges the class's observational skills. She then says, "You seem to know how things work at school and you have identified that what is happening to George is bullying. What can be done about it?" A class discussion takes place and suggestions are noted and written up on the board. The following points emerge:

1 George could sit with a group of other students, and maybe try to make friends with kids like himself.
2 He could tell a teacher or a prefect.
3 He could tell the cafeteria staff.
4 He should avoid the cafeteria, as this is sure to happen to him again. "Why go looking for trouble?" the students ask.
5 He could laugh it off, clean up the mess, and be cool, and then maybe he would be accepted.
6 He could be assertive and state, "I don't like it when you hit me because it makes feel bad."
7 He could take up a martial art to learn how to protect himself better.
8 He could leave and go to another school.
9 George should hit one of the boys who bully him.

Step 5: feedback and extra information are provided

This initial response demonstrates that although the students see what happens (they understand the dynamics and power relations), they also accept it as "just the way things are" and do not think anything can be done about it (they feel a sense of powerlessness). When faced with a marauding and potentially menacing group of powerful adolescent boys, what can anyone do, they think? At this point, the students often feel a sense of anxiety. They would like to come up with a better solution. The teacher needs to extend their understanding of what is going on and to assist them to do this.

Some specific information to show that they are not alone in feeling this way can be provided on the board or via an overhead. They can be told that, in one research study (Adair et al., 2000):

1 79 percent of students who witnessed bullying did not tell an adult (parent or teacher) about it;
2 half of those who witnessed such incidents did not think bullying could be stopped or had no solutions for dealing with it; and
3 students are sometimes willing to try to help if it is a friend or someone they approve of who is being victimized, but not if the person is neither a friend nor someone they regard highly.

Step 6: improved strategies and solutions are developed

At this point, the students can be asked to discuss these points:

• Do the above research findings reflect their experiences?
• If not, what are their experiences?

Students frequently respond that this is pretty accurate. Most students do not tell if they are being bullied, and bystanders do nothing to support them. Generally, they say that it sounds as if those bullying George are well organized (they moved in, did the damage, and moved out without being caught). They are a force to be reckoned with and would probably victimize anyone who went to George's rescue. It is also observed that if George is picked on in the cafeteria as described, he is probably an "easy target" and this would happen on other occasions when the opportunity arose. The bullies would probably even seek him out (as may have been the case in the cafeteria). He would be picked on in the playground, on the way to school, in the corridors, at the local shopping mall, and wherever he went.

This is a pivotal moment in the lesson. The teacher can challenge the students by asking the following question: "In all your suggestions, you have given George the job of finding a solution to the bullying. You suggest he find some friends, take up a martial art, or not come to the cafeteria. Do you think it is the job of the victim to find a solution? Would you expect a victim of a violent robbery to go and arrest the perpetrator or stop going to the place he was robbed to avoid any further incidents? Do you have any more ideas about how to deal with the bullying incident more effectively?"

The students are then asked to work in small groups and use this new information to brainstorm and come up with further strategies and solutions. They make the following suggestions:

1 Some of the students present could help George clean up the mess.
2 He should be assertive and voice his disapproval: "I think what you just did sucks and I won't tolerate it again … ."

Step 7: steps 4 and 5 are repeated until the participants are satisfied with the strategies and solutions

A useful tool for effective teaching is to develop an understanding of an issue by approaching it in a variety of ways. At this point, in order to help them dig a bit deeper, the teacher reframes the bullying event by tapping into the students' imagination and combining it with their lived experiences.

1 They are given some more information.
2 A task is set that is designed to elicit new responses.

First, the information: The teacher explains at this point that certain areas in a school can be difficult to patrol and that it is unclear whose responsibility it should be (the prefects? the teachers? the cafeteria staff?) (see "Can We Tell Where Bullying Will Occur?," Chapter 1). Do they think anything should be done about it?

Secondly, the task: the teacher sets about getting the students to reconstruct what happened by:

1 drawing a map and creating a picture of the cafeteria; and
2 asking for more information, who was there, and what roles the various "participants" took on.

First, a map is drawn and the cafeteria described. The food service area is at the front of the cafeteria. The cash register is located at the far end of the area which consists of a sliding counter for students to push their trays along as they select their lunches. This is logically ordered, with soup and starters first, followed by the day's selection of main meals (including hot food and sandwiches), and desserts consisting of yoghurts, fruit, and health food bars. Drinks can be obtained beyond the desserts and just before the cash register. Halfway up the right-hand side of the cafeteria there are service areas where leftover food is dumped in bins, cutlery and plates are put in separate containers, and dirty trays are stacked on a trolley. There are doors and windows down the full length of the other side where students can go out onto a patio where there are wooden tables and benches.

The room is long and four tables wide. The tables can seat 12 students and have benches of equal length down each side. Tables and benches are immovable and bolted to the floor. There are 10 rows of tables (meaning the cafeteria can seat 480 students). The school has two lunch hours (11:30 to 12:30, and 12:30 to 1:30). There are four or five staff behind the counter.

The teacher then attempts to tease out the drama and has the class fill in the missing details prompted by these questions:

- When does George have his lunch?
- What has he been doing?
- Where does he decide to sit?
- Who are the boys who bully him?
- What were they doing before he arrived?
- What do they do to him?

The time of our episode is halfway through the first lunchtime. Many students have eaten their main meal and are starting on their health food bars, yoghurt, or fruit and chatting with their friends or taking their trays and rubbish to the service area. George arrives late for lunch, a bit dishevelled and by himself. His last class was physical education which he does not like—he is not an athlete— and he was asked to stay behind to put away equipment. Academically, however, he is a top student, particularly in math, science, and computing. He is small for his age. He has a group of like-minded friends but is very independent and spends a lot of time absorbed in what he is doing rather than socializing. He is reading a book as he helps himself to some food. A group of boys who are sitting at a bench by one of the doors to the patio notice him come in. They have been talking with some girls who have just left. They see

> George enter and two of them, Maurice and Billy, smile at each other conspiratorially. George heads to the back of the cafeteria and chooses an empty table where he plans to read his book and eat his lunch. When he has just sat down, Maurice signals Billy and looks toward four other friends and they get up rowdily and move toward George. They sit down at his table and make remarks about him always swotting. One grabs his book and says, "Let me see that." They throw it around and George tries unsuccessfully to get it back. It lands finally in his soup. As they leave, Billy "accidently" bumps George (and looks towards Maurice who gives a barely perceptible smile). The tray tips spilling George's pie, potatoes, and drink onto the floor, and George falls off the bench. "Oh George, you are so clumsy," says Tim and laughs.

The teacher asks who else is there.

> There are a number of other people present from George's class. There is Max who does not like what is going on but does not particularly like George. Sitting with Max is his friend Ishmael. He does not want to get involved. Geraldine is sitting in the middle of the room with Fran and Beth. Geraldine thinks George is quite nice and is angry when she sees what the boys do to him but feels confused.

The teacher asks what Geraldine might be feeling:

> - These boys have a lot of power but the teachers do not seem to mind their behavior.
> - They seem to be having fun.
> - Things got spilled but perhaps that was accidental.
> - Boys often act like that and get a bit rowdy.
> - It all happened so quickly, there was hardly any time to get involved even if you wanted to.

Fran and Beth just watch with amusement, and when Maurice and his friends leave they call out, "See you later."

There are some prefects in the cafeteria but they are sitting at a front table and Maurice's girlfriend, Ann, is a prefect. She was talking to Maurice and left shortly before George arrived.

The teacher asks what any of these students could have done. Billy and Tim are the two boys who did all the "dirty work" while Maurice just egged them on. Everyone is afraid or in awe of Maurice's crowd. They are popular with the other male students as well as the teachers and the girls, whereas George is a bit of a loner.

The teacher suggests they use a "freeze frame" to analyze what happens. As Maurice and the other boys move towards George, the pause button can be hit.

What are all the students in the cafeteria doing?

> George looks up quizzically as if he is about to realize what is going to happen. The girls in the middle look apprehensive. The prefects look the other way. Max and Ishmael are very involved with their food.

If the "video" is allowed to run until Maurice and his gang reach George's table, another freeze frame can be examined.

> George looks frightened. The boys around him are sneering, and being active and menacing. The girls in the middle look worried. The prefects look down and some are starting to get up to leave. Max and Ishmael are watching George and look perplexed.

Another two seconds into the action, Max half stands but a quick check shows that he sits down again. At the same moment, Geraldine looks to her friends for guidance, but they give none.

The teacher needs to lead the discussion and examine how all the people in the area are drawn into the action. To assist, the teacher should construct a simple diagram of the cafeteria on the whiteboard. Everyone who could be in the immediate vicinity of the altercation should be included on it.

The focus should be on George and his assailants, Geraldine and her friends, Max and Ishmael, and the prefects. A picture can be built up of what each person perceives is going on.

Typically, George will feel isolated and humiliated. He will hear laughter and feel scorned by Maurice and the others at the table. He will feel completely alone, rejected, and very vulnerable. He will be ashamed by his inability to stand up to these boys and perhaps even angry with himself for not being able to prevent it from happening.

Maurice, Billy, and Tim will feel vindicated by the response of others to their actions, especially as Fran and Beth acknowledge them when they leave. Maurice also knows he has immunity because of his relationship with Ann and his popularity with students and teachers.

At this stage, the teacher can introduce the bullying roles identified by the Finnish researcher Salmivalli (1999) to discuss the part played by each member of the scene, and as discussed in Chapter 8:

- bully;
- victim;
- assistant (sidekick);
- reinforcer;
- outsider;
- defender.

It is clear who is the victim. Who are the sidekicks? What about the reinforcers? Maurice is the bully, and Billy and Tim are his sidekicks. The boys who go with them are the reinforcers. Unfortunately for George, he has no defenders (although Geraldine is on the verge). The students who watch are the outsiders, but by doing nothing they may also be seen as reinforcers, as Maurice relies on the compliance of his peers.

Step 8: final recommendations are made

The group has now developed a much better understanding of the nature of bullying, the position of the victim, and the roles of the bystanders. They are aware of the absence of adults, and wonder if there should always be a teacher on duty in the cafeteria. They also think the cafeteria staff should be aware of what is going on and step in when necessary. They come up with the following final recommendations:

1 The school authorities should find ways to patrol the cafeteria and other low-control areas in the school to make sure George or other students are not bullied.
2 There needs to be a teacher on duty.
3 The cafeteria staff should be alert for signs of bullying.
4 It is not alright for Maurice and his friends to treat George or anybody else in this way.
5 Geraldine, Fran, and Beth could have made it clear to Maurice and his friends that their behavior was mean and nasty.
6 Max and/or Ishmael could have gone over to George's table and voiced their disapproval of the bullying.
7 The prefects could have intervened and made it clear that bullying is not acceptable behavior.
8 Any of the students in the cafeteria could tell a teacher and ask for the bullying to be dealt with.
9 Any of the students can make a point of sitting with George.
10 They can tell Maurice and his friends that their behavior is pathetic and that it sucks.

None of these recommendations places the onus for stopping the bullying on the victim. Instead, it rests squarely on the school's safety mechanisms and the development of a prosocial peer group.

Step 9: analysis and overview

This process builds on what students learned about bullying previously and provides them with a vehicle to explore what happens in bullying so that they develop a deeper understanding of how it works.

They are left in no doubt that the bystanders need to become active, that the bullies need to be aware of the disapproval of their peers, and that the victim could do with some support. They are clear that it is not up to the victim to find a way to stop the bullying: they realize that they all need to become part of the solution. But they also know that such change can only occur within a school that does everything it can to be a safe place.

12

Harnessing Student Leadership

Introduction: a tale of two schools

> The boy left the batting crease, having been bowled out on the first ball to the hoots and derisive comments of his school mates. The team came from a school with a very strong sporting heritage. They were the third ranked cricket team in their school yet were still good enough to be playing the top team of the other school. Surprisingly, the game was close and when the batsman in question walked to the crease, the game was finely poised. He was wearing expensive equipment and, despite the tension in the game, even on his way out to bat there were loud and snide comments from his schoolmates. These focused on the disparity between his equipment and his performance: he was being set up for failure.
>
> As he walked away from the crease, the members of the opposite team crowded around their coach and talked in hushed voices about how appalling this treatment was. They were genuinely surprised and shocked that he was being humiliated by those who should have been his community of support. One of this team was Jonah, who understood only too well the derisory group behavior of the other school's spectators. Not so long ago he would have been up there yelling and hissing like them.

If these two sets of reactions can be taken as symbolic of what each of these schools accepts as normal, what else might we infer?

The demeaning and menacing nature of the incident suggests that the batting school has a culture that allows and supports abuse, blame, and shame, while the other school exhibits empathy and compassion. In relation to dealing with bullying, we would probably conclude that the first school was slack and the second vigilant.

In fact, both schools have robust anti-bullying policy statements and programs. On the surface they ostensibly have similar philosophical and practical approaches, and yet based on this single incident there appears to be a huge difference in their underlying cultures. While it would be dangerous to judge either school on the basis only of this one incident, we need to take careful notice of the way students relate to each other.

What we are arguing throughout this book is that however hard it may be, it is essential to develop and implement strategies that make sure that such anti-humane cultures do not predominate in a school. Working within the student culture to create a positive sense of right and wrong and to encourage mutual support of one's classmates is therefore fundamental. In this chapter, we describe a student leadership program that endeavors to harness existing power and influence by providing targeted training and support for student leaders.

Leadership in today's schools: "we don't need no other heroes"

Leadership of any description exhibits the primary characteristics of power and status. Leadership may be defined as a "process of organizing ... through negotiation, to achieve acceptable influence over the description and handling of issues within and between groups" (Hosking and Morley, 1991: 241). Hosking and Morley argue that people's identity can only be constructed through their relationships with other people. In other words, people need others (through a response or as a reflection) in order to determine how they act in particular roles. This is how they "construct their social order (or culture)" (ibid.: 239). Leadership can also be defined as "an influence relationship among leaders and followers who intend real changes that reflect their mutual purposes" (Rost, 1993: 102). The literature on leadership in the business context identifies it as coaching, enabling, encouraging, facilitating, inspiring, modeling, stewarding and visioning (see Parry, 2001), as compared to the more traditional management role which is hierarchical and controling.

In this chapter, we argue that, below the surface (deep structure), all forms of leadership contain the same characteristics and that it is how the power and status of leadership are used (on the surface) that defines what kind of a leader someone is (Figure 12.1). Positive leaders use their power in a positive fashion. They benefit from what they do and also make a positive contribution to the society of which they are a part. Negative leaders misuse and abuse their power and status.

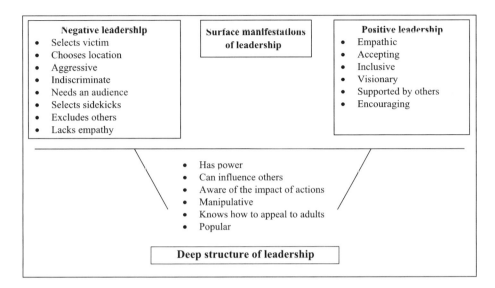

Figure 12.1 *Deep structure and surface manifestations of negative and positive leadership*

Those who bully are often negative leaders. They use their power and status in an antisocial fashion not only to subjugate their victims but also to create a web of manipulation and control within their immediate peer group. When this bullying dynamic is flexed, it spreads from the classroom and beyond into the school and wider community. Maines and Robinson's definition of a bullying amplifies this point and helps explain how people use bullying to meet their needs: "[A bully is] a person behaving in a way which might meet needs for excitement, status, material gain or group process and does not recognise or meet the needs and rights of the other people/person who are harmed by the behaviour." (1992a: 18).

The issues of actively participating in and leading group processes, securing material gain, and creating and participating in enjoyable, exciting events (particularly in adolescence) are driven by fundamental biological and social needs and are perfectly normal. It is the lack of recognition of others' rights or feelings and resulting abusive and disrespectful treatment that make the behavior of bullies antisocial and negative. We argue that if a school recognizes the leadership qualities not only of its positive and obvious leaders but also of its negative and sometimes hidden leaders (as bullying is often hidden), and provides a platform for them to experience success, there are likely to be positive outcomes for the individuals involved, their classmates, and the school as a whole.

In this chapter, we give a template for a leadership program that is based on one developed at Mark Cleary's school, Colenso High School, in Napier.

The school provides a course that acknowledges and gives direction to the leadership skills of natural leaders during their first two years at school as a way of creating an ongoing positive and safe school climate. Traditionally, it is the good and prosocial students who are targeted for leadership opportunities. However, in this case the school also recognizes the power and status of the anti-leaders and creates an equal space for them. As a result, each year, four students (two boys and two girls; two prosocial and two antisocial) are chosen by each class for the leadership program. The prosocial students have had years of experience of academic and social success, and this selection is a further confirmation of their skills and status as leaders. In comparison, the antisocial students have often been in trouble, are familiar with failure and the disapproval this usually brings, and do not usually regard themselves as good at anything. This recognition of their status and potential as leaders comes as a complete surprise to them. Contrary to expectations, in the program they are not difficult and disruptive but, instead, usually rise to the challenge and are able to reframe a plethora of negative skills and attributes into more positive ones. Not only do they benefit, but their classmates and the school do as well. It is a case where "grasping the nettle" pays dividends.

These students are identified first by their form teacher who uses the Strathclyde triangle to map out each class (see Chapter 8). The triangle shows a victim–bully continuum, which is also a passive–active continuum. The same qualities of action, energy, power, and status cluster at the active end of the continuum where both the prosocial and antisocial leaders sit. These characteristics are in themselves the driving force of both types of leader: it is just their application and expression that have differing social impacts. The purpose of the social mapping of classes is to give each teacher a good understanding of the individual personalities and peer groupings within the class, so that they can identify the opinion-leaders, frontiers-persons, power-brokers, *and* the bullies, as well as the more passive members.

Class social dynamics are not straightforward. Bullies run on fuel that is a high octane combination of power and prestige, and because they act in powerful ways they often believe they are popular. However, while Salmivalli's figures (Salmivalli, 1999) show that 80 percent of students support the bully, Pikas (1989) has found that those who seem to give support to the bully do not feel comfortable, whether they are active or passive. The apparent support that bullies receive must contribute to their perception that they have a lot of friends (Johnson and Lewis, 1999), but although they have status they are seldom popular. Research indicates that in analysis the bystanders tend not to nominate that person as their friend (Hargreaves, 1967; McLean, 1994).

The main purpose of leadership training is to create a safe classroom and school environment. By selecting students who bully to take part in a leadership program, they are immediately reframed in a positive light. Behavior that has always got them into trouble, or about which they are secretive, suddenly ceases to be the focus of the school's response to them. Instead, they start to get positive feedback and to be noticed in a context of approval, and as they relinquish their hold on manipulation as a means of influence, they are likely to become more attractive to their peers. As leaders they can have prosocial rather than antisocial influence, and their sidekicks often move with them.

In addition to a general improvement in social climate and classroom safety that results from leadership programs, trained leaders can take on other useful roles:

1 They can be assigned specifically to help with conflict resolution, along-side their classmates.
2 They can form the core of an anti-bullying team.
3 They can aid and embody a process of team-based teaching, learning, and classroom management that fully empowers the students. In this sort of set-ting a team approach can be more thoroughly introduced and sustained, encouraging constructive learners within a resilient social environment.
4 When they are older, they can become peer mentors (see Chapter 14).

Traditionally, secondary schools conduct their leadership training with prosocial students at the beginning of the last year of schooling. We have explained why it is important to train those who are antisocial as well, and we have also found that it is better to put time and energy into developing leadership qualities in the first two years of secondary school.

While there have been many positive aspects to traditional leadership pro-grams, they have generally failed to recognize the influence and power of the key members of the peer group. Because of their age and inexperience, a num-ber of these students will also be oblivious to the influence they have, and some, especially those who are not succeeding academically, may view teacher intervention as a threat to their hard-won and jealously guarded leadership. For others, their power within the peer group is the one thing that is positive in their lives. Our challenge is to help these leaders develop and channel their skills to ensure that they and their classmates are successful.

The purpose of this training program, therefore, is to harness the abilities of both positive and negative leaders; to reframe the negative as active, ener-getic, and powerful; and to encourage leadership potential through teaching new skills in a positive, experiential learning environment.

The leadership program

The leadership program aims to help students (in their first two years of sec-ondary schooling) refine their existing leadership skills in the hope that they become more thoughtful in the way they exercise leadership within the peer group, particularly at school. Four of the most powerful students from each class are selected by teachers and peers and receive initial training.They are given opportunities to use their leadership in formal situations with ongoing supervision and support in the hope that they will begin to have an enhanced positive influence on the way the class group interacts.

Colenso is a decile 2 school with a large multi-ethnic population (30 percent indigenous Maori, 3 percent Pacific Islanders, 4 percent Asian) in a low-socioeconomic status community with high unemployment and a strong gang presence. It is known to have a caring teacher population, to be innovative, and to seek educational processes that meet the needs of its students.

The training program on which this template is based was developed by Outdoor Education teachers at Colenso High School who have the enhancement of student leadership as a key curriculum outcome.[1] The teachers in this department are committed to a constructivist philosophy, have a strong background in adventure education, and use many elements advocated by Project Adventure.[2]

During the training program, the leaders are given an opportunity to gain a deeper understanding of leadership, harassment, bullying, and conflict, as well as the chance to become more familiar with approaches such as No Blame and conflict resolution strategies.

Key objectives of the program

- To give formal recognition to existing leadership and influence within the class group.
- To discuss what leadership is, how it works, and what it can do.
- To help leaders identify their personal style of leadership.
- To allow leaders to reflect on whether this personal style is useful.
- To help leaders become aware of leadership behavior and its influences, both positive and negative.
- To give students an opportunity to practise their leadership.
- To provide opportunities for students to develop understandings of the complex social dynamics that operate in emerging adolescent groups.
- To introduce the students to positive role models who will be able to provide ongoing support.
- To empower leaders to act to help create a positive learning environment.

The process

1 Leadership selection.
2 Initial training session.

3 Weekly meeting format.
4 Follow-up training.

Leadership selection

The selection process begins near the end of the first 10-week term. The delay is deliberate as it gives students and classes a chance to become settled.

The following letter is sent to form teachers to begin the process.

Leadership in Year 9/10

With half the term gone it's overdue for us to identify the *"real leaders"* in our junior forms so that we can channel and use their energy and influence to ensure that our classrooms are more effective learning units.

We need to identify those students who are seen by their peers as attractive, fun, and powerful. While many of these students will stand out and be easy to recognize, sometimes these students are unproductive in the classroom and can, from our perspective, actively undermine what we are trying to do. It is important that we recognize the influence these students have over the tone of the class and that we use our skills to help them develop their natural leadership.

Once identified, all the nominated students will undergo a leadership-training course where their skills, energy, and talents will be developed and focused towards providing positive influence.

Please discuss this with your colleagues who teach the form class and come up with four nominations [two boys/two girls]. Hand the nominations to your dean by [date].

Before this occurs, teachers need to be briefed on a device such as Hargreaves's (1973) use of sociometry in the classroom (Sullivan, 2000: 96–105); and McLean's (1994) development of relationship maps (see especially Chapter 8; and Sullivan, 2000: 103–5, 220–2) so that they can map out the social dynamics of their class.

The form teacher coordinates the selection and encourages the choice to be made from those who have exhibited leadership. Two boys and two girls from each home/form class are chosen by their classmates and teachers.

How to identify the leaders
• Explain the program to the class and ask students for their opinion/nomination.
• "Map" the class using a passive–active continuum. (A leader cannot be passive!)
• Look at the way the more active students relate to their peers.

Nomination Class:	Girls	Boys
	1	1
	2	2

The teachers are encouraged to involve the whole class in the selection, making sure that the aims and objectives of the program are fully explained and that everyone understands what type of person is needed. The aim of the selection process is to ensure that the genuine leaders in the class are chosen. The following issues need to be considered:

- Who has the power and influence?
- Who are the recognized leaders?
- Who is the most popular and is fun to be around?
- Who has the most friends?
- Who is the most feared?

A Typical Group of Leaders from One Class

Shelly: Academically confident, popular, and well liked. Surrounded by friends. Involved in a large number of extracurricula activities (music, debating, drama, soccer, and underwater hockey). *Chosen by both teachers and students.*

Marty: Academically confident, a musician (plays guitar in a rock band) and a very promising rugby player. He's enthusiastic and competitive and has a small but strong friendship group. *Chosen by both teachers and students.*

Gina: Bright but often fails to complete school work. Is the queen bee of the class surrounded by followers. Is very talkative and often makes smart comments to teachers. She has already been suspended from school for three days after verbally abusing a relief (substitute) teacher. *Nomination opposed by two of her teachers who do not want her rewarded for bad behavior. The form teacher insists that she be part of the program as her influence is obvious.*

Jonah: Slight, a good athlete but refused to be in any of the school sports teams. He rarely finishes his schoolwork, despite having obvious ability. He is always surrounded by three or four other boys who are negative about school and are already experimenting with antisocial behavior. Many of the boys look for Jonah's approval before they participate in any activity. He actively excludes other boys in the class from being part of the group. *He is the most popular choice of the students but not of the teachers. The form teacher and level dean reluctantly agree to his inclusion. They are fearful that he will disrupt the training sessions.*

Once selected, each student receives a letter of invitation to attend the training session. It helps if an off-site venue is used and that the senior student school leaders are involved.

Initial training session

All the selected year 9 students attend the training session (in this case there are 20). It is essential that the teacher and senior student leaders are well briefed before the day and are skilled in the delivery. Here is a typical timetable for this junior leadership training session:

Time	Year 9	Facilitators
9:00–9:30	Ice breakers	Teacher, senior students
9:30–10:00	Explanation of the day's program	Three teachers
10:00–11:00	Leadership styles activities	Teachers and senior students
11:00–12:00	Leadership and team-building activities	Teachers and senior students
12:00–1:00	Lunch	Mentors
1:00–2.15	Problem-solving	Two teachers
2.15–2:45	Putting it into action	Two teachers

Ice breakers

The students participate in a number of fun de-inhibiting activities. In the first, an article such as a soft ball or a rubber chicken is thrown around the group. The teacher starts it off by saying their name and the name of the student they are throwing it to ("Mark to Clare"). That student then throws it to someone else ("Clare to Stacey"), and so it goes on. The use of names is important: those present get to know each other, the adolescent aversion to using first names is addressed, and humor and fun start to enter into the activity. Other games can be used as well.[3]

Explanation of the day's program

The details of the day's activities are then presented to the participants by the teacher responsible for the program or the school's principal. This will include a short overview of what leadership is all about and why the school is undertaking the program.

Leadership styles activities

The following leadership styles are described and explained by the teachers:

- authoritarian;
- laissez-faire/permissive; and
- authoritative.

Ahead of time, the senior students have prepared a series of short role plays to illustrate these styles. A scenario is presented:

> Rewi, a year 12 student, is walking down a corridor one day and notices that a year 9 girl is being jostled against a wall and that her lunch money is being taken off her.

The same event is played out by the seniors three times, each one showing a different leadership style.

- In the first (authoritarian), Rewi rushes over, yells at the offender to stop immediately, threatens to report the incident to the principal, and grabs the offender's hand and wrests the money out of it.
- In the second (laissez-faire/permissive), Rewi looks away, then comes back slowly, says, "I guess you guys can handle this," and wanders off. He winks at the offender—he's friends with her older brother.
- In the third (authoritative), Rewi asks if the girl is OK, requests that the offender returns the money to her and apologizes, says, "It's not cool to take people's money," and states he will let the year 9 dean know about the incident, making it clear that he means it.

The students are then broken into groups to discuss what they saw. They take turns trying out similar role plays, to see how each style feels. At the end of the session the teachers lead a discussion of the advantages and disadvantages of each style, and focus on authoritative styles, with their characteristics of clarity, encouragement, fairness, and restoration.

Leadership and team-building activities

To provide practical opportunities for students to experience leadership and team-building, the students are put into groups of four to six. These groups are each given the same task—to build the tallest tower using paper straws, for example.

The teachers and senior students observe and let the students carry out this activity on their own as much as possible, but help if asked. The students have to work out how to build the tower, the best way of going about it, how to include each other, and how to intervene if it starts to go wrong.

Afterward they all talk about how their processes worked, who did what, whether they succeeded, what would have worked better, and if they managed to work well together and why.

Lunch

The lunch break can be used as a positive learning time by inviting local community and business leaders to share lunch with the students. Lunch is best taken in class-based groups, including the four leaders in training, their form teacher, one or two of the senior leaders who worked with the class group in the morning, and an outside community leader. The form teachers are responsible for organizing the guests, and each of the trainees and senior students is given a task to help make the lunch a success. The students have the opportunity to talk with the invited guest as well as describing what the program is all about.

Problem-solving

After the break the students work in different small groups of four to six and are given a number of problem-solving activities to undertake. The first is an obstacle course. An imaginary river is drawn with chalk or laid out with ropes, and the students are given certain equipment to cross it. Each group might be given three tyres and three planks, and they are told that they cannot touch the floor (the river bottom) on their way across and they have to work out together how to do it. The planks and tyres do not span the river.

Once they have completed this task, they can be encouraged to discuss their solutions and strategies and to talk about what worked and what did not.

Next they are given problems for which they need to find strategies and solutions.

"We Have a Problem"

1 Your friends ask you to skip school for the afternoon.
2 You know who is stealing money from the teacher's desk.
3 You are invited to a friend's house at lunchtime and told that there will be drugs and alcohol available.
4 You know that someone in your class is always being left out and is very unhappy.
5 A friend confides in you that she is being abused by her stepfather.

Each group addresses a different problem and they each respond and then try to work out the best way to handle it as a group. After the activities, they are given the opportunity to talk about their discussion, whether they felt they came to a good decision, and whether they had their say. In a very controlled manner, each member is given the opportunity to give their view on whether anyone dominated the group during the problem-solving exercises, and how. The students are asked what worked well and what did not. They are then asked to relate their experiences to the earlier styles exercise. The aim is for the students to identify the changing nature of leadership and how different styles can be used in different situations.

> *Debriefing*: We recommend the use of the Project Adventure debriefing format that is based on four basic questions:
>
> 1 What did we do?
> 2 Why did we do it?
> 3 What did we learn?
> 4 How can we apply this in our daily lives?

The students usually arrive at the following conclusions:

- They realize they can talk about issues with their peers and find solutions.
- They realize that they are not alone.
- They learn that if something dangerous, harmful, unfair, or wrong is occurring, it is good to act responsibly.
- They realize they can refer problems to adults and that they do not have to handle things alone.
- They learn that there are always solutions.
- They learn that leadership is not about being a hero or being in charge. It is about helping to change the social dynamic.

Putting it into action
The teacher with responsibility for the program explains how leaders can lead by example and role-modeling. When someone is being bullied, if they intervene, the bullying is likely to stop. If they have bullied others in the past and now stop behaving as a bully, the bystanders will notice and shift in relation to the victim as well.

The teacher can also explain how the leaders can take on particular jobs such as being in anti-bullying and anti-harassment teams. These teams are points of contact for other students and are not elite exclusive groups. They help maintain safe classrooms and give an anti-bullying message.

The teacher can also explain how these leaders need to try to include others in their prosocial activities so that social responsibility becomes the norm throughout the school. The problem-solving and team nature of the position is emphasized, as well as the fact that the leadership program is one of the school's strategies to maintain health.

Each class group of four is told that they will help their own class develop a class charter. Their form teacher will help them do this, and they will have to overcome obstacles such as negative attitudes and sabotage when they undertake the task in their own class.

Weekly meeting format

Typically, students are very positive at the end of the first training session. It is essential that there is immediate and high-quality follow-up to ensure that the momentum is not lost. The next session needs to involve the form teacher in preparation for a report back to the class and the organization of the class charter. It is essential that the form teacher promotes a team-building approach. Some of the leaders will not be used to this sort of inclusion and collaboration and will still have some strong reservations about what is going on. They may well have been involved in bullying behavior themselves and may be feeling vulnerable. The adults should emphasize how important they are to the success of the project.

Teachers need to identify specific barriers to the success of the project:

- Who are the students most likely to bully or harass?
- Who are they most likely to target for this?
- How can the leaders take positive action to ensure that these behaviors do not take place?

The four leaders need to develop strategies that will be useful in gaining the support of friends and potential allies in the class.

At this stage the form teacher should establish a regular meeting time for the leaders. The first few meetings would involve planning and then debriefing over the class charter (see Appendix 4), while later other issues can be discussed as they arise. These could include helping new class members settle in, addressing specific cases of bad behavior or disruption to the learning environment, and the development of cooperative and group-learning strategies.

Follow-up training

The teacher in charge of the program needs to organize at least two full training sessions at which the students are given more information about leadership and how to handle difficult problems and situations. One session can be devoted to explaining and practising the No Blame Approach to bullying. Another can deal with harassment.

It is essential that these follow-up sessions give the students opportunities to ask questions and to raise issues of concern.

Jonah enters the leadership program

Among the group of 20 leader trainees are Gina, Marty, Shelly, and Jonah. Jonah is very surprised when he is chosen for the leadership program. In fact, he thinks there must have been a mistake and that he has misheard. By the next morning, he is starting to believe it is true, and every time he acknowledges this he feels a warm glow start off in his body and move up to a smile on his face. He tries very hard to hide how excited he is starting to feel, and is nonchalant with his friends. He masks his feelings with a dismissive stance but withdraws from teasing a boy who is frequently the butt of his sarcasm and ridicule, pretending that he has forgotten something in his locker.

The next day he arrives on time at the program venue, feeling quite nervous and unsure of himself. He wonders again why he is there and thinks that perhaps after all there has been a mistake. He nods to some of the students he knows and they all go in and sit down on comfortable couches or on cushions on the floor.

First they play a game. He thinks this sounds as if it will be pretty lame and stupid. But soon he starts to enjoy himself and he finds it fun. The students around him suddenly feel almost like friends, and he does not feel separate from them.

He listens to the explanation of what the program is all about and starts to feel interested. He is still surprised to have been chosen, but begins to see why he might have been selected.

When they work in a group with a senior student, he gets very excited and tries hard to help build the tallest tower. He starts to yell at one of the other students whose straw is on the wrong angle and in fact is in danger of dislodging part of the tower, but he stops when someone else says it is OK and suggests a way to move the offending straw instead. He gets agitated when another student starts to take over a move and Jonah goes to elbow him out of the way. When one of the others says it is a good idea, he stops and watches what is going on.

In the discussion about leadership styles, he feels intimidated by the long words but gets his tongue around "authoritative" and enjoys the feel of saying it.

Lunch is fun. The food is really good and he enjoys talking to the guest who sits at their table. She is an elderly nun who has walked the length of the country (1,000 kilometres) on a peace march, has nursed the victims of war in Afghanistan, and now runs a shelter for homeless people in the city. Jonah is glad he gets to talk to her rather than the winner of the Young Farmers' Competition who is the guest at the next table. The students at that table, however, find it exciting to hear about how he encourages volunteers to work on his farm and learn about biodynamics, and how he has increased crop yields because of his irrigation and crop-cycling system that is now being trialed in Ethiopia and India. Jonah hears all about all the other guests afterwards.

In the afternoon, they have to do an obstacle course, in different groups from the ones they were in during the morning. Jonah finds it easy to take part and he enjoys showing off his physical prowess. He feels proud of his agility. When he is halfway across, he notices that one of the girls is having difficulties and he stops to help her. As he does so, he pulls himself up short in wonder, but gives her a hand and tells her where to put her feet. By the time he gets to the other side, he has helped three other students and is aware of how his whole group has got across. He is no longer aware only of himself.

They then talk about some difficult situations. Jonah's group focuses on the problem, "You know who is stealing money from the teacher's desk." They argue vehemently about the problem. Should they tell/shouldn't they tell? Who should they tell? Should they tell the teacher? Should they speak to the thief? Should they tell the school principal? Jonah finds it very interesting to hear so many different opinions. And when he thinks he knows for sure how to handle it, he then hears another opinion and feels less sure. In the end, they decide together that one of them should approach the student who is taking the money, and suggest to him that he own up to the teacher and give her back the money.

They feel this is the fairest thing to do: it gives the student a chance to make things right, both with the teacher and by returning the money. It gives the teacher a chance to act authoritatively with the student, and for the issue to be closed satisfactorily. Jonah learns that there are many ways of dealing with a problem, that it is a good idea to listen to the opinions of other people, and that it is best to do whatever seems most likely to achieve the fairest result. If the purpose is to stop the thieving and restore the teacher's money, then the course they choose together seems the best. Jonah realizes that he can think like this about many things that happen in his life.

For Jonah, being in the leadership program had the following effects:

- He was singled out, not for something wrong he had done (as was usual) but for something positive.
- He was in effect given a new identity and a new chance.
- He learnt about being part of a team.
- He realized that others have useful things to say that are worth listening to.
- He felt good when he did something that was good.
- He started to feel for the first time that others liked him.

By the end of the year, in the height of summer, he becomes the boy in the story with which we open this chapter. He recognizes the derisory behavior of the other team's "supporters" and knows he could have been one of them. Now he is shocked by it. After being in the huddle with his team mates and coach (for now he is also in the cricket eleven), he goes after the boy who leaves the pitch in tears and walks with him off the sportsfield.

Notes

1 We are indebted to Phil Kay and Jason Pearson of Colenso High School for much of this information.
2 Project Adventure is an American organization of educators who are committed to using outdoor activities as a teaching and learning tool. Their website is: http://www.pa.org/
3 There are many readily available resources to assist in the planning of such sessions. See Project Adventure, for instance.

13

Experiential Learning through Social Theater

If bullying needs an audience, let's put on the play

When we take part in or witness a piece of powerful drama, we come to understand the perspective of individual participants, what they are thinking, what they are feeling, and what personal power they possess (or don't). And as characters interact and events intersect, a sort of dance begins and if we are open and carefully listen, watch, and feel, we can learn a lot. Using social theater to create and deconstruct instances of bullying is a very powerful way of getting inside "the beast." If an act of bullying (or a series of acts) is likened to a play, then there are usually not two but three types of central roles:

1 the perpetrator(s);
2 the victim(s); and
3 the bystanders, who can choose to:
   (a) become actively involved in the bullying;
   (b) encourage the bullying;
   (c) watch;
   (d) walk away;
   (e) have an undefined role; or
   (f) take the part of the victim(s).

In this book, we argue that bullying is a dynamic event or series of events and that although the central roles appear to belong to the bully and the victim, if bystanders as individuals and as a group claim their power (which they have often just by force of numbers), then they can halt the bullying. The question in response to this statement is, of course, "Then why don't they?" The purpose of this chapter is to answer this and other important questions. It does so by using social theater to get inside the various roles in their many forms, to explore the dynamics of bullying, and to develop strategies for defeating it. In order to do this, we have created an organizational template and we show how it works through recounting the events of a fascinating case study.

A Template for Using Social Theater to Address School Bullying

Step   1 Preparing for the workshop
Step   2 Getting established
Step   3 Identifying bullying scenarios
Step   4 Writing a script
Step   5 Performing the drama
Step   6 Discussing the drama in order to understand what is happening
Step   7 Identifying the emotional content of the drama and writing alternative dramas
Step   8 Taking on roles and making alternate dialogues to create better solutions

Steps 5 to 8 can be repeated once or twice in order to find better solutions.

Step   9 Coming out of role and resolution
Step 10 Student evaluation
Step 11 Facilitator reflection, self-evaluation, and follow-up
Step 12 Performance to other members of the school (optional)

Using social theater in the school: a case study

This case study is based on a successful workshop carried out by Keith Sullivan and Mark Cleary with a group of 12 16- and 17-year-old year 13 students in a multiethnic New Zealand high school. For the first half of the workshop, Keith was the only adult present. Mark took part in the afternoon session. The workshop started at 10:00 A.M. and finished at 2:30 P.M. and consisted of three sessions.

The aims of social theater are to assist participants to:

- generate a consensual definition of bullying;
- identify common bullying scenarios based on participants' experiences and observations;
- write up and act out a selected drama; and
- use the dramatic process to develop effective anti-bullying strategies.

Step 1: preparing for the workshop

Choosing a venue

The first consideration was to find the location. The school's audiovisual suite was ideal. It was a large, soundproof, windowless empty space away from the rest of the school. It had wide, carpeted steps and space to sit, spread out, or move around in. A few pieces of school furniture (desks and chairs) were stacked in a corner. It suited our purposes well.

Step 2: getting established

Step 2 focuses on creating a sense of group cohesion, and aims:

- to explain the purpose and processes of the workshop;
- to establish that this is a safe place to explore the nature and effects of bullying in an honest, interactive, and realistic fashion; and
- to generate a definition of bullying.

Establishing rapport

Once the group was gathered together, Keith explained that the purpose of this workshop was to explore bullying through creating and acting out typical school bullying scenarios.

He initiated a "getting to know you" conversation, introduced himself, and asked students to introduce themselves. He enquired about their hopes and aspirations and engaged with them, creating rapport and building trust. He was also quietly establishing his credibility and authority so he would have control over the day's proceedings. He found the students receptive and interesting. It was a public conversation so they learned new and interesting information about each other.

In this group, there were six girls and six boys. Two were exchange students, Paolo from Italy and Pieter from Germany. A boy and a girl (Maui, who wanted to be an actor, and Reihana, whose goal was to work in the airline industry) were indigenous Maori. The rest were New Zealand Europeans. Takis was a cellist, Mitch a talented athlete (a New Zealand schoolboy soccer representative), and Mike intended studying politics at university. Katy, Lucy, and Maria wanted to study art and graphic design, and Caroline tourism. Sharon wanted to become a teacher.

Discussing and defining bullying

The students split up into four groups of three (of their own choosing). The groups were gender-specific, comprising two of three girls and two of three boys. Keith provided them with large sheets of paper and pens and asked them to brainstorm about bullying for 10 minutes and to come up with a set of characteristics. He walked around offering them biscuits while they worked.

One of the girls' groups reported back first. They articulately described three characteristics of bullying which they wrote on their sheet of paper. Keith thanked them and asked for contributions from the other groups (aware that this first group could have come up with all the characteristics alone). They each wrote their responses on a piece of paper as they delivered their findings. Together they identified the following characteristics:

- acting superior;
- being insulting;
- unwanted physical contact;
- intimidation;
- emotional bullying;
- it can be oral/verbal;
- mental abuse;
- pressuring people;
- sexual abuse, overtones, or language;
- intentionally making someone feel bad/uncomfortable;
- lowering someone else's self-esteem;
- body language (for example, giving the finger can be an implicit part of ongoing bullying);
- leaving someone out;
- misuse of power;
- repetitive.

They summarized what had been written, that is, that bullying can be physical or psychological, and that it is repetitive, menacing, and a misuse of power. Everyone had a partial understanding about bullying and the session acted to clarify what bullying is.

This process took an hour, provided a foundation for the rest of the workshop, and reinforced that this would be a safe environment in which to explore some sensitive issues.

Step 3: identifying bullying scenarios

The purpose of this step is to encourage the students to think up some bullying scenarios that can be used for role play. This maintains a high level of investment in the material by the students, and a reinforcement of their understanding of bullying.

After a short break, the groups discussed and came up with typical school bullying scenarios.

Students were asked to form into four groups of three, but mixed this time. They were asked to discuss bullying and to describe a bullying scenario they were familiar with. This is what they wrote:

1 *The canteen scenario (Reihana, Takis, Paolo)*. John is a third former who is fairly well-off. He goes to the canteen on a daily basis. When he purchases his goods, a group of kids hassles him for food and spare change. He is reluctant to give them anything but is bullied into it.
2 *The sleazy scenario (Maria, Katy, Mitch)*. Jim and Zac make Olivia feel uncomfortable with rude and inappropriate sexual jokes. They take it too far and lift up her skirt when she walks past and hug her against her will. It makes her feel like shit. She feels stink [embarrassed] about telling anyone about it.
3 *The ridiculing scenario (Lucy, Mike, Pieter)*. Bob sits outside every day at lunch and Ned starts ridiculing him, which makes everyone laugh at his expense. No one sticks up for him for fear that they will replace him as victim.
4 *The "crack" scenario (Caroline, Maui, Sharon)*. David (handicapped) walks into the basketball courts and gets "the crack" [a hard punch] for no apparent reason from Brad.

Step 4: writing a script

In step 4, students choose one bullying scenario to make a play about.

This group selected "the sleazy scenario" about sexual bullying. The students were asked to number off as one or two (that is, there were six ones and six twos). All the ones gathered in the bottom right and the twos in the top left-hand corner of the room, so that they could work apart. Each group consisted of three boys and three girls. They were told to develop a script in two stages:

• to discuss the scenario and write down their thoughts; and
• to write a short but realistic script based on their ideas.

In both groups, a director naturally emerged.

Step 5: performing the drama

In step 5, the students perform the bullying dramas.

The drama

Maui took on the role of director (and commentator). The first scene is set in the evening and features Adam telephoning Heidi. Scene 2 takes place the following day at school and also includes Adam and Heidi's respective friends, James and Michelle, and an unnamed female teacher. The group used four plastic chairs as their props.

Scene 1: Sunday night. All is quiet when Heidi gets an unusual call. Take 1.

Adam: Hello, is Heidi there, please?
Heidi: Yes, this is Heidi speaking.
Adam: Hey Heidi. This is Adam. How you going? I've noticed you around school. I find you very attractive. Do you wanna go out sometime?
Heidi: Na.
Adam: Why?
Heidi: 'Cause I don't like you.
Adam: F**k you then, bitch (hangs up).

Scene 2: Monday morning. A very awkward situation in class. Take 1.

Heidi and her friend Michelle are sitting toward the back of the class. Adam and James are sitting behind them continuously throwing spit balls at Heidi's head and smirking and laughing. James is egging Adam on. The teacher is writing on the board with her back to the students, completely unaware.

Heidi: (loses her temper and turns around and says to Adam) Stop it, w****r!
Adam: (smirks and laughs)
Teacher: (turns around, says to the boys) Stop that! (to Heidi) Don't use that language in my class!

The bell rings to signal the end of class. As they move out of the classroom, Adam shoves Heidi up against the wall. She bumps her shoulders and head. James and Michelle are close behind. Michelle shouts at Adam, "Leave her alone!" There is a lot of jostling. It's all a bit too close and feels very threatening. Heidi runs off crying to the toilet.

 The students had a quick "dress rehearsal" and then performed it dramatically and fully.

Step 6: discussing the drama in order to understand what is happening

Step 6 gives students the opportunity to discuss the drama immediately after it has been performed, in order to get a sense of its dynamics, to identify the nature of the bullying, and to start thinking about strategies.

Everyone agreed that the play was about sexual harassment but were confused about the rights and wrongs of what happened. They knew that it was nasty but didn't know how to change things. They decided on the following strategy:

Strategy 1: Heidi needs to make Adam feel better
Generally, the students felt that Heidi had been cruel to Adam when he asked why she did not want to go out with him. One girl suggested she should have said that she did not want to go out with him now, but perhaps she would in the future. Most did not feel comfortable with this strategy. More exploration was needed!

Step 7: identifying the emotional content of the drama and writing alternative dramas

Step 7 is intended to develop a deeper understanding of the nature and dynamics of the drama.

Everyone had either performed in or watched the drama and the group had come up with an initial but inadequate solution. In the earlier steps the students had called on their own resources (such as the selection of a director and the writing of the drama) and had made the process work. Now they were stuck and needed some help. Keith decided to approach things from a different angle and said to Sharon (who had played Heidi), "I am going to ask you what it felt like as Heidi when Adam phoned you." The following dialogue developed:

Sharon develops strategy 2: between passivity and assertiveness
Keith: Heidi, how did you feel when Adam asked you out?
Heidi: Well, I was surprised when he phoned me up out of the blue. He is in two of my classes but I don't really know him. It felt creepy.
Keith: How did you feel when he was abusive to you?
Heidi: I felt awful! Really awful! He swore at me!

This dialogue provided a new perspective and Keith decided to develop another angle and asked Sharon to speak as herself.

Keith: Sharon, did your experience as Heidi feel accurate? Would it have happened like that?

Sharon: Yes, it felt real. I know some people would have handled it like Heidi did but I would have done it differently.

Keith: What would you have done?

Heidi: I wouldn't have been so harsh. I would have let Adam down more gently.

Keith: What would you have said?

Sharon: Well, probably something like, "Hi Adam. Thanks for calling. Look, I don't want to go out with you. I have a boyfriend already and everything is sweet."

Keith: OK, let's do the first scene of the drama again and see how it feels.

Scene 1: Sunday night. All is quiet when Heidi gets an unusual call. Take 2.

Adam: Hello, is Heidi there, please?

Heidi: Yes, this is Heidi speaking.

Adam: Hey Heidi. This is Adam. How you going? I've noticed you around school. I find you very attractive. Do you wanna go out sometime?

Heidi: Hi Adam. Thanks for calling. Look, I don't want to go out with you. I have a boyfriend already and everything is sweet. I have to go now. 'Bye.

The facilitator strategically stops the dialogue

The other main character in this scene is Adam. Keith decided to build on Mike's intuition in the role of Adam and as himself.

Keith: Let's stop it there and ask Mike a question. Mike, how does that feel for you in your role as Adam? Is the new response from Heidi likely to change Adam's reaction?

Mike: I'm not certain how Adam'd react. Heidi's new response is less of a put-down than just saying "Na" that she didn't like him. As Adam, I would have still been angry and probably still aggressive and abusive. Perhaps not as much though!

Keith: Mike, I am going to interview you now as Adam and I want you to answer my questions as you feel Adam would respond.

Keith: Adam, can you tell me about your conversation with Heidi on Sunday night?

Adam: Well, it was embarrassing. I telephoned Heidi to ask her if she wanted to go out with me. My mate James was there [new information] and she dumped on me, said she didn't want to go out with me, and that she didn't even like me. Stupid cow!

Keith: So how did that make you feel?

Adam: Pretty crap! I don't wanna talk about it.

Keith: When she turned you down, you swore at her. You said "F**k you then,

bitch" and hung up on her. Was it OK to do that?
Adam: She deserved it.
Keith: (to Mike) Mike, do you want to change anything Adam's said?
Mike: No, I'll leave it.

A dialogue for problem-solving
Keith suggested they try this new dialogue.

Scene 1: Sunday night. All is quiet when Heidi gets an unusual call. Take 3.
Adam: Hello, is Heidi there, please?
Heidi: Yes, this is Heidi speaking.
Adam: Hey Heidi. This is Adam. How you going? I've noticed you around school. I find you very attractive. Do you wanna go out sometime?
Heidi: Hi Adam. Thanks for calling. Look, I don't want to go out with you. I have a boyfriend already and everything is sweet. I have to go now. 'Bye.
Adam: F**k you then, bitch (hangs up).

Although Mike had chosen to use the same abusive sentence to finish the dialogue, he was not as convincing or as angry as in the original drama. He looked slightly uncomfortable.

Checking things out with the characters
Keith then asked Heidi and Adam (in role) how this new dialogue felt.

Keith: Heidi, can you tell me how this dialogue felt compared to the first one?
Heidi: Well, Adam was still abusive to me so I didn't feel great but I didn't bad mouth him so it's his problem if he reacts like that.
Keith: Adam, how was this second dialogue for you?
Adam: I felt angry and still swore at Heidi but I didn't feel as bad because she was nice to me.

Checking things out with the audience
Keith then asked the audience for feedback to involve them in the problem-solving/strategy development process so that different opinions would emerge, points would be elaborated, and conversations become richer. "So what did you think about the second dialogue? How was the new strategy different? Would it work?" Keith wrote the dialogue on the board and got students to work in pairs (taking turns being Heidi and Adam), trying out Sharon's new dialogue to come up with new strategies.

The students acted out and discussed the two dialogues. They were still ambivalent, but now knew why. They felt that although Heidi could have been nicer to Adam, by calling her out of the blue and then quickly turning nasty, he did not really deserve kindness. They also felt strategy 1 was misleading and dishonest. Heidi did not want to go out with Adam so why pretend she might, as going by his present performance, when he found out he would turn nasty. Further to this, Adam was aggressive and sleazy. The group decided Heidi was within her rights to respond bluntly but she also needed to protect herself, and neither of their two strategies did this. They came up with another strategy.

Strategy 3: Heidi needs to be assertive

The group talked some more (with input from Keith) and decided that a better strategy was for Heidi to be assertive rather than aggressive and rude. She could tell Adam she did not want to go out with him in a neutral but firm voice. The students were sure that he would want to know why, be persistent, and keep pushing for an answer. They agreed that Heidi did not have to give a reason. She could politely but firmly repeat that she did not want to go out with him (the broken record technique). They stated that if Heidi lost her temper or became abusive back to Adam (which she may feel justified to do), this would somehow give Adam legitimacy to continue and even escalate his abuse and give him an excuse to harbor long-term resentment.

It was underlined that Heidi was not responsible for creating this problem, but it was seen as important that Heidi and other girls in this familiar situation be able to develop verbal self-defense strategies. The following mini-dialogue was created:

Adam: Why don't you want to go out with me?
Heidi: I don't want to go out with you.
Adam: But why don't you want to go out with me?
Heidi: I don't want to go out with you.
Adam: But why? Do I smell? Do you think I'm a jerk?
Heidi: I don't want to go out with you. I'm going now. Good-bye.

There were suggestions that Heidi could say things like, "It's nothing personal," or "I know you're a nice guy," but the group decided that this made things unclear, that Adam might think she did want to go out with him and was playing hard to get. It was important to give a clear message, to be neither passive nor aggressive but to be neutral, polite, and firm.

Step 8: taking on roles and making alternate dialogues to create better solutions

The purpose of step 8 is to explore the dynamic of the roles and relationships in more depth to arrive at better solutions.

In this case, step 8 was used to finish with scene 1 and move on to work out the rest of the drama. The students were no longer stuck and were developing better strategies. To achieve this, Keith devised the following questions:

1 We have asked Sharon and Mike if they think this an accurate representation of what could occur and you have heard what they have said. What do the rest of you think?

The students agreed that although the language may seem offensive to an adult audience, the drama as constructed was fairly realistic—although there would always be some variation depending on who was involved. What also became apparent was that the boys were focused on the male point of view (and sympathized with and personalized the rejection), whereas the girls were more able to see both points of view. A way of extending the boys' restricted view was to have them go into the girls' roles, which they did.

2 We have discussed the harassment of Heidi by Adam but it seems to have continued throughout the drama. Is this true? If so, what were its characteristics?

The group felt that in the second scene, the unpleasantness was escalating as a result of Heidi's rejection of Adam on the telephone. They identified the drama as containing three distinct events. These were separated out and analyzed:

Event 1: the telephone call. Adam was initially nice to Heidi because he wanted to go out with her. When she turned him down he immediately became angry and any pretense of being nice disappeared. He used obscene language and was verbally abusive.
Event 2: the classroom harassment. Adam with James's support harassed Heidi by throwing spit balls at her head. This was disrespectful and provocative. When the teacher became involved, her response to the boys was minimal, yet she chastized Heidi for using foul language. By making Heidi angry enough to retaliate, the boys doubly victimized her as they were able to lure the teacher into their web, as if pulling invisible strings.
Event 3: the assault as they leave the classroom. As the students were leaving class, Adam used the opportunity to push Heidi up against the wall, displaying his superior strength and hurting and jeering at her. Her friend Michelle tried to stop him while James gloated. Heidi, hurt and upset, ran to the toilets crying, feeling humiliated, angry, and sore.

Analysing the three events
In relation to event 1, everyone agreed that Adam very quickly turned nasty and there was little Heidi could do to make the interaction end pleasantly. In

relation to event 2, if Adam was asked nicely to stop throwing spit balls, he would have laughed and felt stronger. Building on the students' third strategy (Heidi being assertive with Adam when speaking on the telephone), Keith asked what would happen if Heidi stood up, turned around to Adam and James, and forcefully stated, "Stop throwing spit balls at me!" The students thought this sounded like a good strategy and tried it out.

They discussed how it felt. Those who played Heidi agreed it felt good. Those who acted in Adam's role thought Adam would be tempted to make a smart remark but in a classroom situation might back off (the spit ball attack, like a lot of bullying, occurred under the teacher's nose).

The group was concerned about the teacher's lack of awareness and her inappropriate intervention, and felt this was fairly typical of some teachers. They felt that not only would it happen this way (with Heidi rather than the boys getting the blame), but that it also provided de facto approval for the escalation which followed. Adam was now free to turn from harassing Heidi with pieces of paper to physically hurting her by pushing her up against a wall. Heidi knew the teacher had made her judgment and to go to her about what Adam had done was pointless.

The group was about to try to find a strategy to deal with this, when Mark arrived and decided to act as devil's advocate and defend the actions of the teacher. He argued that her first priority was to maintain classroom control. So we created a revised scenario with the teacher responding to Heidi's assertiveness by taking control. Mark played the teacher and Keith took up Heidi's role. The new drama went like this:

Changing the events

Scene 2: Monday morning. A very awkward situation in class. Take 2.
The students are in the classroom. Heidi and her friend Michelle are sitting toward the back of the class. Adam and James are sitting behind them continuously throwing spit balls at Heidi's head and smirking and laughing. James is egging Adam on. The teacher is writing on the board with her back to the students, completely unaware.

Heidi: (stands up, turns around and says firmly) You stop that!
The teacher: Heidi, please be quiet! Go and wait outside of the room.
Heidi: But he was throwing spit balls at me.
The teacher: No stop! Go and stand outside the room. I'll come and see you in a minute.

Discussion

The students were asked to critique what was presented to them. Keith was asked how he felt as Heidi. He said he was incensed to be treated like this.

Heidi had not been heard! However, what also emerged was that even though Heidi had been told to leave the room, the dynamics had changed. Rather than sitting being attacked with spit balls and feeling exposed and humiliated as Heidi, he felt angry and had been removed from the attack.

Mark was asked why he had done what he did. He argued that the teacher needed to be in control and had to defuse what could quickly become an escalating confrontation. He said his intention was to split the students up and then, after a cooling down period, to talk to those involved and set up a mediation process to find a fair solution.

The students felt this was a good strategy and came up with the following assessment:

1 Heidi had moved from being a passive victim to being angry and active.
2 Although the teacher appeared to be reprimanding Heidi for being disruptive, the intention was to take control and sort things out. The teacher was no longer part of the problem.
3 With the teacher now involved and working towards a fair solution, the school had taken responsibility for solving a bullying problem.
4 These changes would mean that the second part of this scene (the assault) should not occur because the momentum had been halted.

The following ideas also emerged:

1 If the problem had been handled at an earlier stage, the escalation would never have occurred.
2 Getting victims to react so they fall into a web of culpability is a common bullying tactic. So are lies told by the bully's supporters to place blame on the victim. This can be complex and difficult to deal with.
3 Heidi needed support. Michelle tried to give it but against these two mean boys, she could easily become another victim. The students thought Michelle or another friend could have gone to the teacher/guidance counselor/deputy principal to explain what was going on.
4 Once school staff were prepared to tackle the problem, they could perhaps use an anti-bullying strategy such as the No Blame Approach to help reach a solution.
5 Although it was laudable for Heidi to stand up for herself, others may not be able to. It is not the victim's responsibility to solve the problem.

Step 9: coming out of role and resolution

Social theater is often based on lived or observed experiences. In order to get into the roles, the emotions and feelings are often fully taken on. It is therefore essential that the facilitator helps actors to disengage properly from their roles.

We suggest a three-step process:

1 *Coming out of role.* The actor can be moved out of the role by using a short dramatic device, such as: "Heidi, I want you to close your eyes. I will turn you two turns to the right and then one to the left. You will open your eyes you will be Sharon again." The facilitator says, "Welcome back, Sharon."
2 *A final word.* Having moved out of her dramatic persona, she could be asked, "Is there anything final you would like to say about being in the role of Heidi or about the drama as a whole?"
3 *Reintegration.* In order to come full circle, it is useful to return to the starting point of the drama by asking the following question:

> Earlier we described bullying. Throughout our drama we have assumed that bullying was occurring. Does this scenario fit our understanding of bullying?

The group responded with the following:

- There was malicious intent towards Heidi by Adam (supported by James).
- It was repetitive (three incidents occurred).
- It was an abuse of power.
- It involved verbal abuse, harassment, intimidation, pressure, and physical assault.
- Adam bullied Heidi, certain that he would not get into trouble.

The group also decided that, while Adam's bitterness was understandable in scene 1 take 1 when Heidi did not want to go out with him, he escalated the bullying, used physical force, and was so aggressive that his actions implied a threat of sexual violation.

The students had managed to capture the feelings and nature of sexual harassment through their drama and to come up with useful strategies for dealing with it. The session was closed with comments from the facilitator to this effect.

Step 10: student evaluation

> Evaluations provide useful feedback to a presenter and also help students process their learning.

Below are the questions asked and a summary of responses at this workshop:

1. Did this exercise help you to understand more clearly what bullying is?
In varying degrees, everyone found the exercise useful.

2. If so, what did you learn?
- I learnt about how girls feel when guys harass them.
- That it is easy to bully people and if you are bullied there are many options to take.
- Bullying if not solved can get worse. It is important to talk to someone about your problems before it's too late. Talk to someone you trust.
- Bullying can be ongoing, and people may not see what's going on in the full picture unless you tell them.
- Bullying goes deeper than just pushing and hitting, and there are lots of ways to stop it without provoking more bullying. Bullying can be ongoing and will get worse if not dealt with.
- Bullying is wrong and you shouldn't be afraid to tell someone if you're being harassed sexually, physically, or verbally.
- I learned that it is incredibly difficult to get out of.
- Retaliation is not always a good idea.
- Bullying isn't always physical.
- It can go further than name calling and pushing around and can go on over a long period of time.

3. List three things you felt were good about this role-playing exercise
- It put me in a girl's perspective so I won't bully girls now.
- It showed me ways to avoid getting into a threatening situation.
- It was realistic and factual.
- It used pertinent language.
- It was very clear and thoroughly explained.
- It involved everybody.
- You see how things can escalate.
- It is a good way to visualize something before talking about it.
- We got to see what people's responses would be like.
- We got to think more about how to handle bullying.
- It helped us to see problems and how to solve them.
- It was active, and more fun than sitting and listening to a lecture.
- I got a good idea of how it felt to be bullied and be the bully.
- It was fun and interesting, and I didn't feel too embarrassed doing it.
- It helped us understand that we can have some sort of control over a bullying situation.

4. List three things you would change
- Nothing, it was really good.
- Move along a little faster.

- Girls are not always the victims.
- The role play was kind of embarrassing so people were laughing.
- The topic of sexual abuse was embarrassing.
- There could be different scenarios for each group to get a different idea of different types of bullying.
- Not a lot, it was all appropriate, well-presented, and well-thought-out information.
- Costumes and props for our role plays.

5. Any other comments?
- Every class should do such things.
- I thought it was a really cool thing to do and would be good for years 9–10 to do.
- Maybe we could explore how bullying changes for different age groups.
- Although it was an embarrassing scene, people were able to talk about it which was good.
- Food is a brilliant way to get us to do stuff. Brilliant idea [doubly underlined].
- It was a good opportunity to understand how to deal with certain bullying or uncomfortable scenarios.

Step 11: facilitator reflection, self-evaluation, and follow-up

> The facilitator will find it useful to reflect on the day's events by:
>
> 1 noting what worked and what could be improved;
> 2 taking account of the student evaluations and issues that emerged.

The following is a summary of what Keith recorded.

What worked and what could be improved
In terms of my effectiveness, I needed to:

- be shorter and crisper at some points;
- get more students into more roles so that they could feel what was happening and spend less time thinking and discussing; and
- get the balance between action and discussion right.

Taking account of the student evaluations and issues that emerged
I read the student evaluations and reflected on the day's events.

Issue 1: the use of foul language

The use of swear words was an issue but the students wanted to be "authentic" in their scripts. I realized that if I took over and set restrictive rules, the students would withdraw to some extent.

An analysis of the two uses of foul language is instructive.

- Adam used it as a weapon ("F**k you then, bitch"). It needed to be there so we could learn how to deal with it.
- Heidi said "Stop it, w****r!" to Adam in class. Although provoked to say this, it served to get Adam off the hook and made the teacher focus on her instead on what had provoked her outburst.

I was also aware that one male student seemed to "get a buzz" out of swearing publicly at school. When he was placed in Heidi's role (in the girl's perspective), however, he said that he found it very uncomfortable and was surprised at how it made him feel. He became empathic.

I decided:

1 I wouldn't use swearing in social theater with younger classes or in assemblies; or
2 if it would offend people for religious or other significant reasons.

Issue 2: running the workshop

1 Two facilitators with complementary skills (one male and one female?) are better than one.
2 Although the drama worked, two shorter ones with very different themes may have been better.
3 The suggestion of using social theater to portray how bullying changes as students get older is excellent.

Issue 3: follow-up issues

1 The facilitator needs to be vigilant about whether the drama has brought up issues for any participants (such as personal experiences of sexual harassment and/or sexual abuse) and make sure these are taken care of.
2 In relation to the telephone call incident, students asked, "Can the school do anything about things that happen between students out of school? Does the school have any legal jurisdiction, or authority in this area?" One answer is that even if it does not, this incident did contribute to the bullying that occurred in the school and needs to be handled as part of a school bullying problem.

Step 12: performance to other members of the school (optional)

Performing well-developed social theater can be very useful:

• Through performing bullying scenarios to others (younger students or peers), students provide useful information about bullying and show that solutions can be found.
• Social theater can act as a consolidation of understanding for those taking part.
• A clear message is provided that the school takes bullying seriously and that teachers and students have ways of dealing with it.
• The message is provided in the language and lived experience of the student culture and makes sense to the target audience.

If a drama has been created that provides a powerful message about bullying, then this optional step may be useful. The performance context, however, is very different from that of the workshop. Presenting a drama cold to a group of students, many of whom may be cynical and derisory towards any efforts from their peers, is a challenge in itself. The raw emotion of something meaningful may overcome this and engross even the most cynical members of the audience. The help of a talented drama teacher can also be invaluable.

14

Supporting Students through Peer Mentoring

What is peer mentoring?

Peer mentoring is a practical and effective anti-bullying strategy (Cowie and Sharp, 1996). It involves older, more experienced students using their skills and energy to help stop bullying by giving support to younger peers (Smith, 2002). They can do this by:

- assisting victims to recover from and avoid bullying;
- helping perpetrators develop more useful ways of acting; and
- supporting bystanders to find the strength to resist and oppose bullying.

This chapter explains how to develop and run a peer mentoring scheme. A case study of a training session is also provided to show how it is done and to identify important issues that need to be considered.

Peer mentoring and recovering from bullying

When someone has been in an accident and their body has been injured, we accept that time is required for a full recovery, for bones and bruises to heal. When someone has been bullied, they may be physically hurt but will also have emotional and psychological damage (which may be hidden and hard to detect). In Chapter 1, we talk about the trauma which results from bullying and how this can have a downward spiralling effect for the victim. Those who have been traumatized by bullying need to be assisted through a recovery period to return to a normal untraumatized state. When a person is being bullied, the first step is to halt it. The next is to assess the damage and create

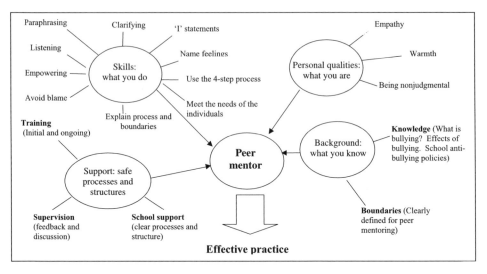

Figure 14.1 *Requirements for an effective peer mentor*

an action plan. This is the job of the school counselor, anti-bullying team, or psychologist. Depending on the length of time, the severity of the bullying, and the personality of the victim, the effects will vary. The victim may have any of the following symptoms:

1 fear that now the bullying is out in the open, their tormentors will make them pay;
2 living in a chronic state of stress and terror;
3 depression;
4 lack confidence;
5 inability to work effectively, have fallen behind academically;
6 truanting to avoid bullying;
7 lack friends;
8 serious thoughts about suicide.

After an initial diagnosis and counseling (and/or the use of the No Blame Approach), the counselor may recommend that a mentoring relationship be set up to provide support and develop strategies to assist the recovery/change process. A similar process can be set up for those who bully or who are bystanders.

Peer mentoring normally includes the following four components:

1 *Befriending.* Being a friend, providing companionship, sharing ideas and activities, perhaps meeting outside of school.
2 *Sharing experiences.* Sometimes those who have been bullied may benefit

from coaching about how school and student cultures work. This can be done by discussion, focusing on issues such as acceptance, expectations, fairness, friendships, and rules (both written and unwritten).

3 *Problem-solving.* Whereas it is not the responsibility of the person being bullied to stop the bullying, it is important for them to learn how to avoid unsafe places and situations, and who they can go to if bullying recurs.

4 *Providing ongoing support.* The mentor provides a safe point of contact and a sense of constancy and reliability. The mentor can give practical help with organizational needs and academic problems.

A peer mentoring program

The following as a template for organizing a peer mentoring program. The stages and steps are as follows:

Stage 1 Initial preparations
Step 1 Creating a program
Step 2 Making students and staff aware
Step 3 A call for volunteers
Step 4 Choosing the peer mentors
Step 5 Contacting those chosen
Stage 2 Training the mentors
Step 1 Training
Step 2 Follow-up
Stage 3 Running the program
Step 1 Matching the mentor and the mentored
Step 2 Carrying out the mentoring
a) Starting off
b) The middle period
c) Finishing off
Step 3 Mentoring support
a) Supervision and a mentor support group
b) Mentoring ethics
Stage 4 Maintaining the program

Stage 1: initial preparations

Step 1: creating a program

In order for a program to be accepted and supported, teachers need to be provided with information and given the opportunity to be involved in its inception and running, and to take part in a critiquing process. Some may feel, for instance, that it is good in theory but ask, "What about the bullying program you tried last year?" Others may think that the responsibility of counseling psychologically at-risk students should not be given to students—that they are too immature for such responsibilities. It is important that such discussions take place, and that all staff are included so that decisions can be made about who will be involved in running the program and how it will work. A trained counselor or psychologist should be in charge, with teachers with skills and enthusiasm also involved.

A time line and a specific structure and processes need to be developed and adhered to.

The following characteristics of effective peer mentoring programs can be used (Beales, 2000):

1 having a clearly articulated philosophical foundation;
2 having a clearly defined procedure for selection;
3 having the central operations run by credible and well-established individuals;
4 attracting enthusiastic and motivated people to run the program;
5 incorporating a method of internal program evaluation.

Step 2: making students and staff aware of peer mentoring and its purposes

At the beginning of the school year, students, and staff (teachers and others) need to be told about the peer mentoring program. What teachers already know needs to be reinforced and built on. Those running the program can discuss progress at staff meetings and send a follow-up memo to all staff (to keep them in the picture). Peer mentoring can be explained to students at school assembly and teachers can be asked to discuss it with their students. Those running the program can visit classes to explain it to students and answer any questions. Here, the nature of bullying can be explained, the school's policies toward bullying reiterated, and the peer mentoring scheme described as a strategy developed to provide assistance to victims, bullies, and bystanders and to help solve this ongoing and universal problem in schools. Information about how extensive bullying is can let those who are being bullied know that there is no shame in getting help. It can also be announced that the organizers are looking for students in the senior school to consider becoming peer mentors.

Step 3: a call for volunteers, nominations, and shoulder-tapping

When everyone has been made aware of the program, it is important to assemble a group of potential mentors. A box can be put in a central place so students can volunteer or nominate mentors. Teachers can be asked for suggestions, and the committee setting up the program can shoulder-tap suitable students who have not been nominated.

Step 4: choosing the peer mentors

A small group of people examine the nominees and create a shortlist. There are several important characteristics to look for in peer mentors:[1]

- a good role model;
- a successful student several years older;
- someone who is prepared to take an interest in others;
- someone who is available, warm, and empathic;
- somcone who is nonjudgmental; and
- someone who has a stable personality and lifestyle.

Candidates need to be carefully screened.

Step 5: contacting those chosen and developing active and reserve lists

Once a final list has been made up, students should be told that everyone on the list is considered worthy but that when someone opts into mentoring, a careful matching process needs to occur. Some will therefore become mentors more quickly, while others will have to wait until they are matched up with a student. How fast the program "takes off" depends upon how it is perceived by the student body. When a system is new and untested, and students are unaware of its effectiveness, a "wait and see" attitude is generally adopted. If, after a "gestation" period, the program is seen as successful, students will start to endorse and use it.

Stage 2: training the mentors

Step 1: training

Training can consist of a series of sessions during lunch hours, afternoons, or evenings spread over a two- or three-week period. Alternatively, a full-day workshop can be held, either during school time or on a weekend. Peer mentoring training should provide information about bullying and skills and structures for effective mentoring. The advantage of a workshop is that students learn a lot of skills in a group situation over a short period of time. On the other hand, spreading the training over a longer period of time breaks the learning up into reasonable "chunks" and allows time for reflection, questioning, and reinforcement of learning.

Step 2: follow-up

Counselors and program organizers need to make certain that mentors receive ongoing support. What they learn through listening, role play, and discussion will be tested when they put their training into practice. Mentors need to meet regularly with a supervisor for debriefing and with other mentors in order to hone their skills.

Stage 3: running the program

Step 1: matching the mentor and the mentored
Experienced facilitators can usually determine whether or not a relationship will work. There are no hard and fast rules, but the following are useful points:

- Those who have been bullied and are now doing well can share their skills and understanding with someone currently experiencing being bullied (it is similar for ex-bullies and bystanders).
- Some students are just good at it. They have a high degree of empathy and problem-solving skills.
- Every peer mentor will have different needs, strengths, and weaknesses. Some who are unsure of themselves at first can, with a bit of experience, become very good at mentoring.

Step 2. Carrying out the mentoring

Starting off
Establishing relationships can be difficult and it is important that the mentor is taught to be encouraging and nonthreatening. At the beginning, what needs to occur is for trust to be established and basic information gathered.

The middle period
The central part of the relationship is about identifying main issues, working on empowering ideas, deciding what actions to take, and putting solutions and strategies in place.

Finishing off
It is important that the mentored student does not become overreliant on the peer mentor. The process needs to support them in making their own decisions rather than tell them what to do. It is also important to provide structure to the process and to indicate well in advance when the mentoring will end. Having a finish is important and symbolizes the mentored person being in charge of his or her life.

Step 3: mentoring support

Supervision and a mentor support group
The mentor will have been given initial training and will have some sense of what to do during mentoring sessions. Doing it in a theoretical practice situation and doing it in the real situation are quite different. The mentor will need support in his or her transfer of learning process and will also need "in-service" training. This can be done through having a regular "information

and maintenance" meeting with the program coordinator and through a mentors' support meeting.

When mentors are active, they will need to meet with their supervisor at least once a week.

Mentoring ethics

A major issue for mentors is that they need to be clear about the rules. This is particularly important in relation to confidentiality. The peer mentoring scheme that was developed at the University of San Diego's Office for Students with Disabilities created a contract which all mentors sign. They refer to this contract as the 12 golden rules of the peer mentoring support group. These rules have been adapted and reduced to seven for anti-bullying peer mentors in the secondary school sector and are as follows:

1 Any matters discussed in the peer mentoring support group are confidential to the group and must not be discussed outside the group.
2 Matters that relate specifically to the person being mentored must be kept confidential for the safety of that individual and the integrity of the process. Issues of concern that arise in a mentoring session can and should be discussed confidentially with one of the program coordinators but should not be part of mentor support group discussions.
3 Mentors will allocate time to attend and take part in peer mentoring support meetings.
4 Mentors agree to arrive on time for all meetings.
5 Mentors will be encouraging and supportive of each other. No put-downs are allowed.
6 The group will follow the direction of the facilitator.
7 Mentors will take turns being facilitator.

Stage 4: maintaining the program

As with everything in a secondary school, regular cycles occur. Every year as one cohort of students in the upper school departs, a new group at the lower end arrives. Within the rest of the school, there will be comings and goings as families move in and out of the district. Similarly, there are movements within a school's staff.

It is important, therefore, that someone (a counselor or a person in a similar role) has the job of maintaining the peer mentoring program and of overseeing the yearly cycle that it goes through. If the job is to be passed on, this should include full training in the running of the program as part of the changeover process. In order for the program to work, to develop its own ecology and safe regeneration, the school administration and teachers need to be informed about and involved to some extent in its process, running, and success.

A case study of a peer mentoring training workshop

This case study is based on a 4-hour peer mentoring training workshop with a group of nine year 13 (grade 12) students at a New Zealand high school. The students selected for the training had previously completed a leadership course and were judged good potential peer mentors.

The training workshop

The purpose of the workshop was to explain what peer mentoring is and to teach the skills required. The workshop was intended to be interactive so as to:

1 enthuse the students about peer mentoring;
2 encourage "ownership" of the peer mentoring program; and
3 draw upon their knowledge about and experience of school culture, as the basis for an effective program.

During the training workshop, most activities were carried out in groups so that group processing could provide the foundation for ongoing and mutual support between participants as the peer mentoring program took shape.

   Schools do not generally have the luxury of abundant free time. Therefore, while it would be preferable to run several consecutive training sessions (to introduce concepts, try things out, have time to review and recapitulate), the reality is that most schools will have to find ways to present maximum information with optimum effect in minimum time. In this case, the training workshop was carried out in three consecutive sessions (with a snack and a lunch break between sessions 2 and 3) during one day, as follows:

Session 1. 10:30–11:00 Introduction and ice breakers
   Balloon game
   Dyads
   (short break)
Session 2. 11:00–12:00 Identifying the major issues
   12:00–12:30 Lunch break (lunch provided)
Session 3. 12:30–2:30 Teaching micro-mentoring skills
   Evaluation of the training session and acknowledgments

Keith ran the workshop with the school's counselor, whom we will call Maggy. The school principal (Howard) participated in the afternoon session. The following is a description of the day.

Session 1: 10:30–11:00 Introduction and ice breakers

> When starting off a workshop, it is important to create a pleasant, cooperative atmosphere and to establish a sense of trust.

First, Keith introduced himself to the students and then using an overhead transparency explained what they would be covering. Next, he ran two ice-breaker activities.

The balloon game

All participants were given a balloon and a small piece of paper. Sitting in a circle, they were asked to write something interesting about themselves, to roll the paper up, insert it into the balloon, and blow it up. The balloons were then thrown into the circle, mixed up, and each student grabbed one. Next, they each burst their balloon, extracted the paper, and read it to the group. They then had to guess who this was about. The last two balloons were burst together. What people had written ranged from general to informative, from serious to funny. This worked well to "break the ice."

Dyads

The students were then asked to pair off with someone they did not know well. They told each other about themselves and then introduced their partner to the rest of the group. This proved interesting and informative, and created a sense of mutual interest and trust.

The students were then given a drink and a chocolate fish (a New Zealand confectionary bar) and they took a 5-minute break.

Session 2: 11:00–12:00 Identifying the major issues

> The purpose of this session is to discuss bullying and come to an agreement about what it is, to discuss peer mentoring, and to brainstorm how participants think they could be most helpful as peer mentors.

The process was designed to provide information and "fill in the gaps." It was also intended to draw upon the knowledge and experience of the participants as members of the student culture in order to create a program that would enable meaningful connections and lead to good practice.

Four questions were posed. Brainstorming threesomes were formed and large sheets of paper provided for recording the findings from discussions (for each question, everyone changed groups). After each brainstorming, groups reported back. The results of the sessions were compiled, typed up, and returned to the students before the end of the workshop. The four questions asked and the responses were as follows:

What is bullying?
- Beating someone up.
- Making someone feel bad.
- Doing it over and over.
- Bullies are bigger and older.
- It is mean.
- The bully is not punished.
- Can be physical or psychological.
- Is against someone who is different (different race, special needs).
- Abuse of power.

What are the effects of bullying?
- Lack of concentration.
- Failure at school.
- Do not want to go to school.
- Have physical and psychological injuries.
- Are scared of things.
- Go into yourself.
- Do badly later [after leaving school].

What is peer mentoring?
- Support network.
- Helping troubled kids.
- Being a buddy for someone in need.
- Helping those mentored realize things can get better.
- Letting them know that there is more to life.
- Being a guide for them.
- Relate to them and share common problems that most students face, for example, peer pressure.
- Being of the same generation.
- Being an equal.
- Being a teacher, guide, coach, or advisor.

What should peer mentors do?/What can we best offer as a peer mentor?
- Someone to take time to help sort out options.
- Find out their interests.
- Encourage them to succeed, congratulate them for doing something good.
- Check with them if everything is OK.

- Discuss the consequences of bad choices, for example, to bully.
- Support.
- Advise.
- Give them options.
- Relate.
- Give them acknowledgment.

This session worked well. It was reasonably fast moving and the students changed groups readily and enjoyed themselves. It was also empowering because, although they as individuals did not have all of the answers, as a group they had most of them. It allowed some misconceptions to be corrected and for understandings to be deepened. Although the session was facilitated by an adult, the peer mentor trainees were able to access their knowledge about what would need to be addressed from their lived experience as members of the school culture.

Structures for peer mentoring
At this point, a number of other fundamental issues were introduced and discussed with the group:

1 When mentors meet those they will mentor for the first time, the coordinator of the peer mentoring program will be present to explain the purpose of peer mentoring and discuss confidentiality.
2 They will meet regularly once a week for 15 minutes during a specified lunch hour and at a specified time.
3 Mentors need to be consistent and fully committed. Some of the students being mentored have often been let down in their lives and a major role of the mentor is to be accessible and to be completely reliable. The trainees were fully committed to this.
4 The coordinator will meet with the mentor individually or as a group on a regular basis (once every two weeks), to provide ongoing support, and to discuss specific issues. The coordinator will also be available if something needs immediate attention, especially at the start of the process while mentors are gaining experience and confidence.
5 The coordinator could meet with the group of mentors on a regular basis (once a month, perhaps) in order to let them discuss things generally (taking into account issues of confidentiality) and to role-play the types of situations that the mentors have encountered so that they can develop and refine their skills.
6 The mentors must be able to identify issues and incidents that are beyond their capability and responsibility, such as physical and sexual abuse, and suicidal feelings, and pass the students in question on to the coordinator.
7 The mentoring relationship will last at least a term (but the students felt

that taking on the role until the end of the year was more appropriate).

Ethics and confidentiality

The important issue of ethics, confidentiality, and the limits of the job were then discussed further. It was explained that confidentiality was central to the relationship between mentor and mentored unless issues arise that concern the health or well-being of the person being mentored. If there is potential danger (such as suicidal thoughts or disclosure of sexual abuse), then the supervisor must be informed. This should be discussed at the initial meeting between the counselor, mentor, and mentored student. The bottom line is that all students are the legal responsibility of the school when they are at school.

For mentors, confidentiality also means that if the need arises, the mentor can discuss specific issues with the adult supervisor but not with other mentors or with anyone else.

Session 3: 12:30–2:30 Teaching micro-mentoring skills

The purpose of this session is to teach basic micro-mentoring skills to the students. This was done by first providing an illustration of how not to mentor and, secondly, how to do it correctly. After having seen good and poor mentoring in practice, students were given more information about what they should aim to achieve and how to do it. Finally, three scenarios were provided for practising.

To mentor or not to mentor—how to do it badly, how to do it well

Keith took on the role of the mentored student and Howard of the mentor. First, they demonstrated how not to do it, and then how to do it correctly.

Take 1: how to do it badly
Keith and Howard came into the room allocated for their meeting. Howard did not tell Keith where to sit and did not welcome him. Howard then got Keith to talk but played with his trouser cuff, picked things off the carpet, looked all around, and kept looking at his watch. When Keith started to explain how he felt, Howard kept interrupting with interjections that stopped him expressing himself and which focused on things that were only slightly relevant to his concern. When Keith talked about having trouble with a teacher, Howard asked who it was and started to deride the teacher: "Oh, Mr Jones. He's a real idiot. I have trouble with him." He then stopped Keith and said time was up, he had to go. Keith was clearly frustrated and let down.

The students commented on the scenario, noting positive and negative aspects as follows:

Positive
- The mentored student was prepared to talk.
- The mentor shared some of his experience.
- The carpet got cleaned. [Humorous comment!]
- The mentor was dressed well. [Humorous comment!].

Negative
- The mentor fidgeted.
- The mentor did not pay attention.
- The mentor criticized a teacher.
- The mentor sidetracked.
- The mentor made irrelevant conversation.
- A mixed message was given: I want to be here/I don't want to be here.
- The mentor could not read between the lines.
- The mentor kept looking at his watch.

Take 2: how to do it well
When Keith came into the room, Howard greeted him, made him feel at ease, showed him where to sit, and explained pleasantly that there was a time limit. Howard let Keith speak and asked for more information without being intrusive. He listened to what Keith had to say and paraphrased it, repeating it back to him. Howard said things like, "That sounds tough. I'd feel pretty awful if that happened to me. I can see how angry you are. Is that what you're feeling? What would you like to do about it? Shall I speak to my supervisor?" He also said that Keith could come back to discuss things further. When they finished, there was a sense of closure and hopefulness.

The students commented on the scenario, noting positive and negative aspects as follows:

Positive
- The mentor warned about the time limit.
- The mentor offered a seat.
- The mentor opened up conversation.
- The mentor engaged in conversation and made eye contact.
- The mentor reviewed/gave feedback/paraphrased.
- The mentored student was allowed to talk.
- The mentored student was listened to.
- The mentor made himself available—he invited the mentored student to come back.
- The mentor offered to talk to his supervisor to ask for help.
- The mentor asked how the mentored student wanted to do things.

Negative
There were no negative comments.

After the scenarios had been played through and discussions taken place, Howard explained to the students that although he and Keith are fairly familiar with counseling and mentoring strategies, they still have to figure things out and practise what to do, and that this type of reflective thinking is important no matter how old or experienced you are. In order to become effective as peer mentors, it is not only OK but also important to think about what could go wrong and to develop role plays to find a variety of solutions.

The group discussed the following useful micro-mentoring skills that they had just witnessed:

- active listening;
- providing useful feedback through paraphrasing;
- using "I" statements, focusing on feelings, and avoiding blaming; and
- supporting people in making their own decisions.

Providing the structure
Maggy, Howard, and Keith then led a wider discussion about the skills required for successful mentoring and how they could structure a typical session. The germs of the discussion were summarized on two prominently displayed whiteboards as follows:

Fundamental Mentoring Skills (What You Do)

- *Listen.* Active listening means that you are involved, not just sitting back and nodding (but you also do not take over).
- *Paraphrasing.* Summarizing. Repeat back what you have heard, and ask if you've got it right.
- *Clarifying.* Ask questions to help yourself and the mentored person clarify the issue.
- *Name feelings.* For example, "You seem to feel angry because the teacher didn't give you a chance to explain. Is this right?"

The 4-Step Process

- *Engage.* Make sure that the mentored student feels comfortable.
- *Opening up.* Ask questions, use paraphrasing, clarifying, mirroring.
- *Focus.* If there is a particular issue to resolve, focus on what the next step might be to resolve the issue. This may involve more dialogue or finding ways to arrive at solutions.
- *Move on.* Finish with an agreement about anything you have resolved to do, and when you will meet again.

Role-playing to practice peer mentoring

It was now time to introduce the students to role play in order to transfer theory into practice, to learn experientially. In three groups and with input from the adults present, they developed three scenarios on which to focus. They were then given the following structure within which to work.

> Instructions: in the role plays, you will be working in groups of three. One student will be the person being mentored. The second will be the mentor. The third student will be the observer/commentator. You need to experience all three roles.

The way it works is as follows:

1 The student being mentored states what his or her concern is.
2 The mentor responds.
   The interaction is ongoing until the issues raised are satisfactorily dealt with.
3 The observer/commentator provides feedback to both participants about the scenario enacted.

> *Scenario 1: The agony of the first-year "geek"*
>
> Curt is a year 9 (grade 8) student who is shy, quiet, and often alone. He is considered a "computer geek." A small group of year 10 boys has been hassling him for some time but Curt hasn't told anyone. These boys trip him up, take his books and throw them around, taunt him, shove him, and take his lunch money. The Deputy Principal has had this brought to his attention by a year 13 girl and has spoken to the boys who have been hassling Curt. They have been made to apologize. Curt is afraid this will make things worse! The counselor has spoken with Curt and decided to pair him with Nick who is in year 12. Nick was bullied for similar reasons to Curt in his first year at secondary school and is now a stable and popular student.

> *Scenario 2: The end of the line for Emily*
>
> Emily is a year 10 student who has no close friends and is always alone. She doesn't follow the dress codes typical for girls in her year, but doesn't win admiration by being a nonconformist either. She is considered stupid, ungainly, and unattractive by her female peer group. Her aloneness has become isolation and her sense of self is being stripped by merciless teasing, name-calling and ostracizing. She is very unhappy and has gone to the school counselor because of how bad she is feeling. The counselor tells Emily about the peer mentoring scheme and offers to pair her with Melanie, a year 13 girl who was once similarly isolated but has now won credibility with a small group of "true" friends.

Scenario 3: An ultimatum for Danny

Danny is a year 11 student with a history of bullying (physical and mental) since he arrived at the school two years ago. This year he bullied a series of year 9 boys, one after another. He is an interesting and intelligent boy with a good sense of humor but he is also troubled. Academically, he is doing very poorly and is disruptive much of the time and at home things are difficult. The Deputy Principal has sent him to the counselor who has suggested peer mentoring. He is paired with Boris, a year 13 student who used to be a bully but is now one of the school leaders. The Deputy Principal has given Danny an ultimatum—either his bullying stops or he will be excluded from school.

Each group develops a role play for the first mentoring session for the protagonists in each of these scenarios. Time should be allowed for each of the students to have the opportunity to take on each of the three roles: the mentor, the mentored student, and the commentator/observer. This is an extremely valuable learning experience. In a supportive environment, the students can learn:

1 how to listen (and how not to listen);
2 how to structure the session (the four steps);
3 the sorts of interactions and dialogues that may emerge; and
4 what works and what does not.

Evaluation
In order to get feedback, students were asked to fill out an evaluation sheet. They were asked the following questions:

1 List three things that you liked about today's training program.
2 List three things that you think would help to improve the training program.
3 Any other comments?

What the students said
Positive and constructive feedback was given. The students expressed appreciation for the skills being imparted. They found working in groups and brainstorming the questions useful and enjoyed the role play as a means of learning peer mentoring skills. It helped them to see what was happening from three perspectives, which allowed them to empathize more and to practise effective communication skills.

Students felt they needed more time to develop their skills and would have liked to work on more varied scenarios. They realized they needed more preparatory training before becoming practising mentors and would need supplementary training after they had gained some practical experience.

An important (and unexpected) issue was that they felt valued and acknowledged when food and drink was provided at no charge to them during breaks and at lunchtime (from the cafeteria).

Acknowledgment

At the end of the workshop, the students were each given a completion certificate by the school principal. The school had also decided that at the end of the mentoring period (in this case, at the end of the school year), each mentor would be given a book or music voucher as an appreciation and acknowledgment.

Note

1 Some ideas in this chapter emerged from discussion and workshops with Marilyn Wright, Guidance Counselor at Napier Girls' High School, Napier, New Zealand. This list of characteristics to look for in peer mentors is Marilyn's idea.

15

Changing the Social Dynamic:
The No Blame Approach

What is the No Blame Approach?

George Robinson and Barbara Maines developed the No Blame Approach[1] as a creative reponse to a bullying crisis they were asked to assist with. They had both worked with children who were struggling in their lives or were considered "difficult" (George as principal of a school for "behavior-disordered" youth, and Barbara as a practitioner psychologist), and their cumulative experiences enabled them to understand the bullying dynamic. They had realized that victims of bullying are not able to make the bullying stop, and that, with a few exceptions, those who bully are misdirected rather than pathological. They were also conscious of the latent power of the peer group and had learned that it is much better for all of those involved in the dynamic to be part of the solution rather than part of the problem. So, instinctively and in response to a real crisis, as well as with a large dose of common sense, they created a humane, pragmatic, and very successful program that is called the No Blame Approach (see Maines and Robinson, 1992b; 1992c; Robinson and Maines, 1997).

The No Blame Approach is radical and ameliorative and models a prosocial response to bullying. Whereas a common reaction is to want to punish the bully or to seek revenge, this approach steps outside of the cycle of blame and thus de-escalates reaction, defensiveness, and denial. Instead of focusing on who did what to whom, and why, it focuses on the feelings of the victim and what the social group around the victim (including the bully) can do to make things better. It is inclusive and socially enabling.

Unlike the restorative justice and conflict management models, this approach can proceed without fundamental agreement about events and issues. The truth is that the victim is suffering, and in order to stop this suffering, blame does not have to be apportioned.

Punishment is a common response to wrongdoing and transgression, but it will not bring a halt to bullying. It usually has the opposite effect: the bully is likely to blame the victim for telling, to bring in other people who support the bully's story, and eventually to escalate the bullying. A climate in which punishment is the response just drives bullying underground. The punishment–blame context is a mutually supportive sustainable environment: the bully will "punish" the victim even more if they themselves are punished. All that punishment does is to sustain this dynamic; and all that fact-finding missions do is to cause the bully to lie and the victim to be blamed and victimized. Most anti-bullying strategies depend on evidence, inequality, and power, and unlike No Blame they address specific incidents, not relationships.

The No Blame Approach forces everyone in the group to reflect on the impact of the bullying behavior. Not only does the facilitator ask for everyone's help in solving the problem, all the participants are given a chance to think about what is really happening as a result of the bullying. The process carefully avoids blaming or shaming the bully and supporters, but gives everyone in the group the opportunity to condemn the behavior. The intention is that the bully, still driven by desire to be a dominant member of the group, will decide to find other more prosocial ways of exhibiting their leadership or retaining their status. The message that needs to be accessed through the process is clear: the group does not condone bullying.

Why does it work?

- The first thing that the No Blame Approach does is to focus on how the victim is feeling. By focusing on feelings rather than on what happened, or who did what, attention is drawn away from blame, cause, and sequence and toward empathy, which is the most powerful catalyst for change in this dynamic.
- The No Blame Approach causes the bully and supporters to think about the impact of their behavior.
- It draws the bystanders and noninvolved students into finding a solution to the problem. They are forced to be involved.
- The group members are asked for their help. The teacher involved makes it clear that it is up to them—it is their process.
- It is a nonconfrontational, prosocial approach.
- No one has to hide behind an untrue picture of what happened as no one is going to be blamed for anything that occurred.

All the participants are given the opportunity to empathize with the victim, the bully perhaps for the first time. The bystanders are given an opening to voice what they may have been thinking but were lacking the confidence to express. This process subtly changes the power structure within the group. The effectiveness of the approach lies somewhere between the encouragement of empathy and the fact that when people do something helpful they usually feel good about it.

Bullying relies on an audience for bullying and support from the bystanders. The No Blame Approach erodes the bully's power base, humanizes the victim, and causes the other students to lose interest in or support for the bullying. The intimidation stops (Young, 1998).

How do teachers feel about it?

The No Blame Approach is popular with teachers and counselors because:

1 it deals with potentially complex situations in a straightforward way;
2 there is no need for extensive and difficult investigations;
3 students see bullying addressed in a constructive, nonthreatening manner;
4 it brings about change quickly;
5 it is easy to use; and
6 it works.

It is also effective because it powerfully reinforces the fact that bullying is a problem that is best solved by those who are enmeshed in the behavior. While adults facilitate the method, they do so by seeking the help of the students and thus empowering them.

The five steps of the No Blame Approach

Although No Blame is a straightforward approach, it is very important that those who use it have a good understanding of the method and are committed to following the steps and maintaining a neutral, inclusive, nonaccusatory attitude. They need to be prepared with bullying knowledge and be clear about the method.

The following is how it works:[2]

The Five-Step No Blame Process

1 Meet with the victim.
   a) Explain the process.
   b) Focus on the feelings that are the result of the bullying.
   c) Ask the victim to consent to the process being used.
   d) Ask for names of students who could be in the group.
   e) Invite the victim to produce a piece of writing or a picture that expresses
      their feelings.
2 Select the group.
   a) Consult with teachers.
   b) Include representatives of the entire group.
3 Hold a meeting with the group.
   a) Explain the problem.
   b) Avoid too much detail and do not apportion blame.
   c) Ask the group members for their ideas.
   d) Leave the outcome up to the group.
4 Review one week later.
   a) Check on the group's progress.
   b) Check with the victim.
5 Follow-up.

The victim's plight comes to the attention of a member of the school's anti-bullying team (through self-reporting, or by being reported by another student, a teacher, or a parent). In response, they decide to initiate the No Blame Approach process.

Step 1: meet with the victim

Explain the process
When the person who is going to facilitate the No Blame process finds out that bullying has occurred, they first thing they do it to talk to the victim.

When the victim has been referred, the facilitator lets them know that the bullying has been brought to their attention and that they want to help sort things out.[3] When the victim has reported the bullying, it is important that the facilitator says that this is a brave and commendable thing to do.

The most important first step in getting on top of the bullying is that the bullying is out in the open. The facilitator needs to explain how the No Blame Approach works.

> One of the pivotal processes is getting those who are bullying and some others in the class or group to understand the effect their behavior or lack of support is having on the victim. The focus is on how the victim of the bullying is feeling rather than on seeking to blame or punish anyone. This needs to be explained clearly to the victim.

Focus on the feelings that are the result of the bullying

The facilitator can talk about how it feels to be bullied, sharing the experience and common human feelings of loneliness that come from being isolated and rejected, assuring them that they are not alone and that bullying can happen to anyone.

  If the victim talks about what happened during the bullying, the facilitator focuses on the feelings. If the victim says, for instance, "They were all laughing at me and making sure I knew there's a party on but that I'm not invited," the facilitator can say, "So you felt really left out and pretty upset."

> At this stage it is crucial not to try to get to the bottom of it. The most important thing is to affirm that it is the behavior of the bullying students that is unacceptable, not the victim's, that he or she has done no wrong and has the right to be left in peace.

Ask the victim to consent to the process being used

The No Blame process is presented as an effective way to deal with the bullying, and it is very important that the victim understands the approach and consents to its use. Victims of bullying feel powerless and can be indecisive; they certainly want to avoid any process that will make things worse. They may need time to think about No Blame, but they usually decide that it sounds helpful. Making this decision themselves is an empowering first step.

Ask for names of students who could be in the group

Without going into too much detail or setting up a cause-and-effect enquiry, the facilitator can gather basic information about what has been happening, who has been doing the bullying, and who has been involved as spectators. There are probably students whom the victim admires or looks up to in the class, and it is important to ask who they are so that they can be included in the group that will be gathered together to take part in the No Blame process.

Invite the victim to produce a piece of writing or a picture that expresses their feelings

The victim is asked to spend some time putting down their feelings on paper that night. Many victims of bullying start diary-writing as a counter to the isolation from their peer group, and so are already adept at expressing how they feel. They may want to write a poem or paint a picture, or use another piece of writing or the lyrics of a song. They are told that these feelings will be shared with the group in an effort to end the bullying.

> *Confidentiality*: It is important to ask the victim what they feel comfortable having disclosed to the group. For instance, in response a victim may state, "You can tell them how desperately sad and alone I feel, how I cry myself to sleep at night but don't mention my nightmares or my vomiting before coming to school each morning."

Step 2: select the group

Consult with teachers

If the facilitator is not the victim's form teacher, then that teacher should be consulted and kept informed about the No Blame process. The teacher will also know the peer group of the victim and may be able to help select those who should be involved so that a balanced student group can be assembled. The teacher may also be able to give some useful background information.

Include representatives of the entire group

> A group of six to eight students is ideal for the No Blame group. They should include the main perpetrator, two main supporters, one or two bystanders, and dominant/assertive class members who may have chosen not to intervene. The composition of the group is central to having a positive outcome. It needs to bring together some of the powerful members of the class as they have the influence and the ability to shape the attitudes of the group. Involving the non-bully popular leaders gives them the opportunity to grasp fully the nature of the bullying behavior and the effect it is having on the victim. Experience has shown that these influential students often do not associate with either the bullies or victims. They may have chosen to ignore or forget about the bullying (if they have seen it), or not to challenge the bullies' behavior as they have nothing to gain by intervening (and have no connection to the victim). The supportive process of No Blame enables them to make a positive connection with the victim, to feel sympathy, and to recognize that as members of the same community, they have a responsibility to act.

Bullies spend little or no time planning their abuse and even less thinking about the impact. They often genuinely see it as being a bit of fun that is supported by the vast majority of the group and are unaware of the disastrous consequences for the victim. If the bullies (eventually) experience some of these feelings, they will be forced to reflect on the impact their behavior is having on their victim.

The bystanders and natural friends or allies of the victim gain confidence through participation and, after hearing that the bullying behavior is not supported, feel more able to contribute positively to finding a solution.

Step 3: hold a meeting with the group

The next thing to do is to convene a meeting with the people involved, allowing at least 30 minutes for the discussion. The victim is not included in this group.

The gathering of the group and the beginning of the discussion must be very carefully managed. A good approach is to visit the class of the victimized student approximately 30 minutes before the end of a lesson (this must, of course, have been prearranged with the class teacher). This makes the purpose of the meeting public: "I'm here to get some help solving a bullying problem that we've become aware of. I need the following people to take part in a No Blame conference [name them]. Just a reminder that the No Blame process involves people who are not directly involved in the bullying."

Some students are likely to feel reluctant to participate, and the facilitator with the support of the class teacher needs authoritatively to insist that the named people participate.

Explain the problem
When the group is gathered, the facilitator explains that there is a problem in the class/group which needs solving and that the facilitator needs their help.

"[Victim's name] is very unhappy and is feeling [summarize feelings]."
"I've got a [poem/story/song/painting] here that [the victim] did for me last night and I want to share it with you."

Avoid too much detail and do not apportion blame
Often at this point, a moment of intense heat is experienced. Teachers need to know that it is likely to occur as group members lapse into defensiveness,

but they should avoid getting waylaid in details about what happened or to apportion blame.

During the exposé of the problem, the bully sometimes reacts by saying something like, "That's not true, I haven't done anything and it's nothing to do with me." The others may look embarassed, uncomfortable, or unhappy.

The facilitator needs to react to this intrusion calmly to keep the meeting on track and avoid falling into the trap of getting into details and evidence. These reactions are typical of the bullying dynamic: the behavior is denied and the bystanders look the other way.

> In order to change the mood of the meeting, all the facilitator has to do is to state explicitly that:
>
> - the victim is unhappy;
> - no-one is being blamed for this;
> - no-one will be punished;
> - it is within the group's power to help make the victim feel happier and safer; and
> - that this is why the group has been called together.

Probably after this the bully will withdraw a little from the group. The interruption has made him or her vulnerable and less able to dominate the group. Already, the desired subtle shift in the group's power structure has begun to take place.

The focus is then shifted back to the victim's feelings. These must be identified as the only indisputable facts in the discussion. "This is how [name] feels and we cannot dispute this. Feelings are the unique property of each individual. The challenge for us is to work out what we can do individually or collectively to change things."

When they hear about the distress the victim has been feeling, members of the group first of all feel relieved that they are not going to be blamed, and often feel genuinely moved by what they hear. They are therefore able to engage fully in problem-solving as part of the group rather than taking up a self-centered defensive stance. They often mention that they have been worried about how the victim has been treated but have dismissed their worries, assuming that the victim has chosen to hang around the abusers.

Sometimes, the discussion will shift to the victim's shortcomings, or to the sequence of events. This information needs to be accepted but managed so that the discussion is not sidetracked. An underlying theme is that we all have shortcomings but that weaknesses and vulnerabilities are not an invitation to abuse! There is a sense of *group responsibility* growing, that can be discussed and reinforced.

It is important that details of the abuse are not focused on, particularly if there is a chance these will be disputed. The "no blame" aspect of the process has to be reiterated. It is useful all the time to focus on the victim's statement and the search for solutions.

Ask the group members for their ideas

Each group member is encouraged to *suggest ways they can provide support to the victim*, saying what they will do ("I will ...").

- It is useful to focus first on one of the more thoughtful confident members of the group to lead the way here.
- The bully can be left to last because they might be negative.
- If a student cannot think of anything, they can be allowed to pass and know that the facilitator will come back to them a bit later in the discussion. This will give them time to think without the spotlight being on them.

When each student has said what they will do, it can be written down on a piece of paper and given to them. This is not meant to hold them to their suggestion but to indicate that it is considered worthwhile.

- The students do not have to promise to do what they suggest.

The solutions students come up with are usually straightforward and logical:

- "He lives just down the road. I'll walk home with him for the next few days."
- "I'll offer to sit with her in math and help her with her work."
- "I'll ask if he want to watch a video with us on Friday night."

The bullies react in a variety of ways:

- They may not have regarded their behavior as bullying and be shocked into stopping.
- They may not have realized the effects of their bullying and decide to do something positive for the victim.
- After becoming aware of how the group is feeling, they may decide the bullying reduces their attractiveness and withdraw gradually from it so as not to lose face.
- They may realize it is more important to be accepted by the group than to be admired or feared for negative behavior.
- They may say, "I'm not going to do anything." (This is a typical bully reaction that should be openly welcomed as a solution that would be most helpful!)
- In order to maintain a position of high status they may take on a leadership role and organize the support being developed for the victim.
- They may deny any responsibility and continue to bully, but in the face of

the changed dynamic and loss of support they may lose their audience and have to stop.
- They may continue with the bullying and need to be dealt with in other, more sustained and "harder" ways. This is the least likely result of the No Blame process.

Leave the outcome up to the group

At the conclusion, the participants are thanked for their support, told that the group will *reconvene in about a week* to discuss progress, and that it is being left up to them to solve the problem. As Robinson and Maines say, "No written record is made—it is left as a matter of trust" (1997: 69).

Step 4: review one week later

Check on the group's progress

This meeting should be short but give time for the students to say what they have done. Mostly the problem will have been resolved as at least some of those involved have done what they said they would do.

> It is less important that all of the students do what they said they would do than that the bullying has been halted.

In the follow-up meeting, the facilitator needs to give positive feedback to the students. In the Robinson and Maines program, the facilitator meets individually with the participants, provides feedback, and reinforces the process. This means that the response does not become competitive. In other situations, facilitators can meet with the group as a whole (excluding the victim) to support their efforts both as individuals and as part of the group.

Check with the victim

The facilitator needs also to meet with the victim separately to check how things are going. This can be done formally as part of the process and less formally as a follow-up in the few weeks afterwards. It is important just to keep in touch so that any lapses into old patterns can be picked up and be given another dose of the No Blame Approach.

Step 5: follow-up

The No Blame Approach may solve a particular situation and bring the bullying to a complete halt. Sometimes it needs to be reactivated. It is at its best when it is supported by a whole-school anti-bullying approach, when other strategies like peer mentoring can be used as a way of supporting the victim, disempowering the bullying dynamic, and preventing it from forming again.

Golden rules of the No Blame Approach

- *Students are surprised that they are not going to be punished.* This leads to a more relaxed empathic response and makes problem-solving much more successful.
- *The victim does not have to do anything differently.* If they had the personal skills and resources to deal with the problem, they would have already dealt with it. Often the victim is made to feel more helpless if asked to adopt strategies to counter the bullying. The No Blame Approach takes the onus off the victim.
- *This is a nonreflective process.* It is important not to ask anyone why they behaved as they did. They will be unable to explain, and may become more alienated, demotivated, or antisocial if challenged. The only thing that counts is that empathy levels are raised.
- *The participants should not be labeled, as this will reinforce the power imbalance that is an essential part of the bullying relationship.* Bullying is about behavior, not personality.
- *Stopping the bullying behavior must be separated from addressing specific incidents such as assaults.* The No Blame approach deals with bullying behavior, whereas specific violent acts and minor rule infringements need to be dealt with formally in accordance with the legal system or school behavior management program.

Two No Blame Approach case studies

The following case studies are based on real events but details have been altered to safeguard the identity of the students involved.

Case study 1: the loneliness of the long-distance runner

Greta was a very talented girl. An exceptional musician, actor, and sportsperson, she was identified as a "top" pupil and had won a national long-distance running event at the age of 13. She was outgoing and friendly, and seemed set for a successful passage through secondary school.

The first signal that something was wrong came when Greta, then in her first year, was late to a small group extension class. When asked where she was, Tina said something about her being unhappy. When the teacher asked why, Tina said that she had been hassled during fashion design. The teacher arranged to see Greta after class and there she revealed that a girl called Louisa had punched her. Fashion design consisted of a mixture of students from several classes and she did not know the girl involved. At the start of class she had been sitting at a sewing machine when Louisa walked in and punched her hard on the arm, berating Greta for sitting in her place. Greta apologized and those nearby laughed. Feeling very embarrassed she moved places. She said the incident made her feel sad and isolated.

The next day the girls looked at her and laughed and she felt even worse. Each time she went to fashion design they laughed at her and called her names, and she felt more and more embarrassed. She dreaded seeing these girls on the way to school and anywhere at all in the school grounds. Eventually, she was terrified and felt totally alone. She returned to the teacher of her small group class and told him what had been going on.

Feeling out of his depth, her teacher sought advice from the school counselor and they contacted Greta's mother. They decided to tackle the problem immediately and to use the No Blame Approach. The teacher was already familiar with it because it was part of the school's anti-bullying arsenal.

The No Blame Approach was explained to Greta and she was asked to write a short piece to explain how she was feeling. The following day she brought in this poem:

I am not wanted. I hate myself for being me.
I want to kill myself, but that would be just as bad.
Why can't I just choose? I can't eat properly, drink, sleep.
I'm just too scared. Too scared.
I don't know why I'm writing.
The people in Bosnia are killing each other
People all over the world are starving.
BUT I'M SCARED!
Just leave me alone. Please leave me alone.
For whatever I did to you, sorry.

Using the No Blame Approach, the teacher assembled a group of six girls from the fashion design class. This included Louisa, a couple of her friends, and three of the girls Greta said she liked or respected. Her teacher decided not to read out all that Greta had written but enough to let them know how awful Greta felt. He explained that no one was going to be blamed or punished but that the school wanted to find a solution so Greta did not continue to feel so unhappy and alone. The group was genuinely surprised and shocked when they realized how bad this "minor" (in their eyes) incident had made her feel. They quickly came up with simple, realistic suggestions for reincluding Greta. These included commitments to be with her at break time and to ensure she was sitting with them in class whenever possible. Another who lived close by said she would go out of her way to cycle home with Greta and touch base in the evening. The bullying group basically agreed to leave her alone.

These suggestions were carried through, and in subsequent contacts with Greta (now a successful university student), she reflected on what had happened. During a recent conversation, she commented that being bullied had been like falling into a black hole or being in a strange nightmare. Once it stopped, she enjoyed her time at secondary school and was very popular and a high achiever.

> *Comment*: The first incident was probably the result of group dynamics and someone pushing the boundaries too far. Certainly, Louisa did not mean to humiliate Greta and was genuinely surprised at the extent of her feelings. She came from a large, boisterous family where individuals had constantly to jockey for position, whereas Greta was the only daughter in a small, nurturing, and gentle family. The incident illustrates powerfully how, in even the most balanced and successful people, feelings of isolation can quickly build up. The use of the No Blame Approach gave everyone a chance to talk and understand each other's points of view. Although Greta was not present, the members of the peer group were given the opportunity to support her without needing to take sides or stand up to anyone. Greta's case shows that bullying can happen to anyone.

Case study 2: Henry's story—when bullying is the only "friendship" on offer

Early one year, computer graffiti was found on the desktop of one of the computers in the computing laboratory. Among other abusive comments was a death threat against Henry.

The culprit (Josh) was quickly identified (the computer file properties said when it had been created and the teacher remembered who had been seated at that terminal). He claimed it was written just as a joke—that Henry was one of his mates. While quick disciplinary action was taken against Josh, the teacher involved was also keen that Henry should have some support. Henry, when spoken with on several occasions, assured his teacher that everything was fine. Josh was his friend and he could handle things. As a result, no action was taken.

A month later, Henry went to this teacher and said, "I've had enough" and asked if he could do something about two boys (including Josh) who were hassling him. He explained that while things had gone well the previous year (his first in high school), his best friend left at the end of the year. Since the start of this year, he felt he had no friends in class apart from the two now harassing him. He explained that most of the time it was fun to be with them but that lately events were getting out of hand. He could only associate with them if he was ridiculed by them and hit and shoved by them. Their only way of including him was to use him as the butt of their energetic but negative behavior.

The teacher suggested using the No Blame Approach to try to solve the problem and Henry agreed. He remembered the approach being explained during a social studies class the previous year. He wrote the following to describe how he was feeling:

> I feel really crappy when Brett and Josh abuse me and beat me up. They say it's just "play-fighting" but they are wrong. It makes me feel really bad about myself and I think it's my fault.
>
> I can't concentrate on work and I dread coming to school each day because I know the abuse is coming. When I am with them I don't say much because they don't care about my opinion or want to know me.
>
> I realize they don't like me near now but whenever one of the group is gone they are cool. It makes me want to feel sorry for myself and ask, Why me?
>
> I don't have anyone to talk to so I just put up with it. Some of their comments make me feel really bad, because some of them I ignore but some just suck. I hate it how they think I suck and that they are better than me.

Henry's case illustrates how an adolescent who may in one situation appear to be resilient and independent can, when circumstances change, become a target of bullying. This happened as a result of his perception (possibly accurate) that he had little choice other than to "hang around" with two boys who then became his tormentors. The relationship between the three boys was complex. Henry was drawn to them because they were in the same class, his old friend had left, and the bullies' disruptive antics seemed like fun. Initially, they welcomed him in, and his other classmates appeared aloof and unapproachable. He lacked skills or confidence so he did not try to make other friends. From his viewpoint, these feelings were borne out when the rest of the class did not intervene to help him when his "new friends" abused him.

The writing is perceptive and suggests that his anti-bullying education from the previous year had given him a way to reframe "play-fighting" as bullying: "I feel really crappy when Brett and Josh abuse me and beat me up. They say it's just 'play-fighting' but they are wrong. It makes me feel really bad about myself and I think it's my fault." He identifies what is happening as abusive behavior not fun. He also realizes the impact of the behavior and that he is blaming himself.

"I can't concentrate on work and I dread coming to school each day because I know the abuse is coming. When I am with them I don't say much because they don't care about my opinion or want to know me." This is a powerful statement about the insidious impact of bullying. Henry recognizes that his tormentors are debasing him and making him feel insignificant. This illustrates how abusers (bullies) objectify their targets.

"I realize they don't like me near now but whenever one of the group is gone they are cool. It makes me want to feel sorry for myself and ask, Why me?" This shows the hold the bullies have on Henry. Sometimes he is valued and included, but then he is discarded and abused again. This is part of the bullying dynamic (see 'Terence's story,' Chapter 8).

This becomes even more obvious during the No Blame Approach meeting held the next day. Before selecting the group, the teacher carefully talked through the class dynamics with the form teacher and others who taught the class. They deliberately chose the two most assertive "bullyproof" boys in the group as well as two others who they felt could possibly become friends with Henry. A carefully selected group of six classmates met during the period immediately before lunchtime in the school seminar room. The perpetrators (Brett and Josh) and four others from the class attended.

At the meeting, the problem was presented to the group in the usual scripted manner: "Thanks for coming to this meeting. I have a problem that I can't solve on my own and I need your help. Henry is feeling miserable and very unhappy. He came to see me yesterday and … ."

At this stage, as often happens, Josh interrupted: "That's not true. We haven't done anything to Henry. He's just a wimp."

After this outburst, the teacher quickly said: "Look, I'm not here to blame anyone. I'm here to try to sort out this problem. Henry has not blamed anyone. Look at this [pointing to Henry's piece of writing]. He's really unhappy, lonely, and feels left out. What I want to know is what can we do about it?" Josh (and Brett) then kept quiet, realizing that by speaking out they had almost admitted bullying Henry.

The group moved on and talked about Henry. The four bystanders were genuinely surprised at how miserable he was. Although they had heard him being abused in class they had assumed that he did not mind. Once they realized this was not the case, and that the teacher was asking for their help, they began to offer constructive ideas. At this stage, each of them was asked for ways they could support Henry. Later on, a number of the other boys in the class not at the meeting also made an effort to befriend Henry and include him in their activities. The outcome was very successful and Henry found he was able to interact with his peers in a positive and normal way.

An interesting offshoot of this particular case was the fact that although the bullies did not change their basic stance, their ability to abuse Henry was eradicated by the support he received from other class members who rejected their behavior. In fact, the bullying escalated into conflict, as other members of the year group became aggressive in their support of Henry. This led to open hostility between Henry's new friends and the bullies. While this was undesirable, it was at least in the open and could not be ignored. Once conflict was present it was clear that bullying, essentially a secretive abuse, was no longer a feature of the behavior and the school was able to apply a range of conflict resolution strategies to put an end to the dispute. This involved mediated meetings where the participants had to articulate and justify their actions. The secrecy and power had been taken away.

Finally, after an episode of out-of-school conflict, a productive parent meeting was called. The parents and boys involved in the hostilities met, and the actions were examined and discussed by the whole group. After this, the conflict ceased. By the end of that year, Henry was no longer being bullied and, because their aggressive behavior was no longer tolerated, the bullying duo had become powerless and isolated. In a move precipitated mainly by his disruptive behavior at home, Josh's parents removed him from the school.

This case illustrates several key elements often present in school bullying. Henry had clearly misread the situation in believing he had no alternative other than to hang out with Josh and Brett. When asked, others in the peer group were supportive and more than willing to befriend him. However, it is also important to underline that at-risk, exciting behavior can seem very alluring to adolescents. We need to be aware of the powerful attraction students who bully can have for vulnerable peers. Bullies often do outrageous, risky things, and appear to be confident and welcoming of others into their group. They appear to offer an exciting outlet for unhappy, isolated students.

Henry took a long time to admit that what was happening was bullying. Despite being offered help after the computer incident, he continued to deny anything was wrong. Often, young people want to solve their own problems and they need to be supported when they do this. If things get out of hand, however, they need to know the school will be there for them.

Notes

1 Barbara and George have produced a tape and a booklet (*Michael's Story*) which provides an excellent example of the No Blame Approach in action and also explains how to use it. This and other materials they have developed can be viewed at: www.luckyduck.co.uk (see also Appendix 1).
2 This is slightly different from the seven-step process described by Robinson and Maines (1997: 67–70); we have altered it a little as a result of experience.
3 The parents can be informed at this point.

APPENDIX 1

Useful Websites

This appendix is designed to provide some starting points for gathering useful information about bullying on the Internet, as well as for locating anti-bullying resources and strategies. The identified websites all contain useful information and most also provide links to other worthwhile websites.

Antibullies is a UK-based website that has links to other UK and international sites, with a good selection of American and Australian sites (http://www.bully.org.uk/).

Bullyproofing our school is a Glasgow-based website built upon the seminal work of Alan McLean (http://www.glasgow.gov.uk/html/council/dept/educ/bullying.htm).
It provides excellent information about bullying and how to deal with it.

Don't Suffer in Silence (http://www.dfes.gov.uk/bullying/). The Department for Education and Skills has created an excellent, interesting, and accessible website to complement the second edition of its major anti-bullying publication, *Bullying: Don't Suffer in Silence* (DfEE, 2000). The original was based on the research findings of the largest bullying research done to date, the Sheffield study, and this builds upon and extends that initial and excellent effort. The report and the website are accessible and very useful and demonstrate the unobtrusive but outstanding handiwork of Professor Peter K. Smith. It provides web pages for pupils, teachers, parents, and families as well as an area of case studies. A copy of the extremely accessible "Anti-bullying pack for schools" can also be downloaded.

George Robinson and Barbara Maines's Lucky Duck website is very good (http://www.luckyduck.co.uk/). Not only do Barbara and George have an excellent philosophy and humane approach to dealing with bullying and other relationship and self-esteem issues, they also produce a mass of useful and inexpensive resources to meet a variety of important needs. Barbara and George are also top-notch presenters and can provide excellent training sessions, not only in the UK but throughout the world.

Keith Sullivan's Anti-Bullying Website (http://www2.vuw.ac.nz/education/ anti-bullying/) provides useful foundational information about bullying based on Keith's 2000 publication, *The Anti-Bullying Handbook*.

Ken Rigby's anti-bullying site "Bullying in Schools and What to Do About It" (http://www.education.unisa.edu.au/bullying/) provides a lot of information and links to a large number of other Australian and international sites of interest. Professor Rigby has written a number of very useful books and a mass of research articles about which he provides information at his site.

No Bully (http://www.police.govt.nz/service/yes/nobully/) provides useful fundamental information about bullying under separate headings "4 Kids" and "4 Teachers and Parents." It is hosted by the New Zealand Police and sup-ported by Telecom New Zealand. The Youth Education Service of the Police has a focus on crime prevention and regards solving school bullying as an investment in preventing crime and supporting safer communities. Central to the website is the Police's own anti-bullying resource, the Kia Kaha program.

The Anti-Bullying Network website (http://www.antibullying.net/) is hosted by Moray House, the University of Edinburgh. In the UK, the anti-bullying movement got its major push from SCRE (the Scottish Council for Research in Education) from which the site developed. Anti-bullying practice has always been of a very high calibre in Scotland and this site is a prime example. The "Young Voices" section is particularly appealing and there are excellent links as well.

The BC Safe School Center is located in Burnaby, Canada, and provides anti-bullying support for schools in the Vancouver area. They have produced an excellent kit for dealing with school bullying and their website is full of use-ful information. Their address is http://www.safeschools.gov.bc.ca/

The Colorado Anti-bullying Project is an excellent site (http://www.no-bully.com/index.html). It provides information for primary, middle, and sec-ondary school students, and for parents and teachers. The information is practical, straightforward, and useful, and has an excellent selection of links.

The LaMarsh Center for Research on Violence and Conflict Resolution (web address: http.//www.yorku.ca/lamarsh/index.html) is mandated to support, conduct, and disseminate the results of research on violence and conflict resolution. It is currently carrying out a number of relevant research projects concerned with bullying and abuse including: The Teen Relationships Project, Bullying and Victimization in Schools, Peer and Media Influences on Dating Violence in Adolescence, and The Problem of Girls' Aggression. The well-known researcher, Professor Debra Pepler, is Director of the Center.

The University of Wisconsin at Milwaukee College of Letters and Science has developed a useful and interesting peer mentoring scheme (http://www.uwm.edu/letsci/edison/pm.html). This website also provides links to other mentoring websites.

APPENDIX 2

School Bullying Questionnaire

Introduction

In order to find out about bullying in a school, it is useful to run a survey. This also serves several other purposes. As the questionnaire defines what bullying is, it lets students know that it is more than just physical abuse. It also means that some data can be gathered that provide a tangible account of the extent and nature of bullying in the school.

It is important that a questionnaire is clear and simple. This is for ease of understanding for those taking the survey; for ease of generating statistics, for those who have to add everything up; and for ease of interpreting, when the information is presented to trustees/governors, staff, students, and parents.

N.B. This questionnaire was written with secondary students in mind, and can be adapted for younger age groups as necessary. Once the questionnaire has been completed, the same basic form can also be used to record the total responses to each question for statistical purposes.

Questionnaire about School Bullying Form/Grade____

Introduction: This school takes bullying very seriously and we wish to know how much bullying is taking place in the school. Bullying can be hitting, kicking, or the use of force in any way. It can be teasing, making rude gestures, name-calling, or leaving you out. Bullying means that these things happened more than once and was done by the same person or persons. Bullying means to hurt, either physically or so that you feel very bad.

This is an anonymous questionnaire. This means that you can answer the questions but you don't have to let us know who you are. There is a blank for your name, however, if you want to fill it in. If you do this, it will be kept confidential. We will not give any information to anyone or do anything without your agreement.

Name: _____ (give your name only if you wish)

1. Are you a boy or a girl? (circle one)   boy   girl

2. How old are you?

3. Which form/grade are you in? (circle one)   3rd   4th   5th   6th   7th

4. Since I have been at school, I have been bullied (circle one of the following):

never   once in a while   often   about once a week   more than once
                                                                        a week

5. I have been bullied in the following ways (tick (√) yes or no for each category):

                                                                        Yes   No
– **hitting (punching, kicking, shoving)** _____
– **a knife or a gun or some kind of weapon was used on me** _____
– **mean teasing**_____
– **purposely left out of things** _____
– **had my things damaged or stolen** _____
– **was horribly sworn at** _____
– **had offensive sexual suggestions made to me**_____
– **had a nasty racial remark made to me** _____
– **received nasty (poisonous) letter(s)** _____
– **someone said nasty things to make others dislike me**_____
– **had untrue and mean gossip spread about me**_____
– **I was threatened**_____
– **had rude gestures or mean faces made at me**_____
– **anything else (write it in here)** _____

6. Since I have been at school, I have bullied someone (circle one of the following):

never   once in a while   often   about once a week   more than once a week

7. I have bullied someone in the following ways (tick (√) yes or no for each category):

                                                      Yes   No

– hitting (punching, kicking shoving) _____
– use of a knife or a gun or some kind of weapon on someone _____
– mean teasing _____
– purposely left someone out of things _____
– damaged or stole someone's possessions _____
– swore at someone _____
– made offensive sexual suggestions to someone _____
– made a nasty racial remark about someone _____
– sent nasty (poisonous) letter(s) _____
– said nasty things to make others dislike a person(s) _____
– made up and spread untrue and mean gossip about someone _____
– I threatened someone _____
– made rude gestures or mean faces at someone _____
– anything else (write it in here) _____

8. Since I have been at school, I have seen bullying take place (circle one of the following):

never   once in a while   often   about once a week   more than once a week

9. I have watched or have heard about the following types of bullying (tick (√) yes or no for each category):

                                                      Yes   No

– hitting (punching, kicking, shoving) _____
– the use of a knife or a gun or some kind of weapon _____
– mean teasing _____
– someone purposely being left out of things _____
– someone having their things damaged or stolen _____
– someone being horribly sworn at _____

- someone having offensive sexual suggestions made to them _____
- someone having a nasty racial remark made to them _____
- someone receiving nasty (poisonous) letter(s) _____
- someone having nasty things said to make others dislike them _____
- someone having untrue and mean gossip spread about them _____
- someone being threatened _____
- someone having rude gestures or mean faces made at them _____
- anything else (write it in here) _____

10. Tick (√) all places where you have been bullied or have seen bullying take place:

                             have been bullied   seen bullying take place

- in the playground _____
- in the corridors _____
- in the classroom _____
- in the locker room_____
- on the way to school _____
- on the way home from school _____
- on the bus _____
- anywhere else (write in here) _____

11. Where are the "hot spots" where most bullying takes place? Please list these:

    a. _____
    b. _____
    c. _____
    d. _____
    e. _____

APPENDIX 3

An Example of a School Anti-bullying Policy

Rationale

The school actively seeks to provide an excellent learning environment that is safe from intimidation and bullying.

Purpose

The purpose of this policy document is to outline the responsibilities staff, students, and parents have to combat social, emotional, and physical intimidation and bullying.

Definition

Bullying is deliberate, hurtful behavior that is often repeated over a period of time and in which it is difficult for those being bullied to defend themselves.

Guidelines

- Anti-bullying workshops will be run with each year 9 class each year.
- All members of the school community have a responsibility to take some action when they become aware of bullying behavior.
- Staff should treat any report of bullying behavior seriously.
- Staff should first *listen* to the student or students. The student(s) should be

assured that they have acted correctly in reporting the bullying.
- The staff member should next make sure the victim is safe.
- The staff member should then make a brief written summary of the information and pass it on to one of several staff members who have a responsibility for dealing with cases of bullying (the anti-bullying team, including the deputy and assistant principals). This action should be discussed with the student.
- Each case of reported bullying should be assessed by a member of the team and an appropriate response put in place. This, along with the outcomes, will be recorded and filed. The procedures for this assessment and the various responses are available from anti-bullying team members.
- It is important that the staff member checks a week or so later with both the student and the person to whom the information was sent.
- In cases of serious intimidation, parents of both (all) students are to be contacted.

APPENDIX 4

Student Charter

Developing a students' charter

Classrooms that have developed a successful anti-bullying ethos recognize the central role students play in establishing and maintaining this culture. Every individual student needs to feel included, believe they have influence, and feel powerful. The classroom therefore needs to operate on democratic principles. A useful tool in building on this approach is to give the class an opportunity to develop a charter that will encapsulate the developing culture. As in the development of an understanding of bullying behavior, the process of gaining commitment to the charter demands that the students are given plenty of opportunities to reflect on, discuss, and practise the principles that have been adopted. This is an ideal activity for student leaders to take control of as it gives the students themselves an opportunity to identify what is important to them at school.

An example of the process is the following charter that was developed at Colenso High School. The student leaders in each class led a discussion on the rights they should have as students in the school and also corresponding responsibilities. Each of the student leaders worked with a group of six other students to come up with a list of five important rights they believed they should have. They then took each right and developed a subsequent responsibility. The leaders next led a class-wide discussion that identified five key rights and responsibilities that were then submitted to the student council. The student council collated every class's effort and developed a concise set of beliefs that was selected and returned to the classes for discussion and modification.

The result was:

> ## Students' Charter
>
> ### *"This is our place and it belongs to all of us!"*
>
> **These are our Rights:**
>
> 1 We all have the right to learn without disruption.
> 2 We all have the right to aim for excellence and to do our personal best.
> 3 We all have the right to be safe.
> 4 We all have the right to expect our possessions to be safe.
> 5 We all have the right to a safe, clean environment.
>
> **These are our Responsibilities:**
> 1 We will not interfere with the learning of others.
> 2 We will not stand in the way of those working to do their personal best.
> 3 We will not harm others either physically or emotionally and we will not allow others to do so either.
> 4 We will not interfere with other people's possessions.
> 5 We will care for OUR PLACE and its environment.

There was little dissension and the students agreed that it was a good guiding statement.

However, while there had clearly been wide consultation, it was evident that many students saw it as removed from the reality of their lives. To provoke discussion and to provide opportunities for the students to develop a greater commitment to the charter, a series of worksheets was developed that aimed to engage the students, to make them think about strategies they would use when confronted with everyday abuses of the charter, and to make them better prepared to stand up for their rights.

What follows is an example of one such worksheet, which can be adapted to address the other paired rights and responsibilities.

Rights/Responsibilities Worksheet 1

Right   **Responsibility**
We all have the right to learn   **We will not interfere with the**
without disruption.   **learning of others.**

Read the **right** *and the corresponding* **responsibility** *taken from the* **School
Students' Charter** *and complete the following activities:*
1 Rewrite the "Right" in your own words.

2 Give an example of a situation when you might need that right.

3 Give a specific example of how the right has been broken in the last term.

4 Think of other examples of this right either being ignored or being important.

5 Rewrite the "Responsibility" using your own words.

6 Give an example of when you might need to exercise this responsibility.

7 When others are disrupting your, or the class's learning, what can you do?

8 What would stop you acting responsibly?

After completing the sheet on your own, discuss your answers with three other
students. As a group, come up with a combined list of ways in which learning
can be disrupted.

Develop a number of strategies that would be useful for students to use to stop
others disrupting learning.

Work out a role-play of someone acting out and disrupting the learning of others, and act out two or three of the strategies that would help them solve the
problem.

References

Adair, V.A., Dixon, R.S., Moore, D.W. and Sutherland, C.M. (2000) "Ask your mother not to make yummy sandwiches: bullying in New Zealand secondary schools," *New Zealand Journal of Educational Studies*, 35(2): 207–21.

Astor, R.A., Meyer, H.A. and Behre, W.J. (1999) "Unowned places and times: maps and interviews about violence in high schools," *American Educational Research Journal*, 36: 3–42.

Astor, R.A., Meyer, H.A. and Pitner, R.O. (2001) "Elementary and middle school students' perceptions of violence-prone school subcontexts," *Elementary School Journal*, 101(5): 511–28.

Beales, F. (2000) "Youth-at-risk: definition, identification, prevention and intervention: a review of the literature," unpublished report, School of Education, Victoria University of Wellington.

Berthold, K. and Hoover, J.H. (1999) "Correlates of bullying and victimization among intermediate students in the midwestern USA," *School Psychology International Journal*, 29: 159–72.

Besag, V. (1989) *Bullies and Victims in Schools*. Buckingham: Open University Press.

Boulton, M.J. and Underwood, K. (1992) "Bully/victim problems among middle school children," *British Journal of Educational Psychology*, 62: 73–87.

Boulton, M.J., Trueman, M., Chau, C., Whitehand, C. and Amatya, K. (1999) "Concurrent and longitudinal links between friendship and peer victimization: implications for befriending interventions," *Journal of Adolescence*, 22: 461–6.

Brown, B.B. and Lohr, M.J. (1987) "Peer-group affiliation and adolescent self-esteem: an integration of ego-identity and symbolic interaction theories," *Journal of Personality and Social Psychology*, 52: 47–55.

Byrne, B.J. (1994) "Bullies and victims in a school setting with reference to some Dublin schools," *Irish Journal of Psychology*, 15: 574–86.

Chess, S. and Thomas, A. (1977) "Temperamental individuality from childhood to adolescence," *Journal of Child Psychiatry*, 16: 218–26.

Cleary, M. (2001) "Bullying Behaviour in Schools: Towards Better Understandings and

Practice," unpublished Masters thesis, Victoria University of Wellington.

Cleary, M. and Sullivan, K. (1999) " 'On the bus': an action plan for bullyproofing your school and classroom," *New Zealand Annual Review of Education, Te Arotake a Tau o te Ao o te Matauranga i Aotearoa,* 8: 79–96.

Coloroso, B. (2002) *The Bully, the Bullied, and the Bystander.* Toronto: HarperCollins.

Cowie, H. and Sharp, S. (eds) (1996) *Peer Counselling in Schools: A Time to Listen.* London: David Fulton.

Craig, W.M. (1998) "The relationship among bullying, victimization, depression, anxiety, and aggression in elementary school children," *Personality and Individual Differences,* 24: 123–30.

Cullingford, C. and Morrison, J. (1997) "The relationship between criminality and home background," *Children & Society,* 11: 157–72.

Department for Education and Employment (DfEE) (2000) *Bullying: Don't Suffer in Silence – An Anti-bullying Pack for Schools.* London: Department for Education and Employment.

Fonzi, A., Genta, M.L., Menerini, E., Bacchini, D., Bonino, S. and Costabile, A. (1999) "Italy," in P.K. Smith, Y. Morita, J. Junger-Tas, D. Olweus, R. Catalano and P. Slee (eds), *The Nature of School Bullying: A Cross-National Perspective.* London: Routledge, pp. 140–56.

Galambos, M.L. and Turner, P.K. (1997) "Shaping parent–adolescent relations: examining the goodness-of-fit in parent and adolescent temperaments," paper presented at the meeting of the Society for Research in Child Development, Washington, DC.

Galen, B.R. and Underwood, M.K. (1997) "A developmental investigation of social aggression among children," *Developmental Psychology,* 33(4): 589–600.

Goleman, D. (1995) *Emotional Intelligence.* New York: Basic Books.

Hargreaves, D. (1967) *Social Relationships in a Secondary School.* London: Routledge and Kegan Paul.

Haugaard, J.J. (2001) *Problematic Behaviors During Adolescence.* New York: McGraw-Hill.

Hay-Mackenzie, F. (2002) "Tackling the bullies: in the classroom and in the staffroom," *Australia and New Zealand Journal of Law and Education,* 7(2): 87–140.

Haynie, D.L., Nansel, T., Eitel, P., Crump, A.D., Saylor, K., Yu, K. and Simons-Morton, B. (2001) "Bullies, victims and bully/victims: distinct groups of at-risk youth," *Journal of Early Adolescence,* 21(1): 29–49.

Hosking, D.-M. and Morley, I. (1991) *Social Psychology of Organizing People, Processes and Context.* Hemel Hempstead: Harvester Wheatsheaf.

Johnson, D. and Lewis, G. (1999) "Do you like what you see? Self-perceptions of adolescent bullies," *British Educational Research Journal,* 25(5): 665–77.

Kaltiala-Heino, R., Rimpela, M., Marttunen, M., Rimpela, A. and Rantanen, P. (1999) "Bullying, depression, and suicidal ideation in Finnish adolescents: school survey," *British Medical Journal,* 319: 348–51.

Kingery, P.M., Coggeshall, M.B. and Alford, A.A. (1998) "Violence at school: recent evidence from four national surveys," *Psychology in Schools,* 35(3): 247–58.

Kumpulainen, K., Rasanen, E., Henttonen, I., Almqvist, F., Kresanov, K., Linna, S.L., Moilanen, I., Piha, J., Puura, K. and Tamminen, T. (1998) "Bullying and psychiatric symptoms among elementary school-age children," *Child Abuse and Neglect,* 22: 705–17.

Lind, J. and Maxwell, G. (1996) *Children's Experiences of Violence at School*. Wellington: Office of the Commissioner for Children.

Lloyd, N. (1994) "Girls 'hidden bullies' in schools," *Advertiser*, 137(4283): 3.

Maines, B. and Robinson, G. (1992a) *Michael's Story: The No Blame Approach*. Bristol: Lame Duck Publishing.

Maines, B. and Robinson, G. (1992b) *The No Blame Approach* (video and training booklet). Bristol: Lame Duck Publishing.

Maines, B. and Robinson, G. (1992c) *Michael's Been Bullied—A Peer Support Group Method: The No Blame Approach*. Bristol: Lame Duck Publishing.

Marcus, R.F. (1999) "A gender-linked exploratory factor analysis of antisocial behavior in young adolescents," *Adolescence*, 34(133): 33–46.

Maslow, A. (1970) *Motivation and Personality*. (2nd edn). New York: Harper and Row.

McLean, A. (1994) *Bullyproofing Our School: Promoting Positive Relationships*. Glasgow: Strathclyde Regional Council.

Miller-Johnson, S., Coie, J.D., Maumary-Gremaud, A., Lochman, J. and Terry, R. (1999) "Relationship between childhood peer rejection and aggression and adolescent delinquency severity and type among African American youth," *Journal of Emotional and Behavioral Disorders*, 7(3): 137–46.

Nairn, K. and Smith, A.B. (2002) "Secondary school students' experiences of bullying at school—and their suggestions for dealing with it," *Childrenz Issues*, 6(1): 16–22.

Naylor, P. and Cowie, H. (1999) "The effectiveness of peer support systems in challenging school bullying: the perspectives and experiences of teachers and pupils," *Journal of Adolescence*, 22: 467–79.

Olweus, D. (1993a) *Bullying at School: What We Know and What We Can Do*. Oxford: Blackwell.

Olweus, D. (1993b) "Victimization by peers: antecedents and long-term outcomes," in K.H. Rubin and J.B. Asendorf (eds), *Social Withdrawal, Inhibition, and Shyness in Childhood*. Hilldale, NJ: Lawrence Erlbaum Association, pp. 316–26.

Olweus, D. (1995) "Bullying or peer abuse at school: facts and interventions," *Current Directions in Psychological Science*, 4: 196–200.

Owens, L., Slee, P. and Shute, R. (2000) " 'It hurts a hell of a lot …': the effects of indirect aggression on teenage girls," *School Psychology International*, 21(4): 359–76.

Parry, K. (ed.) (2001) *Leadership in the Antipodes: Findings, Implications and a Leader Profile*. Wellington: Institute of Policy Studies.

Pepler, D. and Craig, W. (April 2000) "Making a difference in bullying," LaMarsh Research Report No. 60.

Peterson, L. and Rigby, K. (1999) "Countering bullying at an Australian secondary school with students as helpers," *Journal of Adolescence*, 22: 481–92.

Pikas, A. (1989) "The common concern method for the treatment of mobbing," in E. Munthe and E. Roland (eds), *Bullying: An International Perspective*. London: David Fulton.

Prinstein, M.J., Fetter, M.D. and La Greca, A.M. (1996) "Can you judge adolescents by the company they keep? Peer group membership, substance abuse, and risk-taking behaviors," paper presented at the meeting of the Society for Research on Adolescence, Boston.

Rigby, K. (2000) "Effects of peer victimization in schools and perceived social support on adolescent well-being," *Journal of Adolescence*, 23: 57–68.

Rigby, K. and Slee, P. (1991a) "Bullying among Australian school children: reported behaviour and attitudes towards victims," *Journal of Social Psychology*, 131: 615–27.

Rigby, K. and Slee, P. (1991b) "Dimensions of interpersonal relations among Australian school children and implications for psychological well-being," *Journal of Social Psychology*, 133: 33–42.

Rigby, K. and Slee, P. (1999) "Suicidal ideation among adolescent school children, involvement in bully–victim problems, and perceived social support," *Suicide and Life-Threatening Behavior*, 29(2): 119–30.

Rivers, I. (1995) "Mental health issues among young lesbians and gay men bullied in school," *Health and Social Care in the Community*, 3: 380–3.

Rivers, I. (1996) "Young, gay and bullied," *Young People Now*, 81: 18–19.

Rivers, I. and Smith, P.K. (1994) "Types of bullying behaviour and their correlates," *Aggressive Behaviour*, 20: 359–68.

Robinson, G. and Maines, B. (1997) *Crying for Help: The No Blame Approach to Bullying.* Bristol: Lucky Duck Publishing.

Rost, J.C. (1993) *Leadership for the Twenty-First Century.* Westport, CT: Praeger.

Salmivalli, C. (1999) "Participant role approach to school bullying: implications for interventions," *Journal of Adolescence*, 22: 453–9.

Salmivalli, C., Kaukiainen, A. and Lagerspetz, K. (1998) "Aggression in the social relations of school-aged girls and boys," in P.T. Slee and K. Rigby (eds), *Children's Peer Relations.* London and New York: Routledge, pp 60–75.

Santrock, J. (2001) *Adolescence.* (8th edn). Boston, MA: McGraw-Hill.

Selman, R. (1980) *The Growth of Interpersonal Understanding.* New York: Academic Press.

Shakeshaft, C., Barber, E., Hergenrother, M.A., Johnson, Y.M., Mandel, L.S. and Sawyer, J. (1995) "Peer harassment in schools," *Journal for a Just and Caring Education*, 1: 30–44.

Sharp, S. (1995) "How much does bullying hurt? The effects of bullying on the personal well-being and educational progress of secondary aged students," *Educational and Child Psychology*, 12: 81–8.

Sharp, S. and Smith, P.K. (1994) *Tackling Bullying in Your School: A Practical Handbook for Teachers.* London: Routledge.

Sherman, L., Gottfredson, D., MacKenzie, D., Eck, J., Reuter, P. and Bushway, S. (1997) *Preventing Crime: What Works, What Doesn't, What's Promising. A Report to the United States Congress.* Washington, DC: National Institute of Justice.

Simanton, E., Burthwick, P. and Hoover, J. (2000) "Small-town bullying and student-on-student aggression: an initial investigation of risk," *Journal of At-Risk Factors*, 6(2): 4–10.

Slee, P. (1995) "Bullying: Health concerns of Australian secondary school students," *International Journal of Adolescence and Youth*, 5: 215–24.

Slee, P. and Rigby, K. (1993) "The relationship of Eysenck's personality factors and self-esteem to bully–victim behaviour in Australian schoolboys," *Journal of Personality and Individual Differences*, 14(2): 371–3.

Smith, C. (2002) *B.E.S.T. Buddies (Bettering Everyone's Secondary Transition): A Comprehensive Training Programme Introducing a Peer Buddy System to Support Students Starting Secondary School.* Bristol: Lucky Duck Publishing.

Smith, P.K. (1999) "England and Wales," in P.K. Smith, Y. Morita, J. Junger-Tas, D.

Olweus, R. Catalano and P. Slee (eds), *The Nature of School Bullying: A Cross-National Perspective*. London: Routledge, pp. 68–90.

Smith, P.K. and Sharp, S. (1994) *School Bullying: Insights and Perspectives*. London: Routledge.

Smith, P.K., Morita, Y., Junger-Tas, J., Olweus, D., Catalano, R. and Slee, P. (eds) (1999) *The Nature of School Bullying: A Cross-National Perspective*. London: Routledge.

Smith, P. and Shu, S. (2000) "What good schools can do about bullying: findings from a survey in English schools after a decade of research and action," *Childhood*, 7(2): 193–212.

Sternberg, R.J. (1986) *Intelligence Applied*. San Diego, CA: Harcourt Brace Jovanovich.

Sullivan, K. (2000) *The Anti-Bullying Handbook*, Auckland, Melbourne, Oxford and New York: Oxford University Press.

Sutton, J. and Smith, P.K. (1999) "Bullying as a group process: an adaption of the participant role approach," *Aggressive Behavior*, 25: 97–111.

Sweeting, H. and West, P. (2001) "Being different: correlates of the experience of teasing and bullying at age 11," *Research Papers in Education*, 16(3): 225–46.

Time Magazine (2001) "Society Warning: Andy Williams here. Unhappy kid. Tired of being picked on. Ready to blow. Want to kill some people. Can anybody hear me? How did things get so bad?" Terry McCarthy, March, pp. 12–16.

Trostli, R. (ed. and trans.) (1998) *Rhythms of Learning: What Waldorf Education Offers Children, Parents and Teachers*, Hudson NY: Anthroposophic Press, pp. 30, 44–5, 55, 62, 66.

University of California at San Diego Office for Students with Disabilities (http://orpheus.ucsd.edu/osd/peer.html).

US Department of Justice, Bureau of Justice Statistics, US Department of Education (1998) *National Crime Victimization Survey: School Crime Supplement, Students' Reports of School Crime, 1989 and 1995* (available at http://www.ojp.usdoj.gov/bjs/pub/pdf/srsc.pdf).

Warwick, I., Aggleton, P. and Douglas, N. (2001) "Playing it safe: addressing the emotional and physical health of lesbian and gay pupils in the UK," *Journal of Adolescence*, 24: 129–40.

Whitney, I., Smith, P.K. and Thompson, D. (1994) "Bullying and children with special educational needs," in P.K. Smith and S. Sharp (eds), *School Bullying: Insights and Perspectives*. London: Routledge. pp. 213–40.

Young, S. (1998) "The support group approach to bullying in schools," *Educational Psychology and Practice*, 14(1): 32–9.

Index

academic impact of bullying x, 2, 12, 14–15, 17, 18, 20, 59, 63–64, 85, 90, 95, 97, 101, 104, 133, 200, 229

adolescence ix-x, xv, 2, 7–9, 12, 17, 18, 20, 21, 27–44, 46, 47, 48–53, 64, 82–84, 85, 109–110, 119, 120, 130, 132, 153, 170
  cognitive development 28, 32–33, 34, 39–41, 42, 132
  moral development 40, 49, 52
  personal and social development 2, 20–21, 27–29, 32–33, 34, 40, 42, 46, 47, 132
  physical development 27–29, 30, 31–33, 34, 42, 46, 47, 50, 52, 132

alcohol and drugs xvi, 2, 30, 31, 41, 43, 44, 64, 65–66, 70

anti-bullying policy 66, 76, 81, 87–90, 92, 94, 99, 108, 136, 141–147, 148, 149, 154, 155, 166, 240–241

at-risk behavior/students 16, 17, 18, 35–36, 38, 39, 41–44, 45, 50, 126, 202, 231

Australia xiv, 8, 9, 10, 11, 15, 20–21, 234

authoritarian approaches 36–37, 58, 59, 61, 62, 72–73, 106, 110, 131, 174

authoritative approaches xvi, 36–37, 58, 62, 72, 130–140, 174, 178, 179

blame culture 62, 66, 70–71, 75, 77, 84, 91–92, 109, 135, 148, 165, 216–217

bullies ix, xvi, 5, 6, 7, 9, 15–17, 19–20, 21, 24, 25, 48, 49, 50, 51, 52, 62–64, 73, 77, 85–92, 102, 104, 105, 109, 110, 112–129, 138, 141, 145, 146, 148–149, 150, 152, 153, 158–159, 163, 164, 167, 168, 176, 181, 193, 194, 195, 199, 202, 204, 216–231

bully victims 15–17, 18

bullying
  age differences in 8, 9, 16, 21, 49–53, 116–117, 120, 129, 196, 197, 235
  case studies/stories/anecdotes about ix, xv, 1–3, 27–44, 62–71, 73–80, 85–92, 115–119, 136–139, 151–152, 154–164, 184–185, 213–214, 226–231
  causes of 6, 10, 11–12, 13–15, 18,

62–64, 69, 74–76, 77, 127, 147, 156
appearance 12, 14, 15, 33
class 2, 33
ethnicity 2, 33
gender 2
chaos theory of 3
definition 2, 3–7, 75, 93, 94, 95, 98–99, 101, 106–108, 150–155, 167, 182, 183–184, 194, 195, 207–208, 235, 240
denial of 59–62, 75–77, 83–92, 106
dynamic xi, 15, 17, 24–26, 48, 52, 107, 109, 110, 118, 119–128, 151, 152, 182, 195, 216, 223, 226, 230, 235, 240
effects of bullying xv, 1, 2, 6, 18, 20–26, 43, 66, 70, 78, 96, 98, 101, 104, 112, 147, 150, 184, 199–200, 208, 217, 220, 222, 227–228, 229
    depression 6, 17, 20–21, 43, 96, 200
    fearfulness 6
    loss of self-esteem 18, 20–21, 70, 90
    suicide 17, 18, 20, 41, 42–43, 70–71, 96, 112, 147, 200, 209, 210, 214
    truancy 18, 21, 85–86, 156, 200
gender differences in 9, 11–12, 20–21, 52, 235
hidden nature of
    see secrecy surrounding bullying
homophobic 12, 13, 14, 69
in adolescence ix–x, 7–9, 14, 20–21, 40, 62–64, 82, 116, 120
myths about 102–104
physical 5–6, 8, 11, 12, 14, 15, 24, 65, 69, 88, 107, 153, 184, 185, 191–192, 194, 199, 208, 237
psychological 5–6, 8, 11, 12, 14, 15, 24, 69, 88, 107, 153, 184, 185, 194, 199, 208, 237
prevalence of ix, 9–10, 105, 151, 235

racist 14
rates of 1, 3, 8, 9–10, 16, 116, 120, 151, 154, 202
reporting of 7–8, 23, 58, 62, 63, 64, 67, 80, 81, 82, 83–84, 89–90, 99, 104, 105, 106, 118, 129, 139, 142–143, 149, 158, 195, 219, 228, 231, 240–241
sexual 14, 86, 88, 156, 184, 185–198
special needs 14
symptoms of 12–13, 83, 85, 89
    see also effects of bullying
types of 107, 110, 153
where it occurs 3, 10–11, 50, 90, 100, 159, 163, 201, 239
bullying culture 21, 24, 62–64, 65–67, 68–69, 72, 110, 115–119, 141
bystanders ix, xi, xv, xvi, 6, 15, 19–20, 21, 22–23, 24, 25, 49, 51, 63–64, 67, 84, 96, 104, 109–129, 144–145, 146, 147, 150, 154, 158, 163, 164, 168, 176, 181, 199, 200, 202, 204, 216–231
    defenders 19–20, 113–119, 120, 138, 163
    observers 116
    outsiders 19–20, 49, 113, 114, 116, 163
    reinforcers 19–20, 51, 113, 114, 115, 116–117, 119, 120, 129, 138, 163,
    sidekicks 19–20, 51, 88, 113–114, 115, 116–117, 119–120, 129, 138, 163, 167, 169

Canada x, xiv, 44, 234, 235
charter
    class 177
    school 55, 97, 100
    student 139, 242–244
cliques 36, 38, 68–69, 78
coeducational schools 3, 35, 49, 73, 100
Colenso High School xiii, xiv, 9, 167–168, 170, 180, 242–244

Columbine High School 6, 67–71,
    104
communities 11, 23, 25, 48, 55, 69,
    70, 92, 96, 98, 100, 170, 175
community and bullying x, 2, 22–25,
    66, 70, 92, 93, 108
confidentiality 205, 209, 210, 221
conflict resolution 132, 148, 169, 170,
    216, 231, 235
cooperative and group learning 109,
    139, 177
criminal behavior 6, 16, 23, 24, 25,
    42, 51, 65–67, 96, 104, 139–140,
    148, 226
curriculum interventions xvi, 97, 99,
    108, 129, 148, 149, 150–164

defenders
    see bystanders
dominance x, 17, 21, 38, 50, 51, 73,
    139, 217, 223

Education Review Office (ERO) (NZ)
    80, 81
elite groups/elitism 9, 49, 52–53,
    66–67, 68–69, 71, 176
empathy 8, 15, 17, 22, 34, 38, 40, 46,
    65–66, 68, 111, 114, 124, 128,
    137, 149, 155, 165, 167, 195, 197,
    203, 204, 214, 217–218, 221–222,
    226
ethnicity 33, 39, 46, 111
evaluation 94, 98, 99–100, 108,
    175–176, 182, 194–197, 202,
    214–215
exclusion
    see ostracization
experiential learning 148, 149, 169,
    181–198, 213

family x, 22–23, 27, 34, 35, 36, 37,
    42, 46, 48, 60, 63, 68, 70, 233
friendship 16, 17, 20, 21, 30, 31, 32,
    36, 38, 43, 46, 65–66, 67–68, 79,
    88, 112, 118, 121, 126, 147, 152,
    157, 158, 160, 168, 172, 200, 201,

228–231

Harris, Eric 67–69
hidden nature of bullying
    see secrecy surrounding bullying

ice breakers 173, 178, 183, 206, 207
individuation 2, 17, 34, 37, 38, 41,
    47, 49, 50, 51, 52, 53, 64, 120
intimacy ix
intimidation 2, 23, 71, 82, 91, 96,
    184, 194
isolation 2, 5, 12, 20, 21, 27, 46, 50,
    52, 67, 68, 71, 75–77, 79, 86, 89,
    96, 115, 121, 137, 213, 220, 221,
    227, 228, 231

Kia Kaha 9, 26, 153, 234
Klebold, Dylan 67–69

leadership xvi, 9, 15–16, 49, 50, 52,
    64, 65, 66, 95, 96, 108, 109, 114,
    116, 117, 119, 122, 125, 139, 149,
    165–180, 206, 217, 221, 224, 242

mediation 231
murder/killings 6, 67–71, 104,
    111–112

New Zealand xiii, xiv, 3, 8, 9, 10, 11,
    12, 35, 42, 65–67, 71, 81,
    100–101, 103, 108, 140, 150, 151,
    153, 154, 182, 193, 206, 234
New Zealand Office of the
    Commissioner for Children 1,
    151
New Zealand Police xiii, 26, 234
No Blame Approach xvi, 26, 58, 108,
    118, 129, 134–138, 149, 170, 177,
    193, 200, 216–231, 234

ostracization/exclusion 2, 11–12, 20,
    50, 52, 71, 76, 85, 86, 136, 141,
    147, 213
outsiders 67–71
    see bystanders

parenting styles 36–37, 72

parents x, xi, xv, 7, 12, 19, 22–23, 34, 35–37, 39, 40, 47, 50, 55, 60, 64, 68, 70, 75–77, 78–80, 81, 82–92, 96, 97, 98, 99, 105, 108, 115, 136, 142, 158, 219, 227, 231, 233, 235, 240, 241

passivity 168

peer mentoring xvi, 16, 52, 108, 120, 149, 169, 199–215, 226, 235

peer pressure xv, 28, 31, 42, 66, 132, 208

peer relations xv, 9, 17, 30, 32, 35–38, 48–53, 113, 116, 119, 121–128, 132, 133, 153

peers/peer groups x, xvi, 2, 7, 11, 14, 15, 16, 17, 19, 21, 27, 32–34, 35–36, 37–38, 39, 40, 41, 42, 46, 47–48, 49, 50, 51, 52, 64, 73, 105, 109, 110, 116–119, 120–129, 136, 137, 138, 143, 146, 147, 150, 163, 164, 167, 168, 169–170, 176, 198, 216, 220–221, 231, 233, 235, 240, 241

permissiveness 36–37, 59, 72, 73, 80–81, 106, 131, 174

Piaget 39

power x, 5, 12, 15, 16, 20, 25, 48, 64, 109, 110, 116, 117, 118, 166, 167, 168, 169, 172, 181, 231

power imbalance 7, 9, 12, 15, 17, 21, 24, 25, 49, 73, 77, 82, 110, 114, 117, 118, 148, 153, 157–158, 184, 194, 217–218, 220, 226

primary school ix, x, 27, 30, 34, 35, 36, 39, 44, 45–47, 48, 49–50, 73, 75, 130, 142

problem-solving xvi, 92, 132, 135, 142, 173, 175–177, 179, 189–190, 201, 204, 216, 217, 221–226, 227, 230

problems and disorders xv, 30–31, 32, 41–44

prosocial behavior xv, 16, 51, 83, 91, 92, 111, 119, 120–121, 124, 128, 132, 148, 164, 168, 169, 176, 216,

217

provocative victims 18–19, 111, 139, 147

reinforcers
    see bystanders

restorative justice 148, 216

risk-taking 38, 41–42, 50

role models 36, 132, 139, 166, 170, 176, 203

role play 174, 181–198, 209, 210–211, 212, 213–214, 244

safe schools x, xi, xvi, 2, 8, 23, 46, 51, 53, 56, 57, 59, 60, 62, 66, 67, 71, 72, 78, 81, Part III, Part IV, 243

Santana High School 6, 69–71

Santee 6, 69–70

Scandinavia xiv, 93

schools' reaction to bullying 7, 22–25, 55–71, 72, 77, 79–80, 82–92, 117–118, 193, 198, 231

secondary schools, culture of xv, 10–11, 27, 39, 45–53, 95, 109, 130–131, 133, 138, 142, 206, 209

secrecy surrounding bullying 5, 6, 7–8, 12, 13, 62–63, 64, 67, 71, 82, 84, 87, 106, 110, 114, 118, 141, 152, 153, 167, 168, 217, 231

sexual abuse 14, 31, 37, 65–67, 194, 196, 197, 209, 210

Sheffield Project 56, 58, 94–95, 233

shootings
    see weapons

sidekicks
    see bystanders

single-sex schools 2, 3, 35

social theater xvi, 149, 181–198

sociometry 120–128, 133, 171

Steiner, Rudolf 33

Strathclyde triangle 120, 125–128, 168, 171

students
    finishing students xv, 48, 49, 52–53, 66–67, 97, 99, 169, 173–175, 178, 199, 202, 206

first-year students xv, 48–50, 51, 73–78, 85–92, 115, 116–117, 169, 171
    groupings 35–36, 38, 40, 48–53, 64
    middle students xv, 48, 49, 51–52, 62–64, 78–80, 169, 171
suicide 42–43, 67, 112, 209, 210
    see also effects of bullying

Taradale incident 65–67, 71, 119
teachers xi, 11, 23, 33–34, 36, 37, 39, 40, 45–48, 50, 55, 59, 60, 62, 64, 69, 72–81, 96, 110, 130–140, 142, 151, 157–164, 171–177, 205, 210–211
teachers and bullying xi, xv, xvi, 2–3, 7–8, 11, 12, 13, 15, 17, 19, 48, 50, 58–62, 72–81, 82–84, 85–92, 94, 95–97, 103, 105, 115–116, 117, 136–140, 141–148, 149, 168, 186, 191–193, 198, 201–202, 217–231, 240–241
teaching styles 72–81, 110, 130–140
    see also authoritarian approaches; authoritative approaches; permissiveness
team approach to dealing with bullying 94–100, 137, 143, 146, 147, 148, 169, 176, 200, 219, 241
team building 174–177, 178–179
temperaments 33, 40

truancy 30, 85
    see also effects of bullying

UK xiii, xiv, 8, 10, 11, 20, 56, 93, 233, 234
USA xiv, 6, 9–10, 11, 42–43, 44, 67–71, 93, 140, 234, 235

victims ix, xvi, 2, 5, 6, 7, 11–12, 13–15, 17–20, 21–26, 31, 49, 50, 51, 63, 64, 65–67, 73, 75, 78, 83–84, 85–92, 99, 102, 103, 104, 105, 107, 109, 110–114, 116–117, 119, 120, 121, 139, 141, 142, 143, 144–147, 148, 150, 152, 154–164, 167, 181, 193, 195–196, 199–200, 202, 204, 205, 216–231, 241
    see also bullying, case studies/ stories/anecdotes about; bully victims; provocative victims
Vygotsky 40

weapons 6, 42, 67–71, 104
websites xvi, 95, 233–235
WHO ix
whole-school approach xv, 55–58, 60, 62, 64, 66, 71, 72, 93–108, 149, 226
Williams, Charles Andrew (Andy) 69–71

zero tolerance 58, 60, 61–62